Edge Networking

SCIENCES

Networks and Communications, Field Director – Guy Pujolle

Cloud Networking, Subject Head – Kamel Haddadou

Edge Networking

Internet of Edges

Khaldoun Al Agha
Pauline Loygue
Guy Pujolle

WILEY

First published 2022 in Great Britain and the United States by ISTE Ltd and John Wiley & Sons, Inc.

ISTE Ltd
27-37 St George's Road
London SW19 4EU
UK

www.iste.co.uk

John Wiley & Sons, Inc.
111 River Street
Hoboken, NJ 07030
USA

www.wiley.com

Library of Congress Control Number: 2022941477

British Library Cataloguing-in-Publication Data
A CIP record for this book is available from the British Library
ISBN 978-1-78945-068-2

ERC code:
PE7 Systems and Communication Engineering
  PE7_8 Networks (communication networks, sensor networks, networks of robots, etc.)
SH3 The Social World, Diversity, Population
  SH3_12 Communication and information, networks, media

Contents

Introduction

I.1. The Edge

The Internet of Edges, the subtitle of this book, is the formulation in simple terms of a new generation of networks: an infrastructure of communications and services that is realized at the edge of the network. The Internet of Edges is an interconnection of Edge networks. There are three levels of Edge networks: Skin networks, Fog networks and Mobile/Multi-access Edge Computing (MEC) networks. Skin networks connect clients to each other on the far edge, and the network nodes that support services are within a few meters of the users. Fog networks are more for company use. In a sense, they are replacing local area networks. However, their structure is a little different since the objective is to connect the company's employees to a small data center located within the company. MEC networks originate from the Edge networks of telecommunications operators. These are the networks using 5G and connecting customers to an operator's data center located very close to a 5G antenna. We have represented an Internet of Edges in Figure I.1.

Skin, Fog and MEC networks can themselves be participatory networks or not. A participatory network is built by interconnecting the electronic machines of its participants, which can be a user's terminal, a nearby box, a drone, a robot or a vehicle, etc. Participatory networks are distinguished from other types of networks by their totally distributed aspect. A non-participatory network is a network where services are centralized in a cloud, usually far away, to which customers must connect to obtain a service. In participatory networks, all services are distributed, whether they are infrastructure services or application services. The distance between the user and the data center hosting the service is comparable to the range of Wi-Fi communication. The machines that participate in the network bring their resources and host services that will be available to all users of the network.

Edge Networking,
by Khaldoun AL AGHA, Pauline LOYGUE and Guy PUJOLLE. © ISTE Ltd 2022.

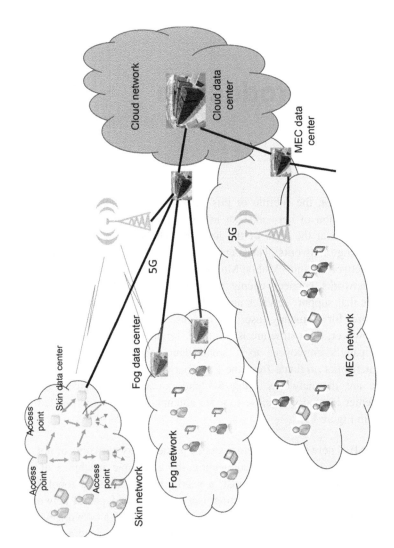

Figure I.1. *An Internet of Edges. For a color version of this figure, see www.iste.co.uk/alagha/networking.zip*

The participatory Internet is a participatory network using a fully distributed Transmission Control Protocol/Internet Protocol (TCP/IP) environment. It is a new paradigm that brings together autonomous direct communications between mobile nodes and the concept of Edge Computing. The user of the participatory Internet is no longer a consumer of the environment's resources but, on the contrary, participates in the realization and life of the digital infrastructure of this new Internet concept. The network is alive; it forms and deforms itself according to its participants. It replaces the classic Internet while using the same protocols in a distributed way and more or less powerful Edge data centers. IP compatibility allows it to connect or disconnect from the Internet without altering its operation. Of course, disconnection can stop some services that require centralized Internet servers. On the other hand, the participatory Internet allows mobility, independence, autonomy, instant deployment and strong security. The participatory Internet is perfectly applicable to companies to manage their information system and their applications while bringing increased security to their IT environment. The participatory Internet is very well suited to telecom operators by allowing immediate extensions of their network. This new concept is also very interesting for integrators by facilitating the introduction of mobile digital infrastructure to customers who need it. The architecture related to the participatory Internet is designed to realize a new world of mobility. It adapts to vehicular networks and is expected to become the standard for the mobile Internet that is bound to emerge with connected vehicles. Many forecasts show that drivers will switch from driving to connecting to the Internet as soon as the vehicle becomes autonomous. As a result, the amount of data flowing through the Internet from mobile devices could reach almost the same value as that from fixed customers. The participatory Internet is also suitable for robot networks, drone networks and all networks in which humans, machines, or objects are in motion. It is particularly suitable for tactical cells and smart spaces. This new paradigm of the participatory Internet is associated with *ad hoc* and mesh technologies in hybrid mode and with data and application processing at the Edge. It is an integral part of the digitization of enterprises and will be integrated into Edge environments that have two other components: the MEC and Fog. These two other components are characterized by more powerful and totally fixed data centers.

The new Internet of Edges generation with participatory networks can be referred to as the uberization of telecommunications since it allows the creation of a network using only machines belonging to users, whether they are the general public or companies. However, this architecture based on participatory networks can also be implemented by telecommunications operators through their users with their smartphones or their Internet box. An Internet of Edges network based on participatory networks can be created using machines that integrate the TCP/IP protocol stack and hosting servers to provide services to clients connected to this network. The machines can be large servers, small computers, or even smartphones. Any electronic device with a processor, memory and network interface is suitable to participate in the creation of a participative network. This network can be interconnected to other networks with gateways to globalize it. The interconnection can be made with other participatory networks but also with more classical Internet networks. In the latter case, a user can go and look for centralized services on the Internet.

Currently, the global Internet works well and satisfies many needs, but it also consumes many resources because of the distance of users from the data centers that have the functions and data needed to provide the services requested. To send a message to its neighbor, the message must travel long distances to reach the server and return to the sender's neighborhood. This also leads to the creation of huge and energy-consuming data centers that are difficult to control and secure. The idea of deglobalizing the Internet makes it possible to use nearby resources to provide a service, like Airbnb or Uber, where anyone with a resource (house, car, etc.) can offer it to enrich the accommodation or transportation offer.

In the rest of this book, we will take an in-depth look at the Internet of Edges but also the reasons for its introduction to easily achieve the digitization of businesses and the industrial world. We will also examine the other two components of Edge Computing, the MEC and the Fog, and their cooperation with the level closest to the user, the Skin level, with a particular interest in participatory networks.

I.2. The digitization of companies

The digitalization of business and industry is the main reason for the extension of digital infrastructures, especially at the edge, whether it be through MECs, Fog data centers, or the participatory Internet, which is located at the level closest to the user.

We have represented in Figure I.2 the different elements of this digitization from networks to applications.

At the digital network level, we find the three main components based on virtualization: Software-defined networking/Network functions virtualization (SDN/NFV), 5G and Cloud-Native technologies. The participatory Internet is also part of digital networks and can use virtualization techniques and be associated with 5G. It can also use the solutions provided by Cloud Native.

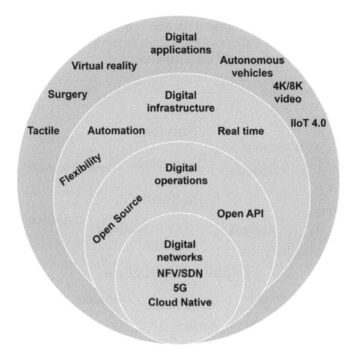

Figure I.2. *The digitization of companies. For a color version of this figure, see www.iste.co.uk/alagha/networking.zip*

Digital operations are increasingly in demand for automation to enable cost reduction by having autonomous networks that can automatically handle the configuration, control and management of the digital infrastructure. Open Source represents the second way to lower the costs of infrastructure. It is necessary to move towards open application interfaces so that network and application modules can be easily interconnected, with the possibility of marketing more efficient proprietary modules that could replace the open-source modules. At the top level of the digital experience, there are real-time applications and generic applications that enable easy implementation of services, optimizations and reliability. Finally, at the highest level, the digital services that can be expected from the entire infrastructure such as high-definition video, applications that bring the virtual such as augmented reality, intelligent applications for the city, building or home, autonomous vehicles, tactile services such as remote surgery and finally the Internet of Industrial Things to realize applications of Industry 4.0.

Overall, three levels are defined in the new IT environments: the digital infrastructure, the platforms and, at the highest level, the services. Figure I.3 describes the IT environment of companies and the industrial world.

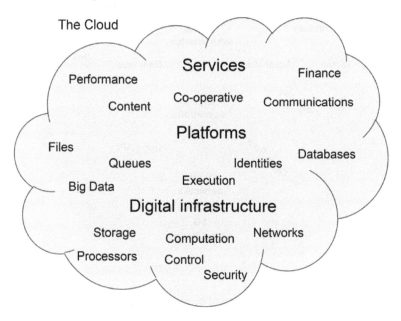

Figure I.3. *The IT environment of an enterprise*

At the level of digital infrastructure, there are two sub-levels: the technical infrastructure composed of hardware, mainly data centers of various sizes, antennas and cables, whether fiber optic or wire cables. The second sub-layer corresponds to the digital software infrastructure, which gathers all the functions of the infrastructure, such as routing, switching, firewall, signal processing, etc.

The layer above forms the platform on which the applications run. This platform is made up of software that enables the simple development of services. Finally, the highest layer, the services layer, contains all the virtual machines that will provide services to the users of the digital infrastructure.

I.3. The different levels of the Edge

Edge Networking is a subset of Edge Computing that comprises the data centers located at the network's edge. Edge Networking deals with the digital infrastructure consisting of infrastructure and application services. These services are integrated into data centers that form a distributed multi-cloud. Three categories of data centers make up this distributed multi-Cloud: the MEC, the Fog and the Skin, as shown in Figure I.4.

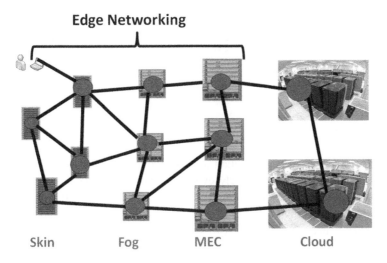

Figure I.4. *The different levels of Edge Computing and the Cloud Computing. For a color version of this figure, see www.iste.co.uk/alagha/networking.zip*

The MEC is the telecom operators' version of virtualizing all the equipment between the customer and the data center: the processes related to the antenna, but also the intermediate equipment such as the Internet boxes. The Cloud-Radio Access Network (Cloud-RAN), and its evolution into the Software-Defined-RAN (SD-RAN) for dynamic management of the sharing of physical layer functions, is part of this MEC environment of Edge Networking.

The Fog represents the data centers of companies that are positioned on their premises and that allow the virtualization of the Local Area Network (LAN) and Wide Area Network (WAN) access equipment and, of course, all the company's business processes. It can be virtualized on a MEC data center if the company outsources its IT and networks to an operator. The Fog allows the realization of virtual Customer Premises Equipment (vCPE) and the support of SD-WAN.

The Skin is a new vision, watched very closely by some of the big Web companies such as Google, which sees an opportunity not to leave room for operators and companies to develop by themselves on the Edge. Indeed, this solution would allow the introduction of proximity marketing which is the future of advertising. The Skin allows tracking of a customer wherever they are, and with a very good knowledge of their instantaneous environment, it is easy to send them customized advertising. Each customer receives a different advertisement than other users. Proximity marketing represents a completely personalized solution to advertising.

These three tiers of Edge networks will co-exist in a distributed multi-cloud. In addition, some companies and organizations will trust their carrier to manage networks and applications from the MEC, others will want to keep control of their IT and network and others will want to be able to set up mobile smart spaces like those found in civil security, events, or mobile worksites.

I.4. Conclusion

The two concepts of centralization and distribution alternate over time, moving from one to the other approximately every 10 years. Centralization arrived in the early 2010s with Cloud Networking and SDN to enable simplified controls and intelligence that was only known to be done centrally. The 2020s should see a return to distribution with an overlay of the two solutions between 2020 and 2025.

This distribution should come back with the paradigm of participatory networks and the Internet of Edges based on participatory networks. The Internet of Edges is a concept that takes up the basic properties of the Internet as they were defined at its birth with a distribution of powers to allow a strong resilience and good security by avoiding points of high sensitivity and distributed management.

In the rest of this book, we will examine the current state of Edge networks coming from the 2010s thinking and reaching maturity and the transition to next-generation distributed networks that will be dominant from 2025.

I.5. References

Aazam, M., Harras, K.A., Zeadally, S. (2019). Fog computing for 5G tactile industrial Internet of Things: QoE-aware resource allocation model. *IEEE Trans. Ind. Inform.*, 15, 3085–3092.

Ahmed, A. and Ahmed, E. (2016). A survey on mobile edge computing. *10th International Conference on Intelligent Systems and Control (ISCO)*, Coimbatore, India, 7–8 January 2016.

Ahmed, E., Gani, A., Khan, M.K., Buyya, R., Khan, S.U. (2015). Seamless application execution in mobile cloud computing: Motivation, taxonomy, and open challenges. *Journal of Network and Computer Applications*, 52, 154–172.

Ahvar, E., Orgerie, A., Lébre, A. (2019). Estimating energy consumption of cloud, fog and edge computing infrastructures. *IEEE Transactions on Sustainable Computing*, 1–12. doi: 10.1109/TSUSC.2019.2905900.

Anttalainen, T. (1999). *Introduction to Telecommunications Network Engineering*. Artech House, Norwood.

Byrne, P. (2017). *Computer Networking*. Larsen and Keller Education, New York.

Clark, M.P. (1997). *Networks and Telecommunications: Design and Operation*. Wiley, New York.

Comer, D.E. (2013). *Internetworking with TCP/IP Volume 1: Principles, Protocols, and Architecture*, 5th edition. Prentice-Hall, Hoboken.

Czarnecki, C. and Dietze, C. (2017). *Reference Architecture for the Telecommunications Industry: Transformation of Strategy, Organization, Processes, Data, and Applications*. Springer, Berlin.

Davies, D.W. and Barber, D.L.A. (1973). *A Communication Networks for Computers*. Wiley, New York.

Elkhodr, M. and Hassan, Q. (2017). *Networks of the Future: Architectures, Technologies, and Implementations*. Chapman & Hall, London.

Fajjari, I., Aitsaadi, N., Pióro, M., Pujolle, G. (2014). A new virtual network static embedding strategy within the Cloud's private backbone network. *Computer Networks*, 62(7), 69–88.

Frahim, J. and Josyula, V. (2017). *Intercloud: Solving Interoperability and Communication in a Cloud of Clouds*. Cisco Press, Indianapolis.

Freeman, R. (1999). *Fundamentals of Telecommunications*. Wiley, New York.

Goralski, W. (2017). *The Illustrated Network, 2nd Edition: How TCP/IP Works in a Modern Network*. Morgan Kaufmann, Burlington.

Hanako, A. (2016). *Communications and Computer Networks*. Clanrye International, New York.

Hérold, J.F. and Guillotin, O. (2015). *Informatique industrielle et réseaux*. Dunod, Malakoff.

Kurose, J.F. and Ross, K.W. (2016). *Computer Networking*. Addison-Wesley, New York.

Lohier, S. and Présent, D. (2016). *Réseaux et transmissions – Protocoles, infrastructures et services*. Dunod, Malakoff.

Macchi, C. and Guilbert, J.-F. (1988). *Téléinformatique*. Dunod, Malakoff.

Mckenzie, V.D. (2017). *Mobile Networks: Concepts, Applications and Performance Analysis.* Nova Science Publishers Inc., Hauppauge, New York.

Musa, S. and Wu, Z. (2017). *Aeronautical Telecommunications Network: Advances, Challenges, and Modeling.* CRC Press, Boca Raton.

Oliver, N. and Oliver, V. (2006). *Computer Networks: Principles, Technologies and Protocols for Network Design.* Wiley, New York.

Peterson, L. and Davie, B.S. (2017). *Computer Networks, 4th Edition: A Systems Approach.* Morgan Kaufmann, Burlington.

Pujolle, G. (2019). *Les réseaux.* Eyrolles, Paris.

Robertazzi, T.G. (2017). *Introduction to Computer Networking.* Springer, Berlin.

Robinson, D. (2017). *Content Delivery Networks: Fundamentals, Design, and Evolution.* Wiley, New York.

Rojas-Cessa, R. (2017). *Interconnections for Computer Communications and Packet Networks.* CRC Press, Boca Raton.

Severance, C.R. (2015). *Introduction to Networking: How the Internet Works.* Create Space Independent Publishing Platform, Scotts Valley.

Tanenbaum, S. (2010). *Computer Networks.* Prentice-Hall, Hoboken.

Valdar, A. (2017). *Understanding Telecommunications Networks.* IET Press, London.

White, C. (2015). *Data Communications and Computer Networks: A Business User's Approach.* Cengage, Boston.

1

Edge Architectures

1.1. The three levels of Edge Networking

The four-tier distributed multi-cloud architecture is becoming the standard. The levels correspond to four types of data centers that form the basis for the digitalization of various companies and organizations. Large data centers symbolize the Cloud with almost infinite computing and storage power. However, these data centers are far from the users with high latency to reach them. Many applications cannot run with these latencies. In addition, the energy consumption per client is very high since the information flows have to pass through many intermediate machines. However, these data centers are indispensable for applications that require power and for particularly consistent storage. The most important data centers belong to the GAFAM companies (Google, Apple, Facebook, Amazon and Microsoft), but also the BATX (Baidu, Alibaba, Tencent and Xiaomi).

For several years, data centers at the edge of networks have become increasingly important for many reasons. Latency allows the introduction of new services that are becoming preponderant for the digitalization, intelligence and security of companies, administrations and public services. For example, Industry 4.0, with IIoT (Industrial IoT), smart grid control, short-latency applications, etc. are examples of these services. These applications have been highlighted by a number of companies. These applications have been highlighted by 5G, which must have an important place in the digital infrastructure of the Edge. Next-generation Wi-Fi should not be forgotten as convergence with 5G has now clearly started. The diagram in Figure 1.1 shows the Edge environment of a network.

Edge Networking,
by Khaldoun AL AGHA, Pauline LOYGUE and Guy PUJOLLE. © ISTE Ltd 2022.

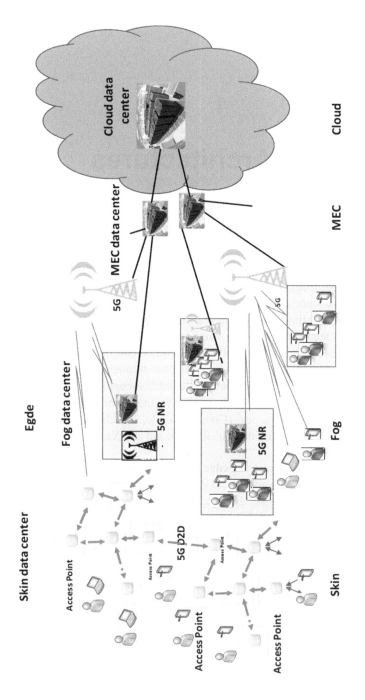

Figure 1.1. *The distributed cloud environment. For a color version of this figure, see www.iste.co.uk/alagha/networking.zip*

Three levels of Edge Computing are being implemented to define a distributed multi-Cloud. The most advanced in its definition and deployment concerns the MEC (Mobile/Multi-access Edge Computing) data centers of 5G operators, which enable the virtualization of numerous telecom devices and the introduction of new services that are well described in the 3GPP specifications and which concern the Internet of Things, mission-critical services with high reliability and very high speeds in mobility.

The second level, defined a long time ago, concerns Fog Networking. The word Fog was introduced by Cisco in 2013. Initially, Fog Computing was used to manage streams from objects to pre-process them before sending them to a central Cloud. Today, Fog Networking is linked to enterprise data centers that virtualize local network equipment such as routers, switches, firewalls, authentication servers and many middleboxes with control and management functions. The vCPE (virtual customer premises equipment) uses Fog data centers.

The third level is the one that is the focus of this book. It has various names that have not yet stabilized, such as Very Edge Networking, the home data center, Mist-Computing or Skin Computing, which we will use in the following. These structures are generally related to the participatory Internet, although we can see star systems around a data center. For a participatory network, the tiny data centers are located very close to the user or even on the user. These are small but powerful servers that support virtualization. These Skin data centers must be light, autonomous and consume very little energy since they can be mobile and follow the users like firemen during a fire. The advantages come from the extremely short latency time, their low energy consumption and their mobility, not to mention their security by disconnecting them from the Internet thanks to their autonomy as soon as necessary.

The four levels we have described overlap, and no one level is expected to be dominant in the future. The distributed Cloud was born from this observation. To optimize performance, services must be positioned as virtual machines (VM) or containers that users need at the right level of the architecture. This level is highly dependent on the application and its performance, control, management and security characteristics.

These digital infrastructure services, whether infrastructure or application services, are divided into microservices encapsulated in virtual machines or containers. We will see in the next chapter the platform architectures and this decomposition into microservices. An even finer decomposition is emerging in the early 2020s with the decomposition into functions. A microservice is, therefore, a set of functions.

1.2. Edge Computing architectures

The three main architectures associated with the services, carried by the data centers of the different levels of the Edge, come from the OIF (Open Infrastructure Forum), the Cloud Native of the CNCF (Cloud Native Computing Foundation) and the EECC (European Edge Computing Consortium). In Figures 1.2A and B, we have depicted the main elements of these three environments.

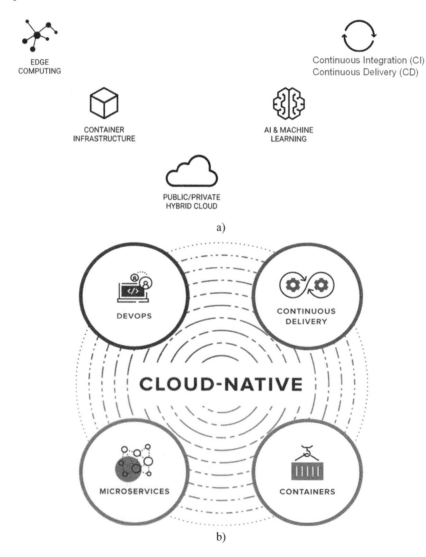

Figure 1.2A. *The basic elements of OIF (a) and CNCF (b)*

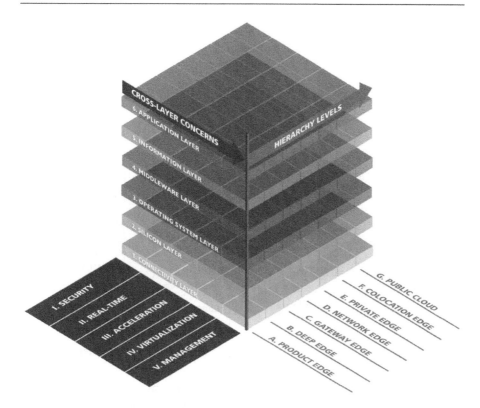

Figure 1.2B. *The basic elements of the EECC (continued). For a color version of this figure, see www.iste.co.uk/alagha/networking.zip*

Notably, the Telco Edge Cloud (TEC) is an initiative that started in 2020 and aims to define an Edge architecture allowing interoperability between operators.

An intelligent digital infrastructure on the Edge requires the deployment of a distributed multi-Cloud distributed framework using 5G and Wi-Fi integration. This generation also relies on infrastructure and application services that must make businesses and organizations more agile, flexible and independent of the web giants. Figure 1.3 shows the evolution of these architectures up to the 2020s that we are interested in here.

In Figure 1.3, looking at the architecture of the 2020s, we see many changes. The physical infrastructure, or technical infrastructure, now contains only three elements: the antennas, optical fibers and data centers. Everything else is virtualized in the data centers. All the boxes have disappeared from this architecture. Indeed, the functions associated with these boxes are virtualized in one of the data centers with urbanization to determine its level Edge or Cloud. This vision of the physical infrastructure is not relevant for participatory networks at the endpoints, which can be mobile and which we will describe a little further on.

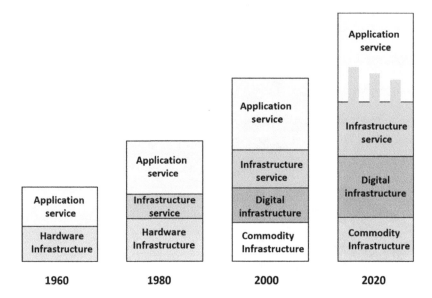

Figure 1.3. *The evolution of architectures. For a color version of this figure, see www.iste.co.uk/alagha/networking.zip*

Above the physical infrastructure is the digital infrastructure, which contains all the functions related to the physical infrastructure to make it work. These are the functions found in boxes such as Wi-Fi boxes, routers, switches, firewalls, etc. Again, these functions are positioned at the different levels associated with Skin, Fog, MEC or Cloud data centers.

Infrastructure services correspond to all the basic functions that can be used by the application services. Infrastructure services are the services provided to meet general requirements, including technical and software solutions, such as interoperability, security, middleware and network or distributed systems services. Infrastructure services also include the management and control of application services. These services are becoming part of the application services as they integrate more and more functions that used to be put directly into the application service but are now available directly to all applications that want to use them rather than being found in parallel at the level of each application.

We are now going to take a closer look at the two most widely used digital infrastructures, which initially came from the major Web industries but now have the support of almost all industries: the OIF and the CNCF.

OIF took over the OpenStack Alliance in 2020. Open Stack is a Cloud management system that is widely used by Cloud providers and operators. However, the Cloud is not enough to define an infrastructure. This is the reason for the birth of OIF: to add to the Cloud and to virtualization the ingredients to build a complete infrastructure.

OpenStack was born in 2010 with the merger of two projects, Rackspace (Storage) and NASA (Compute). OpenStack is developed in Python and distributed under the Apache 2.0 license. The versions started with A, then B, etc. The latest are:

– Queens (2018, 02);

– Rocky (2018, 08);

– Stein (2019, 04);

– Train (2019, 10);

– Ussuri (2020, 05);

– Victoria (2020, 10);

– Wallaby (2021, 04).

OpenStack contains a large number of modules that allow you to build a complete Cloud. Some of these modules are described in Figure 1.4. They include:

– heat: orchestration component;

– neutron: network and addressing management;

– nova: management of the computing resources;

– cinder: block storage;

– swift: object storage;

– glance: disk image service;

– ceilometer: metric-based telemetry;

– keystone identity service.

OpenStack is a complete environment that is increasingly being introduced in commercial software. However, while it supports virtualization techniques well, it needs to be complemented by other open-source Cloud infrastructure software. For example, IOF integrates Magma for Edge infrastructure, offering both cellular (5G) and Wi-Fi services and the OpenInfra Labs. It includes, for example, the Wenjua project that provides services to shorten the introduction time needed to integrate artificial intelligence. The OIF architecture includes, of course, Kubernetes to orchestrate the containers.

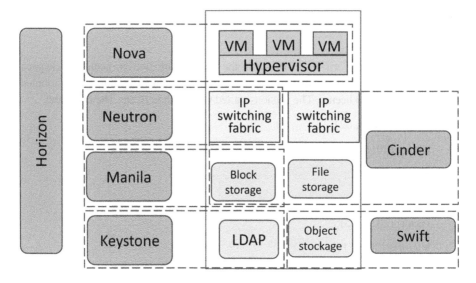

Figure 1.4. *Some modules of the OpenStack open-source software. For a color version of this figure, see www.iste.co.uk/alagha/networking.zip*

The second major architecture is the Cloud Native Computing Foundation (CNCF). This is a project of the Linux Foundation that was founded in 2015 to help advance container technology and align the technology industry around its evolution. Founding members include Google, CoreOS, Mesosphere, Red Hat, Twitter, Huawei, Intel, Cisco, IBM, Docker, Univa and VMware. Today, the CNCF is supported by nearly 500 members.

CNCF technology projects are cataloged with a Sandbox, Incubated and Graduated maturity level in ascending order. The CNCF process incorporates projects as Incubated projects and then aims to progress them to Graduated, which involves a level of process and technology maturity.

The main properties of the CNCF architecture are shown in Figure 1.5.

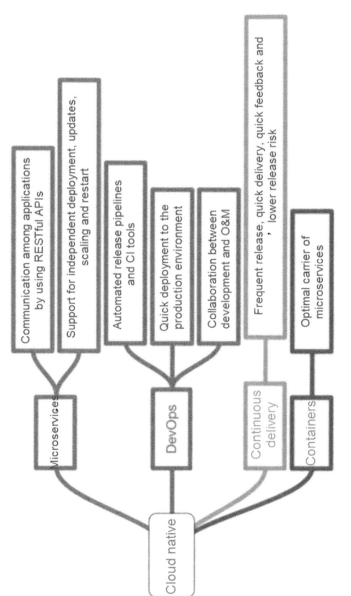

Figure 1.5. *The main properties of the CNCF architecture. For a color version of this figure, see www.iste.co.uk/alagha/networking.zip*

Cloud-native architecture brings the fluidity, resiliency and scalability of Cloud architectures, which contributes to their appeal to organizations that favor a DevOps philosophy. A Cloud-native approach offers the benefits we describe below.

The use of loosely coupled services instead of a monolithic stack. The use of loosely coupled services, instead of a monolithic stack, gives development teams the ability to choose the framework, language or system that best meets the specific goals of an organization or project. The portability of microservices in containers ensures that an organization is not overly dependent on one Cloud provider. The complexity of troubleshooting is reduced since an open-source container orchestration platform like Kubernetes makes it easy to identify a problematic container without shutting down the entire application.

Because microservices operate independently of each other, developers can optimize them one by one for core functionality and ultimately enrich the end-user experience. Using microservices in software development facilitates continuous integration and continuous delivery efforts, reducing the development lifecycle and the risk of human error with automated processes. In addition, a container orchestrator can automatically schedule and allocate resources based on demand to increase efficiency.

The use of microservices for application architecture allows developers to make changes to a microservice or offer new features without affecting the overall application and its availability. The overall CNCF architecture is described in Figure 1.6.

Of the several tens of billions of containerized services in operation by the end of 2021, two-thirds migrate daily. Most of these migrations (70%), take place within the same data center, essentially to cluster and unbundle them with the objective of minimizing energy consumption. Between different data centers, the figure is down to 10%, but the arrival of the distributed Cloud will certainly change the situation.

The process of migrating services and microservices must be optimized and secured in the Edge and Cloud Computing environment. Migrations allow services and microservices to be moved from one level to another, taking into account an urbanization algorithm. These architectures are moving toward a container environment orchestrated by Kubernetes and using CaaS (container as a service) or FaaS (function as a service) techniques in a serverless environment. This environment is deployed on the different levels of the architecture.

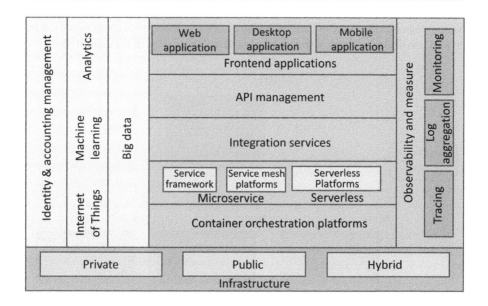

Figure 1.6. *The global architecture of the CNCF. For a color version of this figure, see www.iste.co.uk/alagha/networking.zip*

All modern architectures are moving toward containerization, that is, the use of containers that form the equivalent of virtual machines running on the same operating system, usually Linux. To dynamically allocate resources to the microservices that are encapsulated in the containers, you need an orchestration system that automatically allocates resources. Kubernetes is open-source software that has become essential. Figure 1.7 describes the Kubernetes container orchestrator.

Kubernetes was originally designed by Google and is now maintained by the CNCF. It aims to provide a platform for automating the deployment, scaling and operations of application containers. Kubernetes works with a range of tools to set up containers in a cluster, often with images created using Docker.

Kubernetes defines a set of primitives that collectively provide mechanisms that deploy, maintain and scale applications based on CPU, memory or custom metrics. Kubernetes is loosely coupled and extensible to meet different workloads. This scalability is provided in large part by the Kubernetes API, which is used by internal components as well as by the extensions and containers that run on top of Kubernetes. The platform exercises control over computational and storage resources by defining resources as objects that can then be managed as such. Kubernetes components can be divided into those that manage an individual node and those parts of the control plane.

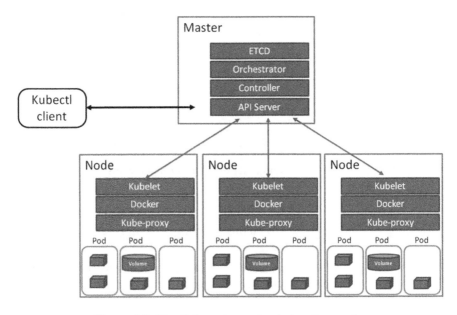

Figure 1.7. *The Kubernetes orchestrator. For a color version of this figure, see www.iste.co.uk/alagha/networking.zip*

Many Cloud services offer a Kubernetes-based platform as a service (PaaS) or infrastructure as a service (IaaS) on which Kubernetes can be deployed as a platform delivery service. Many providers also offer their own Kubernetes distributions.

The basic scheduling unit in Kubernetes is a pod, as shown in Figure 1.7. A pod is a grouping of containerized components. A pod consists of one or more containers that are guaranteed to be co-located on the same node. Each pod in Kubernetes is assigned a unique IP address within the cluster, allowing applications to use ports without the risk of conflict. All containers can reference each other within the pod, but a container in one pod has no way to directly address another container in another pod. If it wishes to perform such an action, it must use the IP address of the pod.

A pod can define a volume, such as a local disk directory or a network disk, and expose it to the pod containers. Pods can be managed manually via the Kubernetes API, or their management can be delegated to a controller that is located in the master node.

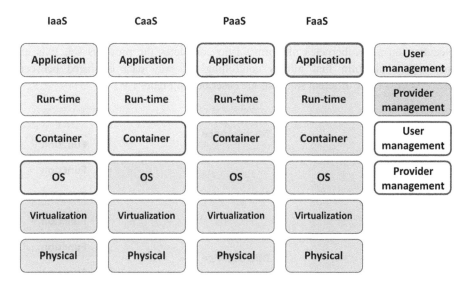

Figure 1.8. *CaaS and FaaS architectures. For a color version of this figure, see www.iste.co.uk/alagha/networking.zip*

Two solutions have been developed strongly since 2020 to complete the environment on top of Kubernetes: CaaS and FaaS. These two solutions are described in Figure 1.8.

The CaaS solution is the one most often seen today. The FaaS solution is expected to become the standard in the coming years. The CaaS solution, as shown in Figure 1.8, requires the digital infrastructure provider to support the hardware, virtualization and operating system, while the customer developing on this environment must support the containers, the runtime environment and, of course, the application. FaaS technology completely hides the containers, so-called serverless techniques, by allowing developers to work with simple functions that form a subset of microservices.

We describe in Figure 1.9 the three solutions for obtaining a development platform. The first one, the most classical so far, concerns monolithic developments on a PaaS platform. The most popular solution today is CaaS, given the breakthrough of containers in Cloud computing architecture. The solution that is starting to gain ground is FaaS which should greatly simplify development on Edge and Cloud platforms.

All architectures today integrate containers and the Kubernetes orchestrator. It is becoming more and more standard to use serverless technology on top of Kubernetes.

On top of this, several open-source solutions are available such as Knative (Cloud-Native serverless). Knative allows serverless deployment of applications and their execution on all Kubernetes platforms. Istio completes the previous set. It is an open-source platform that allows controlling the way data is shared between microservices. These different solutions are described in Figure 1.9.

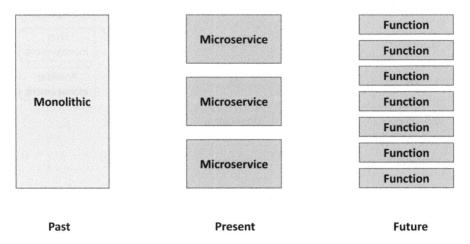

Figure 1.9. *Service architectures. For a color version of this figure, see www.iste.co.uk/alagha/networking.zip*

1.3. Security and domain name system on Edge

Security on Edge will be ensured by solutions provided by 5G and will be based mainly on embedded SIM (eSIM) and the new generation of SIMs: integrated SIM (iSIM). The eSIM is a SIM card integrated into a device (mobile, tablet or connected objects). It is no longer necessary to insert a physical SIM card to allow a device to transmit information using the connections of a mobile network. An eSIM environment is described in Figure 1.10.

The eSIM contains the smartphone's internal component (embedded universal integrated circuit card, eUICC), which allows managing profiles corresponding to specific SIM cards which are managed remotely in the subscription manager–data preparation (SM-DP+) server or even in remote servers through a discovery service offered by a subscription manager-discovery server (SM-DS). This is sometimes referred to as a virtual SIM since the profiles are located remotely and no longer directly in the smartphone's SIM card.

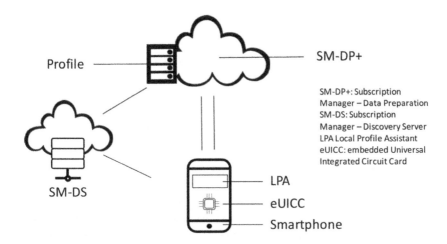

Figure 1.10. *An eSIM environment*

An iSIM card is a miniaturized SIM card with an equally small modem. This assembly is grafted onto the platform that hosts the processor and memory, commonly called the System on a Chip (SoC). The advantage of this solution comes from the integration of a SIM card in each hardware, whether it is tiny or large. In particular, each communicating object will be able to have its own SIM card, which will make it possible to easily introduce a high level of security compared to today, when many objects are very easily attacked because they are protected by software passwords.

The domain name system (DNS) or domain name resolution system is one of the essential building blocks of the Internet today and one of the vectors for spying on and attacking the various Web services. DNS resolution consists of associating a Web address with an IP address in order to route traffic correctly. It is a distributed database system built in a hierarchical manner. DNS servers allow the publication of the correspondence of a DNS address with an IP address through the publication of a DNS zone. But, in order to be able to identify the DNS servers allowing the resolution of a domain, it is essential to have DNS resolvers.

The resolver is the building block for identifying the DNS servers that contain the zone information for a given domain through a recursive search of the DNS servers. Resolvers can be accessible only in a given network, in which case they are identified as private resolvers, or they can be private resolvers, or they can be publicly accessible, in which case they are called public resolvers.

Until now, DNS resolution has been done via the UDP protocol, but several new DNS resolution methods have appeared to complement the initial protocol in order to better secure communications between the resolver and the client, guarantee the reliability of the resolution and allow private resolution. Among the extensions to the DNS protocol that make it more secure is DNS over HTTPS (DoH), which allows DNS requests to be transported via the HTTPS protocol. The DoH protocol is relatively recent and will be integrated via browsers such as Chrome and Firefox.

1.4. The digital infrastructure of the participatory Internet

The participatory Internet is based on a particular physical and digital infrastructure since it can be mobile. The participatory Internet combines Edge Computing with its Skin data centers located close to the users and interconnection of these data centers by a mobile, flexible and autonomous network, the whole forming a distributed Edge Cloud close to the users. The users participate in this flexibility, and their resources are added to the digital infrastructure of the participatory Internet. Participatory Internet infrastructure is described in Figure 1.11.

In the diagram in Figure 1.11, five smart boxes, or Skin data centers, are interconnected by wireless technology such as Wi-Fi, but any technology is possible as long as it allows communication between boxes within an acceptable distance. The boxes contain the digital infrastructure, the infrastructure services and the application services in such a way that even without connection to the Internet, the system continues to function. The interest in this infrastructure also comes from the mobility of the boxes, their possible disappearance without impact on the network and the connection of new boxes, which must be done automatically.

Users can be participants in a tactical bubble, in a smart environment like a smart city, or employees of a company to build the company's digital infrastructure or individuals to build a cluster where resources are shared.

The word participatory comes from the boxes that can be owned by the users, and that participate in the network infrastructure. These boxes are the nodes of the network. They are small data centers capable of managing virtualization to allow the transfer of a service or microservice from one box to another. However, the participatory Internet owes its own infrastructure to be able to detach itself from the central Internet. Since the network is mobile and nodes can appear and disappear, the services included in the infrastructure must be distributed in order to continue to function, regardless of the number of active and interconnected devices. The infrastructure adopts a mesh technology for interconnecting nodes with the possibility of mobility or not. The most interesting case is obviously that of mobility, where all the nodes can move and follow the users as they move.

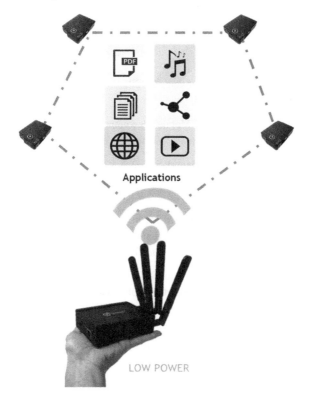

Figure 1.11. *Participatory Internet infrastructure (©Green Communications).* *For a color version of this figure, see www.iste.co.uk/alagha/networking.zip*

The most classical infrastructures of the participatory Internet can be symbolized by the vehicular networks that we will study in Chapter 7. Chapter 4 will also be devoted to the digital infrastructure of the participatory Internet in order to describe it in detail.

1.5. Conclusion

Infrastructure is going digital. While it has taken its place first by the large Cloud data centers, it is now being defined on the Edge and concerns consumer and enterprise users. This new digital infrastructure is positioned on the edges of the network. It must enable users to connect their terminals and provide them directly, quickly and securely with all the functions they need. To do this, these functions are virtualized in data centers to introduce great flexibility, agility and the ability to deploy any service very easily and almost instantly.

1.6. References

Abbas, N., Zhang, Y., Taherkordi, A., Skeie, T. (2018). Mobile edge computing: A survey. *IEEE Internet Things*, 5(1), 450–465.

Ahmed, E. and Rehmani, M.H. (2017). Mobile edge computing: Opportunities, solutions, and challenges. *Future Generation Computer Systems*, 70, 59–63.

Ahmed, E., Gani, A., Sookhak, M., Ab Hamid, S.H., Xia, F. (2015a). Application optimization in mobile cloud computing: Motivation, taxonomies, and open challenges. *Journal of Network and Computer Applications*, 52, 52–68.

Ahmed, E., Akhunzada, A., Whaiduzzaman, M., Gani, A., Ab Hamid, S.H., Buyya, R. (2015b). Network-centric performance analysis of runtime application migration in mobile cloud computing. *Simulation Modelling Practice and Theory*, 50, 42–56.

Ahmed, E., Naveed, A., Gani, A., Ab Hamid, S.H., Imran, M., Guizani, M. (2017a). Process state synchronization for mobility support in mobile cloud computing. *Proceedings IEEE Xplore, International Conference on Communications (ICC)*, IEEE, New York.

Ahmed, E., Ahmed, A., Yaqoob, I., Shuja, J., Gani, A., Imran, M., Shoaib, M. (2017b). Bringing computation closer toward the user network: Is edge computing the solution? *IEEE Communications Magazine*, 55(11), 138–144.

Ahmed, A., Naveed, A., Gani, A., Ab Hamid, S.H., Imran, M., Guizani, M. (2019). Process state synchronization-based application execution management for mobile edge/cloud computing. *Future Generation Computer Systems*, 91, 579–589.

Kraemer, F.A., Braten, A.E., Tamkittikhun, N., Palma, N. (2017). Fog computing in healthcare – A review and discussion. *IEEE Access*, 5, 9206–9222.

Moura, J. and Hutchison, D. (2019). Game theory for multi-access edge computing: Survey, use cases, and future trends. *IEEE Commun. Surveys Tuts.*, 21(1), 260–288.

Open Edge Computing (2022). Open Edge Computing [Online]. Available at: https://www. openedgecomputing.org/ [Accessed 4 October 2019].

Pan, J. and McElhannon, J. (2018). Future edge cloud and edge computing for Internet of Things applications. *IEEE Internet of Things Journal*, 5(1), 439–449.

Porambage, P., Okwuibe, J., Liyanage, M., Ylianttila, M., Taleb, T. (2018). Survey on multi-access Edge computing for Internet of Things realization. *IEEE Commun. Surveys Tuts.*, 20(4), 2961–2991.

Satyanarayanan, M. (2017). The emergence of edge computing. *Computer*, 50(1), 30–39.

Singh, H. (2017). *Implementing Cisco Networking Solutions*. Packt Publishing, Birmingham.

Sun, X. and Ansari, N. (2016). EdgeIoT: Mobile edge computing for the Internet of Things. *IEEE Communications Magazine*, 54(12), 22–29.

Taleb, T., Samdanis, K., Mada, B., Flinck, H., Dutta, S., Sabella, D. (2017). On multi-access edge computing: A survey of the emerging 5G network edge cloud architecture and orchestration. *IEEE Commun. Surveys Tuts.*, 19(3), 1657–1681.

2

MEC Networks

As described in the previous chapters, there are three levels in the Edge. We will describe them in the next three chapters. We will look at how participatory networks fit into these different contexts.

2.1. The MEC level of 5G architecture

Let us start by describing the mobile network environment and then look in more detail at the three sets that make up a mobile network and look at Mobile Edge Computing or Multi-access Edge Computing (MEC). The reason for the change in MEC nomenclature is a broader vision that includes Wi-Fi rather than just 5G.

Figure 2.1 describes the three main parts of a mobile network. The radio forms the transmission from the terminal equipment to the antenna. This part was specified by the 3GPP in Phase 1 in June 2018, and products have been available since early 2020. The architectures of the Radio Access Network (RAN) and Core Network were specified in June 2020, and the products are available as of 2022. Finally, Phase 3, available in June 2022, specifies applications and add-ons to the three parts. The full 5G will, therefore, be available around 2023 for deployment around 2024.

In Figure 2.1, the MEC data center truly represents the 5G revolution by introducing virtualization of all necessary functions in infrastructure and application services. This is the architecture of the digital infrastructure of the 2020s.

Edge Networking,
by Khaldoun AL AGHA, Pauline LOYGUE and Guy PUJOLLE. © ISTE Ltd 2022.

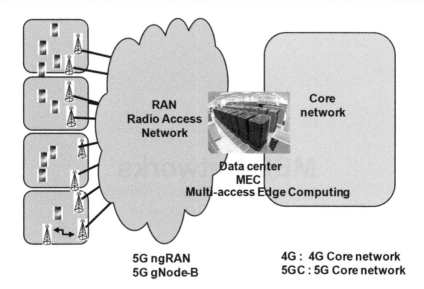

Figure 2.1. *The 5G environment. For a color version of this figure, see www.iste.co.uk/alagha/networking.zip*

The first evolution concerns peak throughput, which is expected to be between 1 and 10 Gbps for all users of a 5G antenna. The second evolution deals with the services available in the context of 5G. In particular, these services deal with the Internet of Things. The objects come from the medical world, home automation, vehicles, cities, etc. These are also services that require very short reaction times, such as real-time vehicle control and finally, services that require very high data rates in mobility.

Figure 2.2 represents the different types of communications supported by 5G. If we start on the left side of the figure, we discover the multi-hop communications that form the basis of participatory networks. In other words, participatory networks allow 5G to be extended: terminals too far from the 5G antenna see their signals pass through intermediate machines to reach the antenna.

This solution could limit the number of large antennas while covering a large area. Participatory networks provide this type of service with routing algorithms between the terminal machines.

Figure 2.2 shows the Device to Device (D2D) or direct communication from a terminal to another terminal without passing through a large antenna. This solution is highly ecological by saving energy, minimizing the flow through the antenna and reducing electromagnetic pollution. Figure 2.2 also describes Machine to Machine (M2M), Machine to Human (M2H) connections as well as the connection of objects represented by medical, home automation, or other equipment. Finally, the figure describes another participatory network that connects vehicles in the form of a vehicular network.

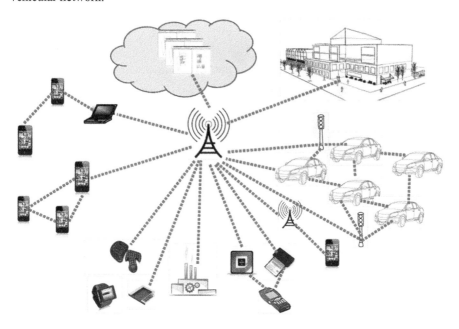

Figure 2.2. *The different 5G accesses. For a color version of this figure, see www.iste.co.uk/alagha/networking.zip*

Figure 2.3 describes the transition from 4G to 5G. In 4G, applications look for a remote data center that is in the core network. In 5G, each access to the core network passes through a MEC data center, allowing very low latencies of less than one millisecond.

In summary, 5G networks are expected to enable the integration of multiple participatory networks or, more accurately, clusters of participatory networks to realize an Internet of Edges.

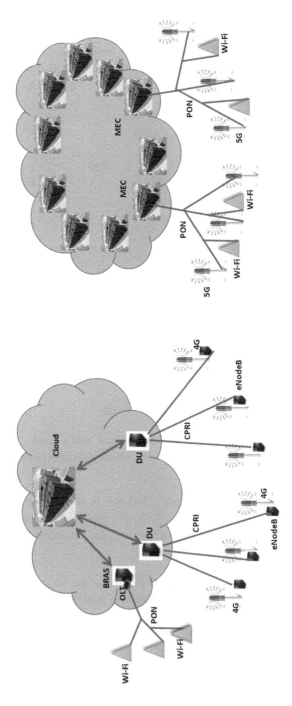

Figure 2.3. *Transition from 4G to 5G. For a color version of this figure, see www.iste.co.uk/alagha/networking.zip*

2.2. 5G

In this section, we will describe 5G, which is an important support for building MEC networks that can include D2D extensions to connect nodes in a participatory network together. The 5G infrastructure also allows Edges to be interconnected with each other.

The 5G radio network is capable of offering very different services, such as connecting objects requiring particularly low data rates and connecting smartphones moving at high speeds of up to 500 km/h. Radio uses a set of new techniques and new frequency bands such as the 3.2–3.8 GHz band or more recently the 24–28 GHz band. The radio access 5G has also been specified for use in free bands: the New Radio Unlicensed (NR-U). This new paradigm will be mostly used in enterprise Fog networks. It gives rise to private 5G networks using the new band being released, which includes all frequencies of the 6 GHz band and a little more, with a total of 1.2 GHz of bandwidth. It is therefore possible in 5G to have licensed exclusive, licensed non-exclusive and unlicensed bands. The 5G system deals with both the licensed and unlicensed spectrum, and in both cases, the interfaces can be shared between multiple operators. This view is encouraged by regulators to optimize the use of frequency resources that are expensive and sometimes underutilized by one operator, while another operator may be overloaded by a lack of frequency resources.

The antenna access technologies developed over many years for 2G, 3G and 4G are complex and varied; a new unified radio interface has been developed that offers flexibility and adaptability. This new unified access interface includes resource blocks and configuration mechanisms to automatically adapt the signal shape, protocols, frame structure, coding, modulation and multiple access schemes. With these resource blocks and mechanisms, the air interface is able to easily support the full range of 5G spectrum bands, traffic, qualities of service and, more generally, the properties associated with the various applications.

The key technology components, shown in Figure 2.4, include new technology for optimizing the use of frequency bands by using specific waveforms, Filtered Orthogonal Frequency Division Multiplexing (F-OFDM), a new multiple access technology, Sparse Code Multiple Access (SCMA), a new error correction code, the Polar Code, replacing the turbocodes, the duplex mode and Massive MIMO. The new air interface design advances spectral efficiency, improves connectivity and reduces latency, facilitating the deployment of new use cases such as the integration of large numbers of sensors in smart cities or the use of virtual reality requiring very high data rates, or the control of autonomous vehicles.

F-OFDM is a fundamental element in operating multiple subcarriers simultaneously in a given frequency band. The technology defines the waveforms; more precisely, it defines different waveforms, access patterns and frame structures depending on the application scenarios and the needs for the realization of service. The solution allows the coexistence of different waveforms associated with OFDM parameters, as illustrated in Figure 2.5. By allowing different parameter configurations, F-OFDM is able to provide an optimal choice of parameters for each service group and thus a better overall system efficiency.

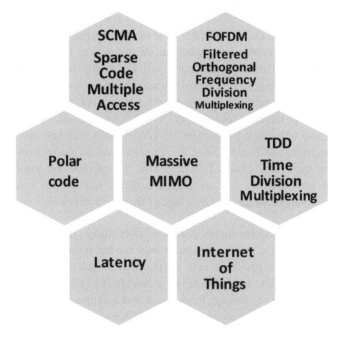

Figure 2.4. *Key technology components of 5G*

Other noteworthy news for 5G is the arrival of Massive MIMO. This technique uses a very large number of antennas allowing the connection of M antennas to K devices where M is very large compared to K. An illustration of this technique is given in Figure 2.6. Massive MIMO is a commercially attractive solution, as it has an efficiency that can be one hundred to one thousand times higher than 4G techniques. The idea is to achieve multiple simultaneous communications using the same time-frequency resource. This technique greatly increases spectral efficiency.

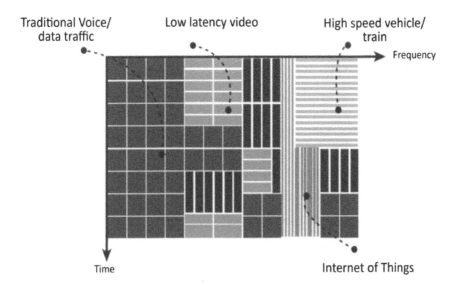

Figure 2.5. *Coexistence of different waveforms associated with F-OFDM. For a color version of this figure, see www.iste.co.uk/alagha/networking.zip*

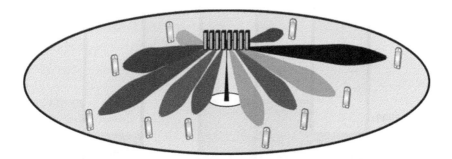

Figure 2.6. *A massive MIMO system. For a color version of this figure, see www.iste.co.uk/alagha/networking.zip*

The main technique of the core network is called slicing, which is a network that forms a slice of an infrastructure. In fact, a slice is a virtual network. The core network is, therefore, a set of virtual networks sharing the same infrastructure. A slice can be:

– a network to connect objects (i.e. the Internet of Things);

– a network to control autonomous vehicles;

– a network to manage industrial processes;

– an MPLS network;

– a network for VoIP.

These types of virtual networks are called horizontal slices.

However, a slice can cover other types of networks which could be the following:

– a network for each major application;

– a network for a large company;

– a network for a small business;

– one network per user.

These types of virtual networks are called vertical slices. In the long term, the 5G core network will be made up of horizontal and vertical slices, as shown in Figure 2.7.

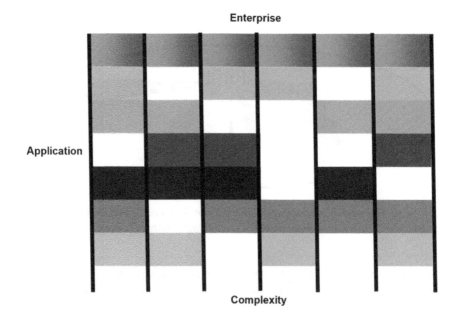

Figure 2.7. *The long-term 5G core network. For a color version of this figure, see www.iste.co.uk/alagha/networking.zip*

One of the complex problems to solve is the urbanization of virtual machines and the global control of the infrastructure network. Indeed, the slices must be isolated to avoid attacks from a virtual network that could destroy the other slices. If the slices are very different from each other, each must have its own management and control system. The slice may also use the same protocols, and, in this case, a common management system is possible, but you have to be sure that the management and control system cannot be attacked. This seems impossible to prove. However, it is necessary to share resources in order to achieve high utilization, which means lower costs. Figure 2.8 shows a diagram produced by 3GPP introducing the large starting slices and the additional slices that will be added little by little. In the long run, there could be a slice set up at the request of a user for a particular service and that is destroyed after use.

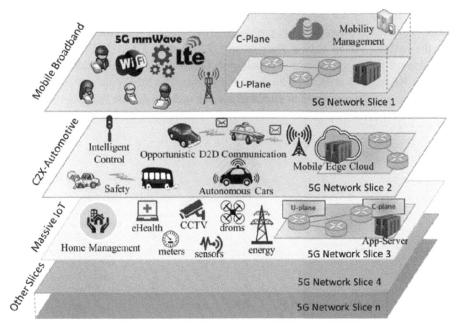

Figure 2.8. *The basic slicing of the 5G core network (©3GPP). For a color version of this figure, see www.iste.co.uk/alagha/networking.zip*

2.3. 5G Edge

The 5G Edge lies between the Fog and the Cloud. It concerns the largest data centers on the Edge by supporting users connected through a 5G link. The MEC data center introduced in this architecture aims to virtualize the entire edge. 5G specifies a new vision of the Edge that goes by the name of Cloud-RAN or C-RAN.

The C-RAN is a proposal made in 2010 by China Telecom to change the access and backhaul networks between the core network and the edge. The C-RAN architecture is cloud-based: all control algorithms are handled by data centers. To realize the 5G architecture, one could have continued to use traditional base station access networks. However, the paradigm of virtualization being there, the C-RAN has followed this revolution with an access network that disappears and is replaced by a solution where the antenna-related functions are grouped in MEC data centers. As a result, the radio signal goes directly to the data center. The radio signal is transferred to the cloud in digital form after digitization of the signal is received by the antenna. The signal processing is done in the Cloud. The original C-RAN is described in Figure 2.9. The terminals are connected to the antennas, which retransmit the signals to a MEC data center where they are processed. The signal is forwarded after reception by the antenna via an optical fiber using a Radio over Fiber (RoF) transmission. Another advantage of the RoF technology is that it can handle very different signals such as 3G, 4G, 5G or Wi-Fi with the same antenna. The MEC data center untangles the signals and determines their characteristics in order to decode them.

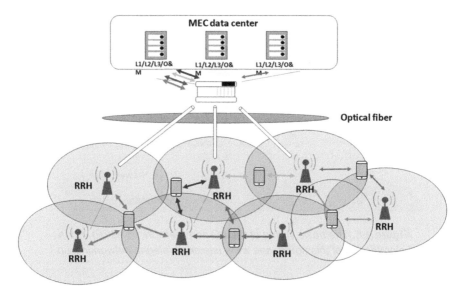

Figure 2.9. *The fully centralized Cloud-RAN architecture. For a color version of this figure, see www.iste.co.uk/alagha/networking.zip*

Other advantages can also be highlighted, such as the low attenuation of the signal on the fiber, so that the data center can be far from the source, up to several kilometers or even several tens of kilometers, to keep the latency time very short. The connection cost is low due to the multiplexing of the antennas on the same fiber. The complexity of the access network is removed, and the data center is managing this complexity with adapted virtual machines. This technology can be found in the cabling of some large stadiums or shopping malls. Also, to reduce costs, several antennas can be multiplexed on the same data center.

The main disadvantage comes from the Fiber to the Antenna (FTTA) cabling that is necessary to realize the communication because the signal bandwidth is important, and its digitization requires a number of samples higher than twice the bandwidth. If the antenna location is not wired, the cost of deploying the optical fiber to connect the antenna can become very important, especially if civil works are required. The optical fiber is connected to the data center by a BaseBand Unit (BBU) and on the other side connected to the physical antenna by a Remote Radio Head (RRH).

The current standardization of the Network Functions Virtualization (NFZ) environment takes into account the C-RAN. The Virtual Network Function (VNF) of the NFV environment for 5G technology, has been defined to allow virtualization of the functions at the antenna level to be deported to a MEC data center. In addition to signal processing, there is also handover management, control of terminal attachment, location determination, etc.

While the C-RAN architecture is an attractive option for countries wishing to develop new infrastructure, it is much less attractive for countries that already have a local loop infrastructure for the RAN. In this case, the proposal is to keep the existing structure and add MEC data centers near the antennas to perform the processing of the application functions. In this case, the signal is processed at the antennas, and the data is sent to the data center via Radio over Ethernet (RoE). The binary data is stored in Ethernet frames to be processed in the data center. There is also the possibility of additional processing at the antenna to retrieve the IP packets and send them to the data center, which in this case essentially processes the application part. This architecture is detailed in Figure 2.10.

Mobile/Multi-access Edge Computing (MEC) has been defined by the European standards body European Telecommunications Standards Institute (ETSI) to take into account very short reaction times between the user and the data center that controls the user's applications. Among the applications that are targeted by this environment, we can mention autonomous vehicles that require latency times of the order of a millisecond, local processing of video images to decide whether or not to transmit them to a video processing platform further away, augmented reality, mobile applications in real-time, etc. Note that the meaning of MEC was changed in 2019 to include not only 5G antennas but also Wi-Fi access points, becoming Multi-access Edge Computing.

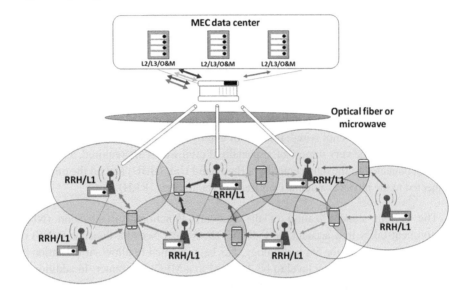

Figure 2.10. *The partially distributed Cloud-RAN architecture. For a color version of this figure, see www.iste.co.uk/alagha/networking.zip*

The MEC provides the equivalent of Cloud Computing on the network edge and, in particular, on RAN, therefore very close to the mobile user. The RAN offers a service environment with very low latency and high bandwidth as well as real-time access to all wireless-related information (radio, location, cell load, intercell change, etc.). The MEC can be seen as the implementation of a Cloud server installed near the user's mobile. The first use is to virtualize the equipment located between the client and the MEC data center in this data center. In addition, it is also possible to virtualize some of the equipment of the private or corporate customers in the MEC data center. For example, the Internet box in the home or the authentication server or the firewall can be virtualized in the MEC.

ETSI defines the MEC environment as described in Figure 2.11.

The Mobile Edge Host includes the following components:

– Virtualization Infrastructure, which provides computing, storage and network resources to run applications on platforms located at the edge.

– The Mobile Edge Platform brings together all the functionalities required to run mobile user applications on a cloud infrastructure. The Mobile Edge Platform can also provide a variety of services.

– The Mobile Edge applications are instantiated on the MEC data center and validated by the management system.

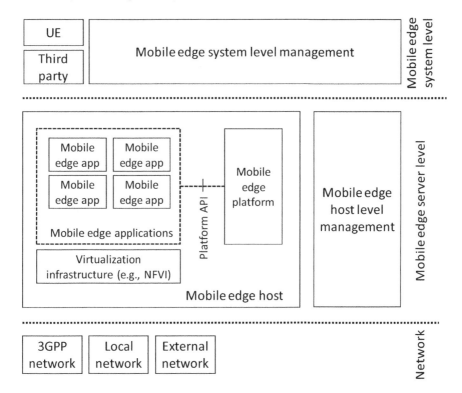

Figure 2.11. *The MEC environment as defined by ETSI*

Mobile management includes management at the mobile edge system level and management at the mobile edge host level:

– The Mobile Edge Host Level Management includes a mobile orchestrator as a core component. It provides an overview of the edge system.

– The Mobile Edge Host Level Management includes the Mobile Platform Manager and the Virtualization Infrastructure Manager. This module also manages the platform applications that support the attached mobiles and the platform itself.

Figure 2.12 shows an eNodeB (4G) or a gNodeB (5G), which is the equipment that processes signals from clients into binaries elements, which in turn generate packets to be sent to the core network. The eNodeB also handles basic mobile network functions such as client attachments, handovers, etc. One of the goals of the MEC data center is to virtualize the eNodeB or gNodeB, that is, to have a software version of the processing done and to run this software in the data center. As a result, the antenna has no more important work to do, just to get the signal from a user and send it back to the data center. The processing of the signal into digital form is done in the MEC servers in the data center as well as all application processing.

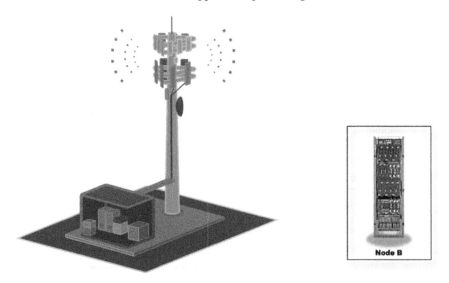

Figure 2.12. *The eNodeB or gNodeB of a mobile network antenna.*
For a color version of this figure, see www.iste.co.uk/alagha/networking.zip

The data center should not be located too far from the antenna because the signals coming from the antenna represent all the flows of all the connected customers as well as the supervision flows. The order of magnitude is 1 Gbps for 4G and 10 Gbps then 20 Gbps with 5G. On a pair of copper wires, it is possible to reach speeds of the order of bps over very short distances, which is why the eNodeB cabinet is located at the foot of the antenna or even along the pole that supports the antenna. To go further, you need to use RoF, which extends the distance to about

20 km, or even much further with high-end single-mode fibers. In other words, the processing of the eNodeB is moved to the data center. This architecture is described in Figure 2.13.

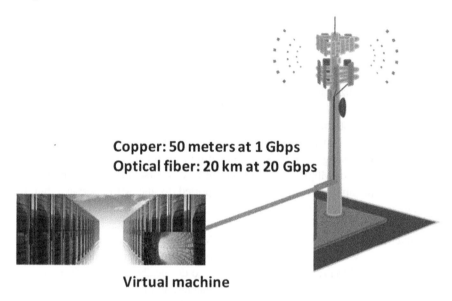

Figure 2.13. *The eNodeB offset in a MEC data center. For a color version of this figure, see www.iste.co.uk/alagha/networking.zip*

The MEC data center is used for many applications that can be virtualized. Overall, all the equipment between the customer and the data center can be virtualized, in particular the Asymmetric Digital Subscriber Line (ADSL) Internet access boxes, Internet boxes, intermediate gateways, etc. The advantage of this solution for an operator is that it does not have to deploy millions of boxes to be maintained and upgraded regularly. The Internet box can easily be customized. In the long run, when smartphones and other tablets are connected all the time, from everywhere, it will be time to virtualize the terminal equipment itself: the functions located in the smartphone will be located in the MEC data center.

Applications that will be impacted by the MEC data center include performance management, augmented reality applications, geolocation management and video stream processing. Video streams from remote monitoring cameras pass through the data center where they can be analyzed to trigger alarms. For example, cameras can count the number of people on a platform and trigger an alarm if a maximum number is exceeded. It is also possible to search for movements on an image, do face recognition or perform Big Data Analytics on several videos to find correlations. Certain streams can be selected for transmission to a central data center where larger-scale correlations can be searched.

MEC data centers will play an important role in enterprise Local Area Networks (LANs) and carrier access networks. Two major impacts are becoming clear: the virtualization of the LAN or Customer Premises Equipment (CPE) and the potential disappearance of these intermediate networks. In the first case, the LAN or CPE equipment is virtualized in the MEC. Load balancers, firewalls, Wi-Fi access points, intermediate appliances, etc., are replaced by virtual machines. In the second case, the LAN or CPE customers have a machine with a SIM card for access to the operator and all the company's customers are directly connected to the antenna. This solution is particularly interesting with 5G since the customer throughput to the antennas and back is several tens of Mbps. The disadvantage is, of course, that the company loses control over the applications which are deported to the MEC servers, but the advantage is that the LAN deployment can be outsourced to the operator.

Another application also classified in the MEC concerns what is called industry 4.0. This industry of the future concerns the control of production means. The objective is to synchronize all processes in order to drastically reduce production costs. This concerns, for example, the production of vehicles, all different from each other, on an assembly line without the throughput being lower than that concerning the manufacture of identical vehicles.

The location of the MEC data center can vary depending on the load or the need to go to the edge by being as close to the customer as possible. The MEC data center can be located on the user's premises by replacing the physical Internet box with a virtualized server supporting virtual machines. The physical box can also be a Home NodeB (HNB) corresponding to a 4G/5G antenna serving a very small cell called femtocell and located in the user's home or company. In this case, we speak rather of Skin data center or home data center or mist data center, that is, a tiny data center in which the access antenna is located. It can also be the Internet box with its Wi-Fi antenna or a broadband gateway with an ADSL modem, a cable modem or a fiber access.

The MEC data center can also be located right next to the antenna, a few meters away, connected by a pair of wires, allowing a throughput of a few Gbps. It can be dedicated to several antennas but at a distance of much more than a few meters. In this case, an optical fiber supporting RoF technology is essential. RoF is a technology in which light is modulated by a radio frequency signal and transmitted over an optical fiber. The main technical advantages of using optical fibers are the very low transmission error rate and the insensitivity to various electromagnetic noises. MEC data centers can also be grouped together in a pool by connecting them via optical fibers so that one data center can be offloaded to other centers if necessary.

2.4. Conclusion

The Edge seen from 5G is taking a strong place in digital infrastructures. Indeed, the architecture aims to digitize companies by offering them data centers capable of managing their IT environment from the network to storage, including all the functions needed to build an enterprise network and take into account applications whether they are high-speed, low-latency or using a very large number of objects. This architecture should allow operators to take a leading role in the new digital infrastructure businesses required for the 2020s.

2.5. References

Al-Roomi, M., Al-Ebrahim, S., Buqrais, S., Ahmad, I. (2013). Cloud computing pricing models: A survey. *International Journal of Grid and Distributed Computing*, 6(5), 93–106.

Antonopoulos, N. and Gilla, L. (2017). *Cloud Computing: Principles, Systems and Application*. Springer, Berlin.

ATHONET (2018). SGW-LBO solution for MEC taking services to the edge [Online]. Available at: http://telecoms.com/wp-content/blogs.dir/1/files/2018/04/MEC_SGWLBO_WP_MWC_2018.pdf.

Barlow, M. (2017). *Data Structures and Transmission: Research, Technology and Applications*. Nova, New York.

Blanco, B., Fajardo, J.O., Giannoulakis, I., Kafetzakis, E., Peng, S., Pérez-Romero, J., Trajkovska, I., Pouria, S.K., Goratti, L., Paolino, M. et al. (2017). Technology pillars in the architecture of future 5G mobile networks: NFV, MEC and SDN. *Computer Standards and Interfaces*, 54, 216–228.

Cattaneo, G., Giust, F., Meani, C., Munaretto, D., Paglierani, P. (2018). Deploying CPU-intensive applications on MEC in NFV systems: The immersive video use case. *Computers*, 7(4), 558.

ETSI (2013). Network functions virtualisation (NFV); Architectural framework v1.1. ETSI White Paper.

ETSI (2014). Network functions virtualisation (NFV); Architectural framework v1.2. ETSI White Paper.

ETSI (2017). Network functions virtualisation (NFV) release 3; Evolution and ecosystem; Report on network slicing support with ETSI NFV architecture framework. ETSI White Paper.

ETSI (2018a). MEC deployments in 4G and evolution towards 5G. ETSI White Paper, Cedex, France.

ETSI (2018b). MEC in an enterprise setting: A solution outline. ETSI White Paper, Cedex, France.

ETSI (2018c). Mobile Edge Computing (MEC): Deployment of Mobile Edge Computing in an NFV environment. ETSI White Paper, Cedex, France.

ETSI (2019a). Developing software for Multi-Access Edge Computing. ETSI White Paper, Cedex, France.

ETSI (2019b). Multi-access edge computing (MEC): Framework and reference architecture. ETSI White Paper, Cedex, France.

ETSI (2019c). System architecture for the 5G System (5GS). ETSI White Paper, Cedex, France.

Hakak, S., Noor, N.F.M., Ayub, M.N., Affal, H., Hussin, N., Imran, M. (2019). Cloud-assisted gamification for education and learning recent advances and challenges. *Computers and Electrical Engineering*, 74, 22–34.

Huazhang, L., Zhonghao, Z., Shuai, G. (2019). 5G Edge Cloud networking and case analysis. *IEEE 19th International Conference on Communication Technology (ICCT)*, Xi'an, China, 16–19 October 2019.

Kim, Y., An, N., Park, J., Lim, H. (2018). Mobility support for vehicular cloud radio-access networks with edge computing. *IEEE 7th International Conference on Cloud Networking (CloudNet)*, Tokyo, Japan, 22–24 October 2018.

Kirci, P. (2017). Ubiquitous and Cloud computing: Ubiquitous computing. In *Resource Management and Efficiency in Cloud Computing Environments*, Turuk, A., Sahoo, B., Addya, S. (eds). IGI Global, Hershey.

Langar, R., Secci, S., Boutaba, R., Pujolle, G. (2015). An operations research game approach for resource and power allocation in cooperative femtocell networks. *IEEE Transactions on Mobile Computing*, 14(4), 675–687.

Lin, L., Li, P., Liao, X., Jin, H., Zhang, Y. (2019). Echo: An edge-centric code offloading system with quality of service guarantee. *IEEE Access*, 7(37), 5905–5917.

Secci, S., Pujolle, G., Nguyen, T.M.T., Nguyen, S. (2014). Performance-cost trade-off strategic evaluation of multipath TCP communications. *IEEE Transactions on Network and Service Management*, 11(2), 250–263.

3

Fog Networks

Fog Computing is also called Edge Computing in a more general framework regrouping the level above (the MEC) and the level below (the Skin). This is a model in which data, computation and storage are concentrated at the edge of the network, in the company, rather than in major cloud providers. The term Fog Computing was introduced by Cisco in 2013 to define this new model allowing objects to connect to edge equipment and be processed at that level before sending the processed data to a cloud data center.

3.1. Fog architectures

Before breaking the Cloud architecture into four main levels (Cloud, MEC, Fog and Skin), it was first highly centralized around large but remote data centers, then decomposed into two levels, Cloud and Fog, as illustrated in Figure 3.1.

In this context, the Fog covers everything that is located on the ends of the network from the edge router, whether it is on the operator side or the enterprise side. If it is on the enterprise side, it is called an enterprise controller. If it is on the operator side, it is called a session border controller (SBC), which today has greater functionalities than those initially defined to secure VoIP and play the role of a SIP firewall.

The word Fog can sometimes be used for small data centers, which we will come back to in Chapter 6 as Skin data centers, where the users are within Wi-Fi or femtocell range of the data center. This case is illustrated in Figure 3.2.

Edge Networking,
by Khaldoun AL AGHA, Pauline LOYGUE and Guy PUJOLLE. © ISTE Ltd 2022.

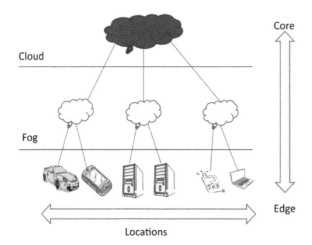

Figure 3.1. *The object-related architecture broken down into two levels. For a color version of this figure, see www.iste.co.uk/alagha/networking.zip*

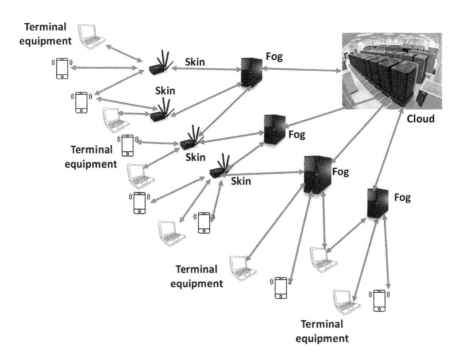

Figure 3.2. *Skin and Fog servers. For a color version of this figure, see www.iste.co.uk/alagha/networking.zip*

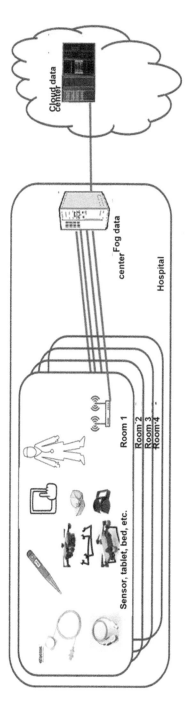

Figure 3.3. *A Fog data center to manage a hospital. For a color version of this figure, see www.iste.co.uk/alagha/networking.zip*

There are many examples of Fog data centers, and one is given in Figure 3.3, which is a data center inside a hospital. In this example, all the sensors and Wi-Fi, Bluetooth or other access points are connected to the Fog data center through a terrestrial cable, wired cable or optical fiber. Through this cabling, caregivers connected to Wi-Fi are able to run a wide range of application software. Objects such as hospital beds are easily mapped, and the location of a bed can be easily found. Patients use another virtual network that is also connected to the Fog server to play games, read or search the Web. These two networks are isolated so that an attack on one network cannot spread to the second network.

A second example is shown in Figure 3.4 with the connection of objects in industrial processes, the so-called Industry 4.0. It is defined for automating production means going toward the personalization of products without a product made in detail costing more than a product made in a very large number of copies.

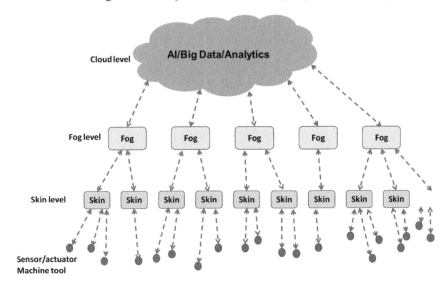

Figure 3.4. *Industry 4.0 processes. For a color version of this figure, see www.iste.co.uk/alagha/networking.zip*

This use case is quite similar to the one discussed in the previous chapter on MEC servers, but instead of having a connection via a telecom operator's antenna to reach a MEC data center, the connection is made here via a network within the factory to access the Fog data center. The network can take many forms, such as a field network, an Ethernet network or a private 5G network.

Smart production allows the customer to interact with the production process by modifying, for example, the values obtained by the sensors in order to produce specific and personalized products. The management system of these measurements or supervisory control and data acquisition (SCADA) is the basis of the new generation of factories.

Decisions, as shown in Figure 3.4, are made at levels similar to those seen previously, that is, in the Skin for very reactive processes such as machine tool control or embedded process execution, in the Fog for processes that use virtualization or processes covering enterprises or the smart city. The Cloud level deals with processes that need a very high capacity of resources.

Other examples could be detailed, such as a Fog server on a train to support connections with customers in the train car, the smart city teeming with sensors to connect to the Fog data center, etc.

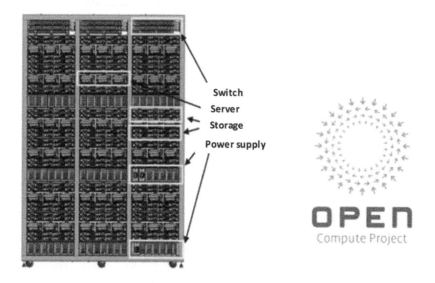

Figure 3.5. *An example of hardware from the Open Compute Project.*
For a color version of this figure, see www.iste.co.uk/alagha/networking.zip

The word Fog has been associated with many data center architectures on the edge of the network. Today, the word Fog is synonymous with an enterprise-related data center. The term white box is used when this data center is built with open-source hardware, that is, hardware whose specifications are public and available on the Internet. The Open Compute Project (OCP) is the main project defining open-source hardware. Original design manufacturers (ODM) companies have these servers or white boxes built in very large numbers, sometimes at costs ten times lower than those of commercial vendors. The white boxes are unbranded servers purchased in large quantities to build data centers. All of the items shown in Figure 3.5 are available, but without maintenance, a problem that companies moving in this direction must consider.

3.2. Fog controllers

Fog data centers usually contain a controller that manages the configurations of virtual machines, that is, services and microservices, when in a centralized architecture. Figure 3.6 summarizes the different cases of controller placement in a virtual network environment. We can see three main cases. The first type of controller is highly centralized and can be used as a software-defined networking (SDN) controller. Knowledge (contextualized information) flows regularly back to this center, which has an almost perfect view of the network resources and is therefore able to configure the network nodes as best as possible. The second solution is to use intermediate machines to replace the edge routers. The edge router does not disappear; it is virtualized in the Fog data center. These machines can be session border controllers (SBCs), a term used more in operator networks, or corresponding network access controllers (NACs), which is the solution recommended by companies. Finally, the last example of architecture consists of positioning the control as close as possible to the user in skin data centers, which are still called femto-data centers. The advantages are obvious: a very short latency time, great agility of this solution allowing to change the virtual machines used in the Skin data centers and a form of network intelligence available close to the user.

This last possibility corresponds to the participative Internet networks, which play on a strong distribution of information to carry out the controls. These controls become essential when the endpoint becomes detached from the other machines.

The three major solutions described above can be mixed by having two tiers simultaneously, or even all four tiers of data centers: some virtual machines can go down to a Skin data center or a Fog data center while others can stay in a central (Cloud) or operator (MEC) data center.

We will now look at Fog servers and data centers with their main virtual machine: the controller. There are, however, other virtual machines in the Fog: those that support the functions of the digital infrastructure of an enterprise such as firewall, middlebox and the authentication and SIP servers, but also the essential and non-essential functions of the company's life grouped in the infrastructure services.

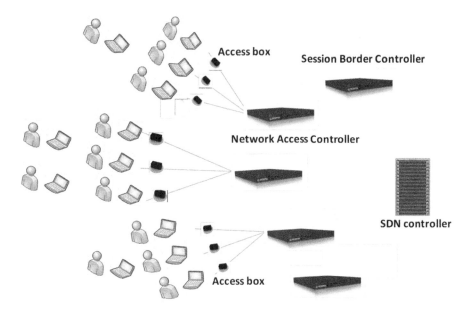

Figure 3.6. *Case study for the location of a controller. For a color version of this figure, see www.iste.co.uk/alagha/networking.zip*

An example of a Fog data center use case is for proximity advertising, which we will examine in this section. First, let's look at the functions that a Fog controller handles. They are shown in Figure 3.7. The first function is the one that supports connecting to the network via Wi-Fi access points, but also any other connection solution, such as cable or Bluetooth. In the control of Wi-Fi connections, which represents the overwhelming majority of cases, the connection includes authentication that identifies the user who connects. This identification is done by the IEEE 802.1x standard, which implies that the authentication server is located in the controller or is directly attached to it. It is possible that the controller only has a proxy and, in this case, the authentication server is further away in the network, in a MEC or Cloud data center. There may be other cases of authorization to initiate a connection, such as filling out a form, which allows us to know the client wishing to connect. Authentications by other means are also accepted, such as assigning a password via his smartphone to authenticate the customer by his mobile number. The authentication by the use of identifiers from other sites, Google, Facebook, LinkedIn, etc., is also a widely used method. The controller then manages the access points (APs). This management can be done at different levels, starting with the lower layers, such as power and frequency used in the AP and moving up to the higher layers that manage the application-level access. The application-level functionalities are very diverse with, for example, the sending of messages by the SMTP server of the controller, the use of a local printer without the client needing to obtain the corresponding driver and the authorization to access a data center from the access point, etc.

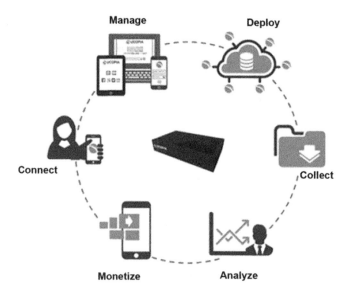

Figure 3.7. *The main functions of a Fog controller. For a color version of this figure, see www.iste.co.uk/alagha/networking.zip*

There is also the collection function, which consists of collecting data to create user profiles. These profiles can help the system to adapt quickly to the customers by having precise information on the usual behavior of the customer. These profiles are also used for proximity marketing actions to send extremely precise and personalized advertisements to a particular user. The marketing message is unique and is sent to one person only. To carry out this marketing and target the user perfectly, it is necessary to have precise information about their geolocation and what they are doing. These profiles must respect the laws in force, which are more or less strong depending on the country and the continent. Globally, the respect for privacy obliges companies that carry out intelligent marketing to destroy the data collected as soon as the customer changes context, for example, when he leaves a shopping mall.

The next function of the controller is data analysis. This analysis is done through tools coming from artificial intelligence and mainly from Big Data Analytics. This analysis makes it possible to determine a whole set of characteristics, in particular by determining correlations that escape humans because the amount of information is so large. The last function is to monetize the information from the analysis, such as optimizing the location of goods for sale in a supermarket. Figure 3.8 describes the proximity marketing process in more detail.

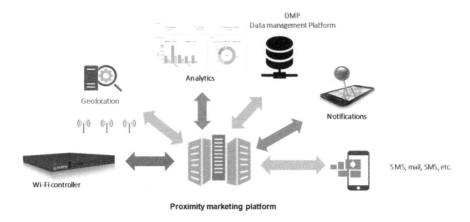

Figure 3.8. *Proximity marketing. For a color version of this figure, see www.iste.co.uk/alagha/networking.zip*

In this proximity marketing, the Fog server contains many virtual machines. The first is the controller itself, and then a machine that handles the precise geolocation of users connected to the Fog server. The controller receives user profiles from Big Data Analytics or other artificial intelligence techniques. A data management platform (DMP) is then used to store, sort and analyze customer data. These solutions allow the development of targeted marketing campaigns with precision. This platform allows for sending notifications to the user through a Bluetooth low energy (BLE) connection or a specific application linked to a store, a shopping mall, or any other environment where advertising is important. Finally, this platform facilitates the purchase of advertising space in a strategic way on all the channels available in the advertising field.

A new path is developing with the Internet of Behaviors (IoB). The idea is to go even further than the profile of a user by seeking to know his behavior and his satisfaction during purchases or simply a passage in a store. In this case, the controller must receive streams of information from sensors or equipment recording behavior. The limitations of these approaches come from the defense of privacy, which should not allow going too far in this direction.

3.3. Fog and the Internet of Things

Now we come to the basic use case of Fog Networking and the Internet of Things (IoT). The number one objective of the Fog is to get closer to the Edge in order to retrieve and process information so that it flows from objects more quickly. A virtual machine can be located in the Fog server to carry out the processing associated with the object, but we can also have a virtual machine to secure the object, a virtual machine to manage the failures of the object, etc. We are going to be interested in the networks which aim to connect the objects on the Fog data center. These networks are also at the center of the participative Internet, which aims to connect all the surrounding objects and to process locally all the flows to control applications ranging from office automation to industrial production through proximity marketing or playful applications.

The networks used to connect objects can be classified into three main categories: short-range networks such as Bluetooth or ZigBee, long-range networks such as SigFox or LoRa, and telecom networks such as long-term evolution for machines (LTE-M) or narrow-band IoT (NB-IoT). The first category is also broken down into two sub-categories: high-speed networks and networks carrying relatively low-speed signaling. In the first sub-category, we find Wi-Fi, which is the simplest solution, but also different versions of Bluetooth, including BLE. In the second, we find ZigBee and 6LowPAN with much lower data rates and very low energy consumption. The ranges of these networks are a few meters, even a few tens of meters in direct view. The networks have more or less important speeds ranging from WiGig at 7 Gbps to Bluetooth, which has a capacity of a few hundred Kbps, and Halow, a new version of Wi-Fi, for objects with data rates ranging from a few bits per second to a few hundred kilobits per second. In the very low-speed solutions to transport commands, but also some data, we find 6LowPAN using the advantages of IPv6.

Long-distance networks include extremely low-speed solutions such as SigFox, which is a proprietary solution, and LoRa, which offers greater openness while remaining proprietary. The access cards require little enough energy to allow two alkaline batteries to last a decade. These solutions are also suitable for transmitting over distances of several tens of kilometers, the flow being very low in these conditions.

The techniques coming directly from the mobile networks of the telecommunication operators are far behind the other two solutions. However, they should quickly become the most used solutions because of their diversity of speeds and their ease of scaling. The first solution is LTE-M, defined during the standardization of 4G, which is being replaced by a second generation represented by NB-IoT. NB-IoT was introduced in the 4G PRO and strongly enhanced in the 3GPP specifications for 5G. We describe in Figure 3.9 these different categories of networks for the IoT.

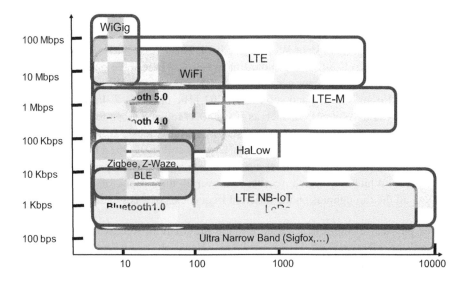

Figure 3.9. *The networks of the Internet of Things. For a color version of this figure, see www.iste.co.uk/alagha/networking.zip*

Fog Networking mainly uses the first two categories concerning long-distance and very low-speed solutions as well as solutions for personal networks or local networks, more precisely networks with a range of a few dozen meters allowing objects to connect directly by wireless links to Fog servers. The storage and processing of the data streams from the sensors take place in these small data centers.

The third category of networks for the IoT can be based on Fog servers via, for example, a private 5G network using the 6 GHz band, but also directly on larger data centers such as MEC data centers. This last solution is deployed through telecom operators who have chosen, at first, LoRa and sometimes SigFox, to fill the gap resulting from the delay in the marketing of 4G and 5G networks dedicated to IoT.

3.4. Wi-Fi in the Fog's digital infrastructure

The primary network technology used in the Fog environment is Wi-Fi to get from the user to the data center. This will also be the case for the connections in the Skin data centers at the base of the Internet of Edges. In the Fog, the Wi-Fi access points are fixed, while in the Skin, they can be mobile.

The IEEE 802.11 working group is responsible for standardizing Wi-Fi networks. To begin with, three types of wireless networks have been proposed: those working at 11 Mbps speed, those at 54 Mbps and those at 600 Mbps. The first is based on the IEEE 802.11b standard and bears the commercial name of Wi-Fi 1, the second on the IEEE 802.11a or Wi-Fi 2 and IEEE 802.11g or Wi-Fi 3 standards and the third on the IEEE 802.11n standard or Wi-Fi 4. These three generations have been succeeded by three new generations: IEEE 802.11ac or Wi-Fi 5, at 2 Gbps, Wi-Fi 802.11ax or Wi-Fi 6 and soon IEEE 802.11be or Wi-Fi 7. In parallel, other Wi-Fi standards have appeared, such as IEEE 802.11ad at 7 Gbps for personal area networks whose commercial name is WiGig. Several extensions have been made with WiGig 2 and 3 up to a hundred Gbps. There is still IEEE 802.11ah for the IoT, with the trade name Halow. Other new features are being prepared with IEEE 802.11af or White-Wi, which reaches an overall throughput of 10 Gps peak, counting all the throughputs on the different frequencies of this standard.

The physical medium is accessed through the Medium Access Control (MAC) protocol for all types of Wi-Fi networks. However, many options make its implementation rather complex. The MAC protocol is based on the Carrier-Sense Multiple Access with Collision Detection (CSMA/CD) access technique already used in wired Ethernet networks. The difference between the wireless protocol and the terrestrial protocol comes from the way collisions are detected. In the terrestrial version, collisions are detected by listening to the carrier. When two stations want to transmit while a third is transmitting its frame, this automatically leads to a collision. In the wireless case, the access protocol avoids the collision by forcing the two stations to wait a different time before transmitting. Since the difference between the two waiting times is greater than the propagation time on the transmission medium, the station with the long waiting time finds the physical medium already occupied and thus avoids a collision. This technique is called Carrier-Sense Multiple Access with Collision Avoidance (CSMA/CA).

To avoid collisions, each station has a timer with a specific value. When a station listens to the carrier and the channel is empty, it transmits. The risk of a collision is extremely low since the probability of two stations starting their transmission in the same microsecond is almost zero.

On the other hand, a collision becomes inevitable when transmission takes place, and other stations start listening and persist in listening. To prevent the collision, the stations must wait before transmitting for a time that allows them to separate their respective transmission inputs. For this purpose, a first very small timer is added, which allows the receiver to send an acknowledgment immediately. A second timer gives high priority to a real-time application. Finally, the longest timer, dedicated to asynchronous packets, determines the transmission time for asynchronous frames.

Wi-Fi networks are defined by a cellular architecture. A group of terminals equipped with an 802.11 network interface card join together to establish direct communications. They form a basic service set (BSS), not to be confused with the base station subsystem (BSS) of GSM networks. The area occupied by the terminals of a BSS can be a basic set area (BSA) or a cell.

The main standards of this working group are shown in Table 3.1.

802.11	Output	Frequency	Bandwidth	Possible flow rate	MIMO	Modulation
First-generation	Jun 1997	2.4 GHz	22 MHz	1 and 2 Mbps	-	DSSS and FHSS
a	Sep 1999	5 GHz	20 MHz	6, 9, 12, 18, 24, 36, 48 and 54 Mbps	-	OFDM
b	Sep 1999	2.4 GHz	22 MHz	1, 2, 5.5 and 11 Mbps	-	DSSS
g	Jun 2003	2.4 GHz	20 MHz	6, 9, 12, 18, 24, 36, 48 and 54 Mbps	-	OFDM
n	Oct 2009	2.4/5 GHz	20 or 40 MHz	72.2 or 150 Mbps	4	MIMO-OFDM
ac	Dec 2013	5 GHz	20, 40, 80 and 160 MHz	96.3 or 200 Mbps or 433.3 or 866.7 Mbps	8	MIMO-OFDM
ax	Nov 2020	2.4 or 5 GHz	20–160 MHz	From 1.1 to 10.5 Gbps	8	OFDM-OFDMA
ad	Dec 2012	60 GHz	2.16 GHz	6.7 Gbps	-	OFDM and *single carrier*
ay	Nov 2019	60 GHz	8.64 GHz	56 Gbps	-	MIMO-OFDM
af	Feb 2014	0.054–0.79 GHz	6–8 MHz	1.8 à 568.9 Mbps	1, 2 and 4	OFDM
ah	Dec 2016	0.9 GHz	-	347 Kbps	-	-

Table 3.1. *The main standards of the IEEE802.11 working group*

As illustrated in Figure 3.10, the 802.11 standard offers two modes of operation: infrastructure mode and ad hoc mode. Infrastructure mode is defined to provide individual stations with specific services over a coverage area determined by the size of the network. Infrastructure networks are established using access points that act as base stations for a BSS.

When the network is composed of several BSS, each BSS is connected to a distribution system (DS) through their respective AP. A distribution system is typically a wired Ethernet network. A group of BSS interconnected by a distribution system forms an extended service set (ESS), which is not very different from a mobile network radio subsystem.

The distribution system is responsible for the transfer of packets between different BSS of the same ESS. In the standard specifications, it is implemented independently of the wireless structure. This is why the distribution system corresponds to an Ethernet network. Another solution is to use the Wi-Fi network itself, which results in mesh networks.

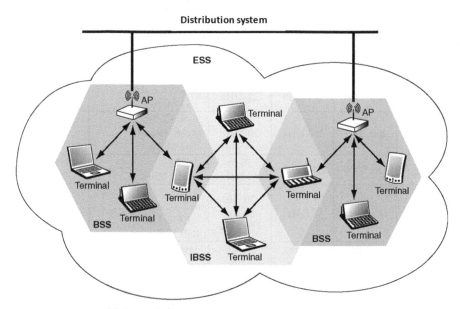

AP: Access Point
BSS: Basic Set Service
ESS: Extended Set Service
IBSS: Independant Basic Set Service

Figure 3.10. *Architecture of a Wi-Fi network*

The ESS can provide individual mobile stations with a gateway to a fixed network such as the Internet. This gateway allows the 802.11 network to be connected to another network. If this network is of IEEE 802x type, the gateway incorporates functions similar to those of a bridge.

An *ad hoc* network is a group of terminals forming an IBSS (Independent Basic Service Set) whose role is to allow stations to communicate without the aid of any infrastructure such as an access point or a connection to the distribution system. Each station can establish communication with any other station in the IBSS without having to go through an access point. Since there is no access point, the stations only integrate a number of features, such as the frames used for synchronization.

This mode of operation is very useful to easily set up a wireless network when a wireless or fixed infrastructure is lacking.

Figure 3.11 describes the frequencies on which the different Wi-Fi are used.

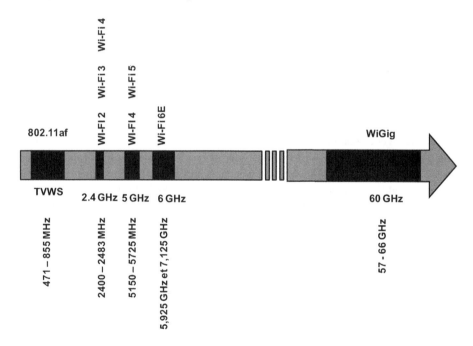

Figure 3.11. *Frequency used for Wi-Fi*

3.5. The new generation Wi-Fi

Wi-Fi has new names since 2018, and we will use them all while indicating the old IEEE nomenclature. Next-generation Wi-Fi starts with the Wi-Fi 5 standard (IEEE 802.11ac) that came to market in late 2013 and exceeds 1 Gbps throughput. This minimum value of 1 Gbps marks the next generation of Wi-Fi. This Wi-Fi 5 standard that we will examine in more detail is complemented by Wi-Fi 6 (IEEE 802.11ax) and the WiGig (IEEE 802.11ad), which takes place on a new frequency band, that of 60 GHz. This last solution is mainly made for the interior of buildings and in a very directive way for the exterior. Indeed, at these frequencies, the signal is strongly disrupted by rain, dust and, of course, all obstacles. It is, therefore, necessary to have a direct view outside with, if possible, good weather conditions or a sufficiently short distance so that the flow remains correct, even in the presence of rain or fog.

The new generation continues with the White-Fi standard (IEEE 802.11af) that uses cognitive radio, that is, the possibility of using frequencies for which there is an owner (also called a primary) that does not use them. To do this, it is necessary to either drastically limit the range to remain in an environment without conflict with the primary, or to have a server that lists the use of frequencies and allows cognitive access points to know where they are being used and to use the available frequencies without risk of interference. The White-Fi standard (IEEE 802.11af) uses the television bands in cognitive radio and is called TV White Space (TVWS) or sometimes Super Wi-Fi.

The new generation of Wi-Fi also has in its panoply the Halow (IEEE 802.11ah), which offers a long-range Wi-Fi of the order of one kilometer, but with much lower speeds. The uses are mainly in the field of connecting objects such as smart electricity meters or health equipment. The Wi-Fi 6 standard (IEEE 802.11ax) is an improvement on Wi-Fi 5 (IEEE 802.11ac) with four times the capacity. The first Wi-Fi 6 products have been available since early 2019. Finally, Wi-Fi 7 is currently being standardized and the first products are to be commercialized in 2022. The corresponding working group is the IEEE 802.11be. Its capacity will still be four times higher than the Wi-Fi 6 version and should globally exceed 100 Gbps.

Wi-Fi 5 (IEEE 802.11ac) is a version of Wi-Fi made to exceed 1 Gbps thanks to multiple antennas that can operate simultaneously on separate lobes. Two solutions have been implemented and complement each other to obtain the announced capacity. The first, quite simple, is simply to increase the width of the transmission channel by using the 5.15 GHz band, which is much freer than the 2.4 GHz band. This band is higher in frequency, and its range is less good. In addition, obstacles also slow down the signals. However, the available bandwidth is 200 MHz, which is significantly more than the 83.5 MHz allocated to the 2.4 GHz band, which allows Wi-Fi channels with a bandwidth of 80 MHz and optionally 160 MHz.

The second solution concerns the directionality of the transmitted signals by using a set of specific antennas. This technique consists in allowing the emission of several communications on the same frequency but in different directions. There is multiplexing in space, hence the name of the technique Space Division Multiple Access (SDMA). Figure 3.12 illustrates this technology.

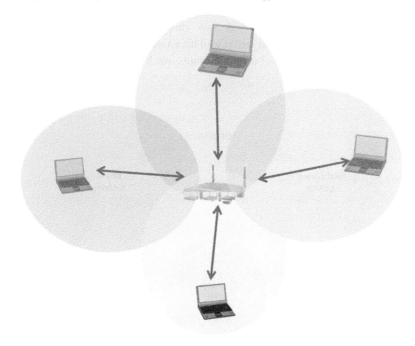

Figure 3.12. *The SDMA. For a color version of this figure, see www.iste.co.uk/alagha/networking.zip*

The SDMA access method uses beamforming techniques that direct the signals in a certain direction, thus creating directional antennas. The antennas allow for multiple directions to be generated simultaneously, allowing communication to multiple clients at the same time. The technique used in Wi-Fi 5 is still called Per-User Unitary Rate Control (PU2RC). The antennas of the Wi-Fi 5 standard allow Multi-User Multiple-In/Multiple-Out (MU-MIMO), that is, connecting multiple clients to the access point antennas. All antennas use the same frequency simultaneously, minimizing interference. In other words, to increase throughput, each directional antenna can be replaced by several antennas with the same directionality, using the same frequency to perform MIMO.

This MIMO technology allows the throughput to be multiplied by the number of antennas, not quite an exact multiplication but almost: the interference increases with the number of antennas but remains relatively small. For example, two physical antennas can give rise to three internal antennas each, so a total of six antennas. These six antennas allow for six simultaneous communications. With these six antennas, one can also realize two MIMO 2×2 communications (two antennas communicating with two antennas of a remote machine) and two simple communications, making six communications in total. One could just as well have three simultaneous communications with, for example, one MIMO 3×3 communication, one MIMO 2×2 communication and one simple communication.

Figure 3.13. *The main characteristics of Wi-Fi 6 (IEEE 802.11ax). For a color version of this figure, see www.iste.co.uk/alagha/networking.zip*

If the peak throughput is 250 Mbps per antenna, with four physical antennas each carrying three antennas, we get 12 antennas. The total throughput is thus 3 Gbps. If, in addition, the bands used are wider, for example, 80 MHz instead of 20 MHz, theoretically 10 Gbps can be exceeded. In reality, as with all Wi-Fi access points, the peak throughput is only reached in exceptional cases where there is no external interference and where the clients are positioned very close to the antenna and distributed in the different lobes. In reality, the raw data rates are often divided by a factor of at least 2, but often much more to obtain the real data rates.

The IEEE 802.11ac group, which standardized Wi-Fi 5, with 433 Mbps per antenna on an 80 MHz band and a two-antenna MIMO per client, claims 866 Mbps per connection with a terminal. With four physical antennas, more than 3 Gbps is reached. With a bandwidth of 160 MHz, double the throughput is achieved. The standard specifies that the number of spatial sectors could be up to eight, which would double the throughput again. This will be the actual case for Wi-Fi 6 (IEEE 802ax). It is clear that the figures given are peak data rates that do not take into account overheads due to controls and management of the access point. As in all Wi-Fi networks, fallback speeds are required when conditions are not ideal. Compatibility with existing standards also requires adapting throughputs in accordance with the standards that have been left compatible.

The goal with the new Wi-Fi 6 standard (IEEE 802.11ax) is to further increase throughput with more and more directional antennas with up to eight directions and thus eight lobes and Multiple User – Multiple Input Multiple Output (MU-MIMO).

A new "target wake-up time" (TWT) feature allows a smartphone, laptop or another device to extend battery life. When the access point transmits to a device, it can tell that device when to put its Wi-Fi radio to sleep and exactly when to wake it up to receive the next transmission. This sleep solution saves a lot of energy since the Wi-Fi radio can spend a lot of time in sleep mode. This property allows connected objects to spend much less energy.

Wi-Fi 6 incorporates new technologies to limit congestion. This is because Wi-Fi tends to slow down significantly in places that are overloaded with users, such as a stadium, airport, hotel, shopping mall or even an office complex where everyone is connected to Wi-Fi. This does not only apply to busy public places but can also apply to homes where many devices are connected to Wi-Fi. To account for these issues, Wi-Fi 6 divides the radio channel into a large number of sub-channels. Each of these sub-channels can carry data for a different device.

This is achieved through Orthogonal Frequency-Division Multiple Access (OFDMA) radio technology. The Wi-Fi access point can talk to several devices at the same time on the same cell, unlike previous versions where only one client at a time was the only solution.

Wi-Fi 6 also brings improvements to the MIMO. This involves multiple antennas that allow the access point to talk to multiple devices at once. With Wi-Fi 5, the access point could talk to devices at the same time, but those devices could not respond at the same time. Wi-Fi 6 brings an improved version of multi-user or MU-MIMO that allows devices to talk back to the wireless access point at the same time.

Another important improvement comes from the possibility for Wi-Fi access points close to each other to transmit on the same channel: BSS Coloring. In the case of Wi-Fi before version 6, the transmitter listens and waits for a clear signal before transmitting. With Wi-Fi 6, wireless access points near each other can be configured to have different colors in a BSS. The color is defined as a number between 0 and 7. If a device is listening to see if the channel is completely free, it may notice a transmission with a weak signal and a different color. It can then ignore this signal and transmit without waiting, which will improve performance in overloaded areas. This solution is also called spatial frequency reuse.

Wi-Fi 6 also brings a much better definition of the beams allowing to make SDMA. This improvement enables having thinner directional antennas preventing fading, that is, avoiding electromagnetic waves arriving at distinct times following multiple routes, including the straight line, the most direct and many bounces on obstacles, before arriving at the receiver.

Wi-Fi 6 access points support WPA3 to increase the security of Wi-Fi networks, but WPA3 support is not a requirement of the standard.

Wi-Fi 6 and previous generations of Wi-Fi use the 2.4 and 5 GHz radio bands. The Wi-Fi 6E operates on the 6 GHz band, which is open in many countries but is being opened in others. This band, located between 5.925 and 7.125 GHz, allows for the full band to be 1,200 MHz, which is large enough to be split into seven new 160 MHz channels with no interference or 14 80 MHz channels. These channels will not overlap at all, which will help to reduce congestion, especially in areas where many networks are operating.

The next generation, Wi-Fi 7 has many new features, as shown in Figure 3.14. Immediately noticeable is a connection to the 5G antennas through a control plane independent of the data plane.

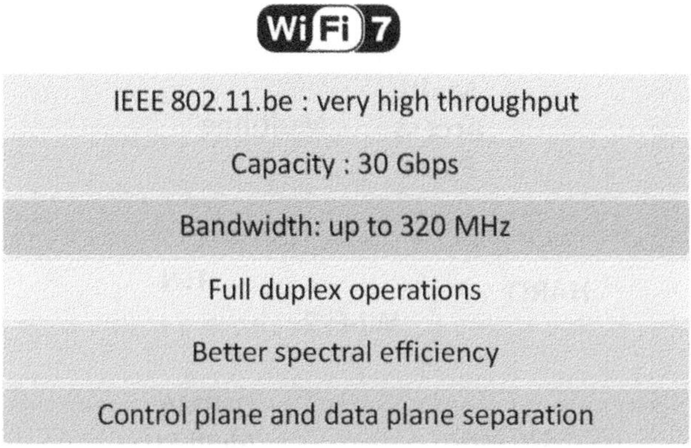

| IEEE 802.11.be : very high throughput |
| Capacity : 30 Gbps |
| Bandwidth: up to 320 MHz |
| Full duplex operations |
| Better spectral efficiency |
| Control plane and data plane separation |

Figure 3.14. *The main characteristics of Wi-Fi 7 (IEEE 802.11be).*
For a color version of this figure, see www.iste.co.uk/alagha/networking.zip

Although the development process is not complete, an analysis of the discussions in the 802.11 working group provides insight into the key innovations of Wi-Fi 7. After reviewing hundreds of proposals for this next generation, the working group members identified key development directions and documented them.

The Wi-Fi 7 version (IEEE 802.11be) will see its number of directional antennas further increased, allowing it to exceed 100 Gbps capacity overall. The main goal of the IEEE 802.11be group is to develop a new Wi-Fi standard that will increase throughput to peak at over 100 Gbps. This comes from an increased number of spatial streams that will reach 16 in the first version of this standard but also supports real-time applications. In addition to these properties, the antennas allow native multi-link operation, channel optimization opening the door to massive MIMO, advanced PHY and MAC level techniques and cooperation of various access points in the same neighborhood. Finally, Wi-Fi 7 introduces some quite revolutionary changes that will form a solid foundation for a new generation of Wi-Fi. Indeed, this standard brings a control plane completely disconnected from the data plane. This new feature will allow for a simple connection to the 5G control plane, which could, in the longer term, allow for a convergence of Wi-Fi and 5G. The Wi-Fi access point could become a cheap 5G access point compared to the cost of 5G components.

Figure 3.15 describes the new features of the Wi-Fi 7 standard, which is expected to be released in 2022.

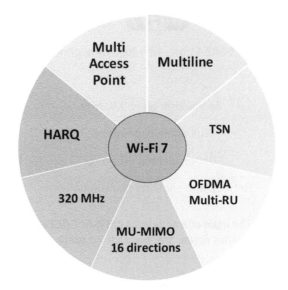

Figure 3.15. *The new features of Wi-Fi 7. For a color version of this figure, see www.iste.co.uk/alagha/networking.zip*

This convergence of Wi-Fi and 5G networks is being examined by a 3GPP working group, the Access Traffic Steering, Switching and Splitting (ATSSS). We will detail this convergence after looking at private 5G in the Fog Networking.

A few words about the next generation, which should be Wi-Fi 8. The IEEE 802.11bf working group gives the first ideas. This future standard defines the modifications to be made to the MAC layer of access control to the medium and to the Directional Multi-Gigabit (DMG) and enhanced DMG (EDMG) techniques to improve the functioning of the detection of the radio signal in the unlicensed frequency bands between 1 and 7.125 GHz and above 45 GHz. This standard should allow stations to inform other stations of their ability to listen to carriers, set up and configure transmissions to perform carrier sense measurements, indicate that a transmission is about to occur, and exchange information about active Wi-Fi networks. These new advances will allow for a much higher quality of service and better use of carriers, avoiding the time-consuming backoff techniques. This standard will ensure backward compatibility and coexistence with older IEEE 802.11 terminals operating in the same band.

After examining the basic line of Wi-Fi from Wi-Fi 1 to 7, let's look at the other versions of Wi-Fi. The IEEE 802ad standard works with frequencies in the 60 GHz range, that is, millimeter waves that do not pass through obstacles. This standard is supported by a group of manufacturers, the Wireless Gigabit Alliance (WGA). The name of the product that has become the standard for personal networks is WiGig, but the basic product could be the tri-band WiGig operating on the 2.4, 5 and 60 GHz bands, thus allowing it to adapt to the environment. The peak throughput is 7 Gbps. The range in the 60 GHz band is less than 10 m, which makes this network belong to the Personal Area Network (PAN) category. The channels used in the basic mode are 57.24, 59.4, 61, 56 and 63.72 GHz. The bandwidths are 2.16 GHz.

To compensate for the high signal attenuation, the WiGig (IEEE 802.11ad) calls for directional antennas that can focus the radio beam within a 6° angle. With this very narrow beam, the WiGig standard is used outdoors between antennas directed in direct view and inside a room, relying on bounces from obstacles to reach the recipient. Indeed, with a 6° beam, the connection between two machines is often complex. Fortunately, there is an option to automatically steer the beam so that the two machines seeking to connect can set up the link with ease.

Two WiGig applications are mentioned in the standard. The first one corresponds to wireless connections for computer peripherals with the aim to suppress the many cables that are lying around. This application also allows the simple sharing of devices. The second application is for wireless-related consumer electronics such as stereo equipment, HDTVs and online gaming systems.

The WiGig products have new extensions with WiGig 2, which again increases the bandwidth quite significantly, and then by the WiGig 3 product, which will have an even higher throughput thanks to a further increase in bandwidth. These elements are shown in the time diagram in Figure 3.16 in comparison to the other technologies that are moving towards very high speed.

The White-Fi technique (IEEE 802.11af) tackles a completely different problem to increase throughput: the use of cognitive radio. It consists of reusing frequency bands that are not used at a given time in the television bands. More generally, recent measurements show that the frequencies between 0 and 20 GHz, despite their scarcity and price, are under-used, often by less than 10%. The only bands that are heavily used are those of the telecom operators, which, thanks to TDMA, CDMA and OFDMA techniques, have excellent utilization rates. The bands reserved for television, located below 1 GHz and for this reason particularly attractive to operators, could allow access points to reach ranges of several hundred meters.

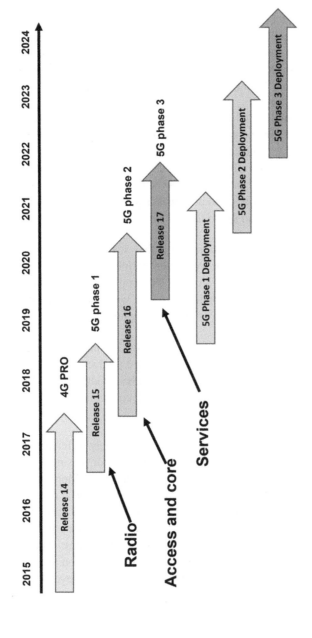

Figure 3.16. *The arrival of WiGig technologies. For a color version of this figure, see www.iste.co.uk/alagha/networking.zip*

The White-Fi standard (IEEE 802.11af), not to be confused with IEEE 802.3af for Power over Ethernet (PoE), is also called TVWS. The term "white space" refers specifically to the frequencies that are not being used by terrestrial television channels. The usable bandwidth in cognitive radio is several tens of digital television channels. The data rates reached can be colossal.

An important issue is how cognitive radio is used. There needs to be regulation by each state to determine the means of use. The main solutions concern how to use free frequencies. There are several solutions depending on the coverage of the cognitive access point. If the band is not occupied at the access point, it can be assumed that it is not occupied within a few meters. In this category, we find Wi-Fi access points inside buildings with limited power to stay inside the building. A second solution is to refer to a bandwidth management server that has the information to determine which bands can be used. This requires a common discipline between the primary and secondary. But for that, will the terrestrial TV operators agree with the White-Fi (802.11af) users? Standardizations are underway in different working groups, such as IEEE P1900, to propose solutions acceptable to both parties. A third, more distant solution could come from the possibility for any device to use a specific sensor that measures interference and indicates to cognitive access points whether or not they can use the frequency.

At the physical level, the method used in the White-Fi (IEEE 802.11af) is fixed subcarrier spacing (FSS) OFDM. The channels used in OFDM can be contiguous or non-contiguous, that is, belonging to TV channels that are next to each other or, on the contrary, separated by active TV channels. A channel contains 64 carriers. Four channels can be selected at 6, 7 or 8 MHz each. In the last two cases, since the data rate per channel is 26.7 Mbps and, as in Wi-Fi 5 (IEEE 802.11ac), at least four directions in SDMA are possible, the maximum basic speed is 568.9 Mbps, with 8 MHz channels.

The media access technique is the same as in conventional Wi-Fi. In addition, classes of service using the Enhanced Distributed Channel Access (EDCA) defined by the IEEE 802.11e standard are available and correspond to the four classes Background, Best-Effort, Video and Voice. A fifth, even higher priority, is added for spectrum listening to determine which channels are potentially usable.

3.6. The next generation of mobile Wi-Fi

Wi-Fi, which is a solution designed for low mobility, will be extended to take into account high mobility with the IEEE 802.11bd standard, which is seen as the successor of IEEE 802.11p. This standard should provide similar performance to 5G, but at a much lower cost. A comparison with the 5G V2X standard for the vehicular domain will be presented in Chapter 7 on vehicular networks.

The future IEEE 802.11bd standard uses the same physical layer clocked at 10 MHz, but also offers optional operation at 20 MHz. The basic coding has been replaced by a low-density parity-check (LDPC) coding. In addition, a 256-QAM modulation option for high-speed applications has been introduced. To address doubly selective channels with a high Doppler effect, the preamble-based channel detection has been improved based on high-density midambles. A dual carrier modulation (DCM) mode and a range extension, already implemented in the 11ax standard, are also offered as an option to increase the transmission range. In DCM mode, the data is duplicated and modulated redundantly on two coherent carriers with half the system bandwidth each, for example, 5 MHz. The transmissions are combined at the receiver using the log-likelihood ratio (LLR) combination. This exploits the frequency diversity to decrease the outage probability at the cost of doubling the transmission time, leading to an increase in channel loading. The coverage extension increases the power of the training sequences by 3 dB to improve the signal detection over much larger ranges. In addition to the 5.9 GHz operation, the 60 GHz millimeter band is also offered to exploit very large bandwidths. However, transmission is limited to a single spatial stream when using the Out of Context of a BSS (OCB) broadcast mode. The structure of the framework has been extended based on the 11ac format. A new preamble, header fields and additional high-density midambles have been added to the IEEE 802.11bd frame.

To increase the reliability of the transmission, the introduction of congestion-dependent retransmissions and grouped acknowledgments in broadcasting on the MAC layer is also considered. As a result, packets are repeated up to three times depending on the channel occupancy rate to avoid congestion. A packet combination similar to the 3GPP HARQ process has been proposed, achieving gains of 3–4 dB for one repetition and 6–8 dB for three repetitions at the link level. Instead of randomly repeating messages, broadcast acknowledgments allow selective repetition for a limited group of users.

This solution should allow Wi-Fi to be able to re-enter the race for control of connected vehicles through performance similar to 5G in this same area but perhaps at much lower costs.

3.7. Private 5G for Fog Networking

Private 5G is an important advancement in mobile networks to allow a private company to connect all the company's equipment to a Fog data center. Initially, the

3GPP was interested in 5G to compete with Wi-Fi by offering LTE-U (Unlicensed), which means deploying 4G on the unlicensed bands that Wi-Fi operates on and then, instead of competing directly with Wi-Fi, making an alliance by allowing a single carrier by aggregating a licensed carrier and a Wi-Fi carrier. This solution is shown in Figure 3.17.

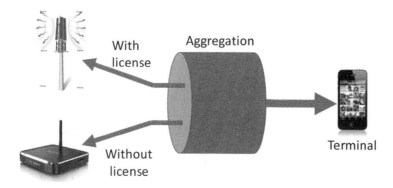

Figure 3.17. *The aggregation of two carriers, one licensed and the other Wi-Fi. For a color version of this figure, see www.iste.co.uk/alagha/networking.zip*

These solutions are obviously interesting but quite complicated to implement, as the packets passing through the licensed carrier have a much higher quality of service than the Wi-Fi carrier. Other solutions have been described in the 4G specifications and extended in 5G, but they are, in general, to the advantage of 4G and 5G solutions by the control that comes from the eNodeB or gNodeB.

The real arrival of private 5G comes from two points: 5G NR-U integrating both 5G NR, Wi-Fi and Licensed-Assisted Access (LAA) and the opening of 4G and 5G to open source.

The opening of the 6 GHz band with 1,200 MHz of bandwidth was a trigger to accelerate the development of a solution to simultaneously integrate 5G NR, Wi-Fi and the first generation of Wi-Fi integration, LAA. The MulteFire had been the first approach to integrate 4G and Wi-Fi by a technique of listening, the Listen Before Talk (LBT), which allows both technologies to compete on the same carrier. However, this solution had poor performance, especially for applications requiring synchronization or real-time execution. The 3GPP specification for 5G release 16 in June 2020 proposes a method to extend the MulteFire solution into 5G NR-U (Unlicensed) technology.

The solution used is always based on LBT, which can come from Wi-Fi 5 or Wi-Fi 6 or from a further enhanced LAA (feLAA) technique or from a 5G NR-U with or without DFT (Discovery Frame Transmission). For each type of access, the LBT technology has different timers and backoff algorithms.

The second approach, which is now taking over, is to introduce private 5G at a relatively low cost through open source. To achieve the introduction of open source into the 5G infrastructure, the monolithic models had to be broken down and replaced with models that integrate many interfaces to disaggregate the base model.

This transition to the open-source model can be seen in Figure 3.18 for the O-RAN project.

This figure shows the traditional model composed of a monolithic environment going from the RRH associated with the antenna to the BBU, which gathers the basic functions of 4G. This model is disaggregated to obtain three pieces with the first interfaces associated with O-RAN. Finally, the layer corresponding to 5G with its open interfaces is presented in the O-RAN version. This last layer includes the RAN Intelligent Controller (RIC), which manages the O-CU (Open Central Unit), O-DU (Open Distributed Unit) and O-RU (Open Radio Unit).

The overall model is shown in Figure 3.19.

The top part of the architecture corresponds to the RIC controller for the non-real-time part, which takes into account the management of the 5G environment. The second layer represents the controller for the real-time or near real-time part corresponding to the control of the data and control plane functions. Then, we find the usual philosophy of data center architectures. The RIC controller is located in the Fog data center in the case of private 5G.

This 5G technology can be coupled with Wi-Fi thanks to the proposals made by the 3GPP working group called ATSSS, which allows the connection of 5G antennas and Wi-Fi access points to the 5G core network, as well as connections made by wired networks, even if these are less and less used. This architecture is described in Figure 3.20.

In this specification, cases are described in detail like the one described in Figure 3.21, where we see the possibility to connect 5G antennas and Wi-Fi antennas to the Fog data center, which is itself connected by an optical fiber to the 5G core network or an Internet network.

We note that objects or machines can be connected simultaneously to a 5G antenna and a Wi-Fi antenna in this last figure.

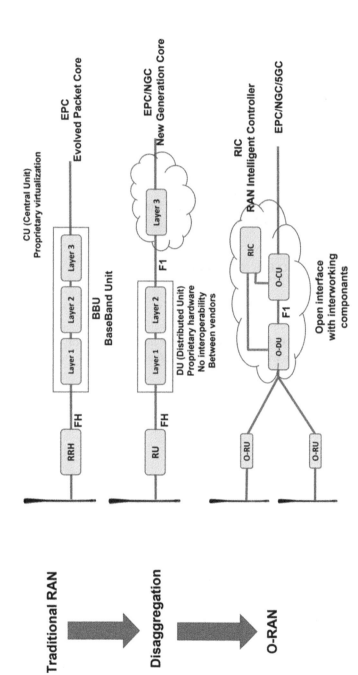

Figure 3.18. *Disaggregation of the base model to O-RAN. For a color version of this figure, see www.iste.co.uk/alagha/networking.zip*

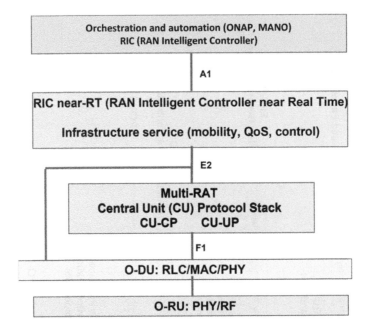

Figure 3.19. *The O-RAN architecture. For a color version of this figure, see www.iste.co.uk/alagha/networking.zip*

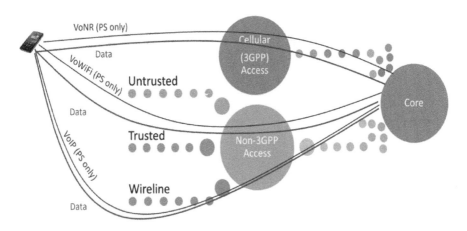

Figure 3.20. *3GPP architecture for 5G and Wi-Fi convergence (©3GPP). For a color version of this figure, see www.iste.co.uk/alagha/networking.zip*

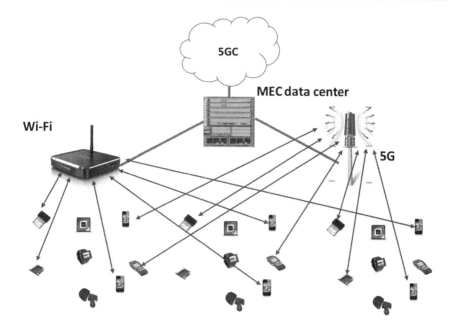

Figure 3.21. *The simultaneous use of 5G and Wi-Fi. For a color version of this figure, see www.iste.co.uk/alagha/networking.zip*

3.8. Conclusion

Fog Networking is an Edge technology that allows companies to go digital while remaining in control of their IT thanks to a Fog data center. This solution should be very successful, even if it lags behind the MEC solutions offered by operators and the Cloud proposals of the major Web companies.

The Fog network is also located between centralized and distributed environments, and the choices range from Wi-Fi/Ethernet LAN to participatory networks to 5G NR-U, which is a rather complex mix integrating 5G and Wi-Fi. The best solution would certainly be a convergence of Wi-Fi and 5G, but it will take a few more years.

3.9. References

Aslanpour, M.S., Gill, S.S., Toosi, A.N. (2020). Performance evaluation metrics for cloud, fog and edge computing: A review, taxonomy, benchmarks and standards for future research. *Internet of Things*, 12, 100273.

Bahman, J., Jingtao, S., Rajiv, R. (2020). Serverless architecture for edge computing. In *Edge Computing: Models, Technologies and Applications*, Taheri, J. and Deng, S. (eds). Institution of Engineering and Technology, London.

Baldini, I., Castro, P., Chang, K., Cheng, P., Fink, S., Ishakian, V., Mitchell, N., Muthusamy, V., Rabbah, R., Slominski, A. et al. (2017). Serverless computing: Current trends and open problems. In *Research Advances in Cloud Computing*, Chaudhary, S., Somani, G., Buyya, R. (eds). Springer, Singapore.

Bao, W., Yuan, D., Yang, Z., Wang, S., Li, W., Zhou, B., Zomaya A. (2017). Follow me fog: Toward seamless handover timing schemes in a fog computing environment. *IEEE Communications Magazine*, 55(11), 72–78.

Bonomi, F., Milito, R., Zhu, J., Addepalli, S. (2014). Fog computing and its role in the Internet of Things. *Proceedings of the First Edition of the MCC Workshop on Mobile Cloud Computing*, Association for Computing Machinery, New York.

Chiang, M. (2017). *Fog for 5G and IoT*. Wiley, New York.

Cicconetti, C., Conti, M., Passarella, A., Sabella, D. (2020). Toward distributed computing environments with serverless solutions in Edge systems. *IEEE Communications Magazine*, 58(3), 40–46.

Dinh, H.T., Lee, C., Niyato, D., Wang, P. (2013). A survey of mobile cloud computing: Architecture, applications, and approaches. *WCMC*, 13, 1587–1611.

Eismann, S., Scheuner, J., Van Eyk, E., Schwinger, M., Grohmann, J., Herbst, N., Abad, C., Losup, A. (2020). Serverless applications: Why, when, and how? *IEEE Software*, 38, 32–39.

Ghobaei-Arani, M., Souri, A., Rahmanian, A. (2020). Resource management approaches in Fog Computing: A comprehensive review. *Journal of Grid Computing*, 18(1), 1–42.

Glikson, A., Nastic, S., Dustdar, S. (2017). Deviceless edge computing: Extending serverless computing to the edge of the network. *Proceedings of the 10th ACM International Systems and Storage Conference*, Association for Computing Machinery, New York.

Hall, A. and Ramachandran, U. (2019). An execution model for serverless functions at the edge. *Proceedings of the International Conference on Internet of Things Design and Implementation*, Association for Computing Machinery, New York.

Jasenka, D., Francisco, C., Admela, J., Masip-Bruin, X. (2019). A survey of communication protocols for Internet of Things and related challenges of fog and cloud computing integration. *ACM Computing Surveys*, 51(6), 1–29.

Mahmud, R., Ramamohanarao, K., Buyya, R. (2020). Application management in Fog computing environments: A taxonomy, review and future directions. *ACM Computing Surveys*, 53(4).

Markakis, E.G. and Mastorakis, G. (2017). *Cloud and Fog Computing in 5G Mobile Networks: Emerging Advances and Applications*. IET Press, Stevenage.

Rafique, W., Qi, L., Yaqoob, I., Imran, M., Rasool, R., Dou, W. (2020). Complementing IoT services through software defined networking and edge computing: A comprehensive survey. *IEEE Communications Surveys and Tutorials*, 1–1.

Rapuzzi, R. and Repetto, M. (2018). Building situational awareness for network threats in Fog/Edge Computing: Emerging paradigms beyond the security perimeter model. *Future Generation Computer Systems*, 85, 235–249.

Stojmenovic, J. and Wen, S. (2014). The fog computing paradigm: Scenarios and security issues. *Federated Conference on Computer Science and Information Systems (FedCSIS)*, Poland, 7–10 September 2014.

Takeda, A., Kimura, T., Hirata, K. (2019). Evaluation of edge cloud server placement for edge computing environments. *IEEE International Conference on Consumer Electronics*, Taiwan, 20–22 May 2019.

Vaquero, L.M. and Rodero-Merino, L. (2014). Finding your way in the fog: Towards a comprehensive definition of fog computing. *ACM SIGCOMM Computer Communication Review*, 44(5), 27–32.

Yi, S., Li, C., Li, Q. (2015a). A survey of fog computing: Concepts, applications and issues, workshop on mobile big data. *Proceedings of the 2015 Workshop on Mobile Big Data*, Association for Computing Machinery, New York.

Yi, S., Qin, Z., Li, Q. (2015b). Security and privacy issues of fog computing: A survey. *International Conference on Wireless Algorithms, Systems and Applications (WASA)*, Qufu, China, 10–12 August 2015.

4

Skin Networks

Skin Networking is a new paradigm that is still not very developed and represents the Cloud floor being as close as possible to the user. Skin Networking is defined as being within Wi-Fi range or within a femtocell. The Skin data center has directly in it the connection antennas of the users, but also of the objects that are within a radius of a few dozen meters. The name Skin Networking is not really standardized, and names like Mist Networking are also in the running. These very small data centers can eventually fit in a pocket and be mobile. The power is obviously reduced by the size and mobility of the equipment. However, many virtual machines can be placed in them. An example of a Skin data center would be a smartphone with very large memory and a large number of multicore processors. It will not be until 2025 that we will see this kind of power in a very small mobile data center. Initially, the Skin data center is a small, powerful hardware environment that is powered either directly or by a battery, allowing it to last all day without a problem. This data center should be able to accommodate all the virtual machines needed to run a home, a small business or a small department of a large corporation.

4.1. The architecture of Skin networks

Skin data centers are located close to the customer, in access points or boxes located on the user's premises. The immediate advantage of small data centers is the extremely short response time to execute a control algorithm and, thus, the possibility to perform operations in real-time. However, this requires equipment with significant resources. Given the decreasing cost of hardware, this solution could be preferred to the Fog. Moreover, with the arrival of femtocells, we might as well take advantage of this to bring some local power to process virtual machines

Edge Networking,
by Khaldoun AL AGHA, Pauline LOYGUE and Guy PUJOLLE. © ISTE Ltd 2022.

that will solve all the connection and processing problems. The solution described in the previous lines forms the basis of participatory networks. Their distributed architecture does not require any link to the Internet. The network can be mobile and strongly secured by the property of not needing a connection to the outside world.

In Figure 4.1, we show a simple configuration of a single Skin data center box. Users and objects are connected on this node with various protocols supported by specialized virtual machines. The box is a small data center where virtual machines are pooled to support network and application services. These services include all the infrastructure level functions that can be found in the literature and the cloud, such as routers, switches, SIP servers, firewalls, etc. In particular, we can find virtual machines coming from the Network Functions Virtualization (NFV) standardization such as Deep Packet Inspection (DPI), Network Address Translation (NAT), Broadband Remote Access Router (BRAS), etc. Of course, all the services and microservices required by the user are included.

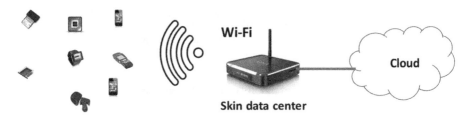

Figure 4.1. *A Skin data center*

4.2. Virtual access points

A data center can support various virtual machines and in particular virtual Wi-Fi access points. The customer has the choice of the access point, which can be in an office, at home or at any other access point with its own specificities. The box can contain a large number of virtual access points, all different from each other and, of course, isolated so that an attack on one access point cannot spread to the others. The exact number depends on the power of the data center and the number of potential users. The throughput for each user is a function of the number of virtual access points, the number of users on each virtual Wi-Fi access point and the Wi-Fi technology used. The virtual access points share the physical antenna with, for example, a token technique to keep the slices isolated. Of course, the capacity of each virtual access point is a function of the number of tokens and is therefore not as large as that of a non-shared access point. However, with the rise of Wi-Fi, each virtual access point can have sufficient capacity. In particular, the use of Wi-Fi 5

(IEEE 802.11ac) and Wi-Fi 6 (IEEE 802.11ax) standards allows each virtual access point to achieve sufficient throughput for all usual and even less usual applications.

The virtual Wi-Fi access point has some flaws! Each virtual Wi-Fi access point has its own signaling frames. If the number of virtual Wi-Fi access points is high, the overhead becomes important. Moreover, the antenna is common, and a radio jamming attack affects all virtual access points.

The access point we describe here concerns a virtual Wi-Fi access point, but it can perfectly adapt to a NodeB, that is, the physical antenna management unit of a mobile network, giving rise to virtual NodeBs. In the case of Skin networks, the box can be considered as an HNB (Home NodeB) or an MNB (Metro NodeB) with important capacities to receive virtual processing machines. More generally, all the functions associated with wireless access techniques can be virtualized and thus provide customized connections. Depending on the software from the virtualized functions, significant advances can be made toward multi-technology access solutions. Figure 4.2 illustrates the case of a virtualized HNB using Wi-Fi frames to transport 4G/5G frames between the end devices and the HNB.

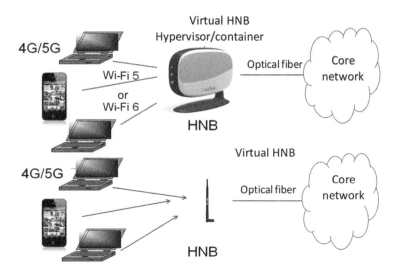

Figure 4.2. *A virtualized HNB. For a color version of this figure, see www.iste.co.uk/alagha/networking.zip*

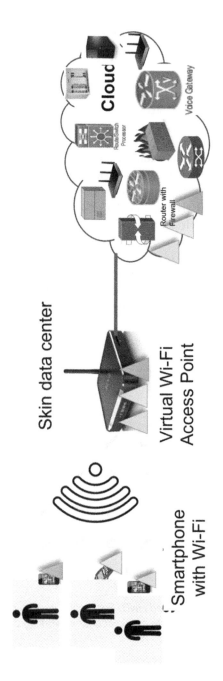

Figure 4.3. *Context of a network around a Skin data center. For a color version of this figure, see www.iste.co.uk/alagha/networking.zip*

In Figure 4.3, we show the context of a virtualized access point that will become one of the foundations of the smart Edge environment. Indeed, the connection of users requires the implementation of antennas and access control functions that are obviously virtualized. Secondly, the infrastructure and ancillary services are available in the box, which allows all necessary processing to be done locally. In this context, a large part of the network intelligence is located at the edge, hence the name smart edge.

Figure 4.3 represents the case of a small data center, receiving two virtual access points, capable of connecting two clients using different operators' networks. Each client has brought its own virtual Wi-Fi access point or HNB back to the box to connect to the network. The two clients do not know each other, and they each have their own personalized access. Of course, other virtual machines can be brought back into the box to manage a particular interface or perform a specific service.

More globally, operators are starting to look at the possibility of deploying their own virtual access points to position themselves in places where their customers might be. For example, a conference room that has a Skin data center could connect all of operator X's customers after migrating an X virtual access point to the data center. This virtual access point is part of the network of operator X and is managed directly by this operator from a MEC or Cloud data center. If the physical access point fails, the responsibility to repair it lies with the infrastructure operator, in our case, the owner of the conference room. Business plans for amortizing the cost of the Skin data center vary widely, from renting resources in the box to putting a virtual machine to charging for time and resources used.

4.3. Participatory Internet networks

The notion of participatory Internet networks refers to the participation of users in the realization of Transmission Control Protocol/Internet Protocol (TCP/IP) networks that can operate completely autonomously and that are able to continue working even without connection to the Internet and its servers. Moreover, nodes can disappear, and others can appear. There is, therefore, no central node in the network since it can disappear at any time. Participatory networks are therefore networks that use users' terminal machines, or machines dedicated to the network, where all processes and protocols are totally distributed. If we add the term Internet, it indicates that the participatory network uses TCP/IP protocols.

This type of network has the advantage of being highly protected from Internet threats since a company can disconnect its network and continue to work in a closed mode without any need for a connection. Only services requiring external servers, such as Twitter or Facebook, can no longer run unless there is an agreement for an internal server to run the application locally. On the other hand, all usual Internet protocols and applications for which there is open source software or not can run in a distributed way. Internal telephony or video, storage, computing and even network applications through virtual machines can run without any external connection. A company that has a participatory network can connect it at certain times to the outside via a gateway and disconnect at other times.

Another advantage of this type of network is its extremely low energy consumption. Indeed, since everything is done directly between clients, there is no need to go and find an antenna or a digital subscriber line access multiplexer and connect to a server that can be located on the other side of the planet to make the connection.

Using the examples in section 4.2, we can build participatory Internet networks by integrating all TCP/IP functions in a distributed manner to allow the network to continue to function even if an outage occurs with the Internet itself. The participatory Internet can be seen as an extension of the Internet or the coverage of a 4G or 5G cell. The participatory Internet forms a local network from different Skin data centers in which the virtual machines needed to create these networks can be located. Many virtual machines such as routers, switches, firewalls or application service machines can be transported to the data centers from a central cloud, a MEC or a local server. The decision to leave a machine in the central or regional Cloud or transport it in the participatory Internet network depends on the characteristics of the service to be obtained and on the evaluation of the resulting traffic.

Figure 4.4 describes the case of an enterprise that would have several boxes to build a participatory Internet network. In this case, the company's virtual Wi-Fi access points must first be transported to all of the boxes, or several virtual access points corresponding to logical networks must be selected, which will themselves be set up according to specific applications such as Voice-over-Internet Protocol, Internet Protocol television, banking access, messaging, file transfer, a business application, etc. The participatory Internet networks are realized thanks to the virtual equipment that is set up in the boxes. It is also possible to add a network for the visitors of the company, but this network must be totally isolated to prevent any intrusion into another virtual network. It allows visitors to the company to connect to the Internet through the company's network without the possibility of an attack.

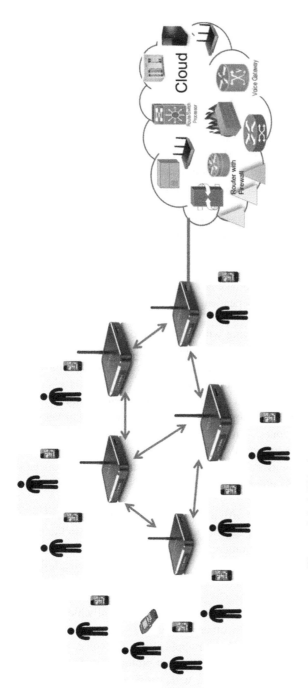

Figure 4.4. *A Skin data center environment for creating a participatory Internet. For a color version of this figure, see www.iste.co.uk/alagha/networking.zip*

Virtual networks can use different protocols such as IPv4, IPv6, Multiprotocol Label Switching, Ethernet, Software-defined Networking (SDN), etc. It is necessary to choose the protocol that is best suited to the application whose flows are passing through the network. There are still only a few commercial products that correspond to this multiple network context that virtualization allows, limiting themselves to a single distributed TCP/IP network to avoid the complexity of slicing.

The connections between the boxes can be wired or wireless using protocols corresponding to the type of network chosen by the user. It can be Optimized Link State Routing Protocol, ad hoc on-demand distance-vector, Transparent Interconnection of Lots of Links or any other protocol developed in this context.

The participatory Internet networks realized in this context offer new possibilities thanks to virtualization. In this case, they necessarily contain a distributed system to control the applications since some boxes can disappear and others enter the network. These participatory Internet networks can also be connected to the Internet itself to take advantage of servers installed in central sites. In this case, there is a loss of independence of the end network.

In the case of a network playing with centralization, it is possible to implement SDN Wi-Fi access points. Indeed, by putting together a virtual Wi-Fi access point and an SDN switch like Open vSwitch, it is possible to send OpenFlow commands from a controller to the Wi-Fi access point. Of course, it is also possible to implement an SDN controller such as OpenDaylight, OpenContrail or FloodLight in one of the boxes to control the other boxes that form the virtual network. In this case, as in the previous ones, some virtual machines can remain in the Cloud or Edge data centers depending on their size and usage rate. With this solution, the independence of the network is lost through, on the one hand, a centralization of the SDN controller and on the other hand the existence of servers in Cloud data centers.

Although forecasts see SDN arriving via core networks, more and more voices are rallying around an SDN implementation from the edge due to the much greater simplicity of automatic configuration. However, this SDN-based solution is only feasible in the case of a fixed-end network. If the network is mobile, fully distributed control systems must be used.

Figure 4.5 illustrates a participatory Internet network in which servers that are Skin data centers connect to each other automatically. They have various virtual machines, such as routers, firewalls and applications for voice, video or business applications. These boxes support all the Internet protocols in distributed mode and offer a large number of functions and a wide range of applications that are also totally distributed.

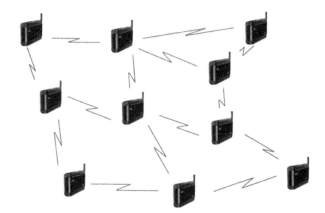

Figure 4.5. *A participatory Internet network*

In fact, a participatory Internet network can take two forms: ad hoc networks and mesh networks, which are grouped under the term multi-hop network. Figure 4.6 describes these two categories of networks.

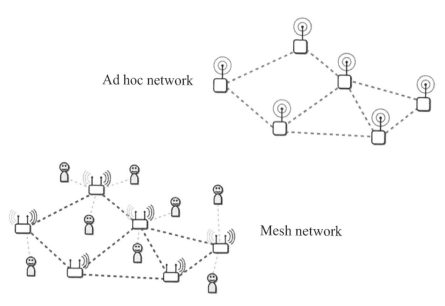

Figure 4.6. *Mesh networks and ad hoc networks*

Multi-hop networks refer to communications that pass through intermediate equipment in the wireless part. The packet is usually stored and processed before being retransmitted to another device, always over the air. When the relays form a mesh network, in which each node is connected to the others by several paths, we speak of mesh networks. The access points forming the mesh network can be fixed or mobile. These stations form a backbone network, usually an operator network or equivalent. The clients of a mesh network are connected to one of the mesh routers, usually through a different access card than the one used by the mesh network itself. In a mesh network, the client does not have any specific software and connects as on a hotspot.

An ad hoc network is similar to a mesh network, except that the routing software is located on the client's terminal. In other words, there are no specific machines in an ad hoc network: it is the clients that form the network. The main drawback of this solution is the strong dependency between the routers and the client terminals. On the other hand, these are networks without any infrastructure since they only have client terminals. They are sometimes called "wild networks" because they can be set up autonomously without an operator. However, it is illusory to think that a customer in Lille could communicate with a customer in Marseille by passing through a few thousand intermediate terminals. The reason for this impossibility is the management of routing tables, which would become immense and highly dynamic as the client terminals move constantly.

The standardization of ad hoc networks has been realized by the Internet Engineering Task Force in the Mobile Ad hoc NETwork (MANET) working group. We will see them in more detail in the chapter devoted to mesh and ad hoc networks.

Another category of networks with relays is formed by the Vehicular Ad hoc NETwork (VANET). These networks are in strong expansion in the automotive industry. This solution makes it possible to connect clients to each other inside a vehicle, the vehicle being a bus, a train or a plane. We will look at some of these elements in the chapter dedicated to vehicular networks.

4.4. Conclusion

Skin Networking is a new domain that extends Edge Networking to the user. The networks that are formed in this context can be centralized around a small data center in the form of a small box. Skin networks can be made up of several boxes by interconnecting them to form participatory networks. In this case, the services are completely distributed since the main objective is to connect mobile machines. The advantage is to obtain solutions with low energy consumption, very low latency and high resilience associated with simple security by detaching the network from the Internet so that there can be no attack from outside the network.

4.5. References

Allam, H., Nassiri, N., Rajan, A., Ahmad, J. (2017). A critical overview of latest challenges and solutions of Mobile Cloud Computing. *Proceedings of the Second International Conference on Fog and Mobile Edge Computing (FMEC'17)*, IEEE, Piscataway, NJ.

Baktir, A.C., Ozgovde, A., Ersoy, C. (2017). How can edge computing benefit from software-defined networking: A survey, use cases, and future directions. *IEEE Communications Surveys and Tutorials*, 19(4), 2359–2391.

Bilal, K., Khalid, O., Erbad, A., Khan, S.U. (2018). Potentials, trends, and prospects in edge technologies: Fog, cloudlet, mobile edge, and micro data centers. *Computer Networks*, 130, 94–120.

Chilukuri, S., Bollapragada, S., Kommineni, S., Chakravarthy, K. (2017). RainCloud – Cloudlet selection for effective cyber foraging. *Wireless Communications and Networking Conference (WCNC'17)*, IEEE, New York.

Dolui, K. and Datta, S.K. (2017). Comparison of edge computing implementations: Fog computing. Cloudlet and Mobile Edge Computing. *Global Internet of Things Summit (GIoTS'17)*, Geneva, Switzerland, 6–9 June 2017.

Drolia, U., Martins, R., Tan, J., Chheda, A., Sanghavi, M., Satyanarayanan, M., Bahl, P., Caceres, R., Davies, N. (2009). The case for VM-based cloudlets in Mobile Computing. *IEEE Pervasive Computing*, 8(4), 14–23.

Li, C., Xue, Y., Wang, J., Zhang, W., Li, T. (2018). Edge-oriented computing paradigms: A survey on architecture design and system management. *ACM Computing Surveys (CSUR)*, 51(2), 39:1–39:34.

Mach, P. and Becvar, Z. (2017). Mobile edge computing: A survey on architecture and computation offloading. *IEEE Communications Surveys and Tutorials*, 19(3), 1628–1656.

Mao, Y., You, C., Zhang, J., Huang, K., Letaief, K.B. (2017). A survey on mobile edge computing: The communication perspective. *IEEE Communications Surveys and Tutorials*, 19(4), 2322–2358.

Mouradian, C., Naboulsi, D., Yangui, C., Glitho, R.H., Morrow, M.J., Polakos, P.A. (2018). A comprehensive survey on fog computing: State-of-the-art and research challenges. *IEEE Communications Surveys and Tutorials*, 20(1), 416–464.

Mukherjee, M., Shu, L., Wang, D. (2018). Survey of fog computing: Fundamental, network applications, and research challenges. *IEEE Communications Surveys and Tutorials*, 20(3), 1826–1857.

Pang, P., Sun, L., Wang, Z., Tian, E., Yang, Z. (2015). A survey of Cloudlet-based mobile computing. *Proceedings of the International Conference on Cloud Computing and Big Data (CCBD'15)*, IEEE Computer Society, Washington, DC.

Perera, C., Qin, Y., Estrella, J.C., Reiff-Marganiec, S., Vasilakos, A.V. (2017). Fog Computing for sustainable smart cities: A survey. *ACM Computing Surveys (CSUR)*, 50(3), 32:1–32:43.

Pujolle, G. (2013). Metamorphic networks. *Journal of Computing Science and Engineering*, 7(3), 198–203.

Satyanarayanan, M. (2017). The emergence of edge computing. *Computer*, 50(1), 30–39.

Shaukat, U., Ahmed, E., Anwar, Z., Xia, F. (2016). Cloudlet deployment in local wireless networks: Motivation, architectures, applications, and open challenges. *Journal of Network and Computer Applications*, 62, 18–40.

Shiraz, M., Gani, A., Khokhar, R.H., Buyya, R. (2013). A review on distributed application processing frameworks in smart mobile devices for mobile cloud computing. *IEEE Communications Surveys and Tutorials*, 15(3), 1294–1313.

5

Ad hoc and
Mesh Networks

Mobile Ad hoc Networks or MANET are an important category of relay networks. The infrastructure consists only of the stations themselves, which act as a transmitter, receiver and router. Routing allows information to pass from one terminal to another without these terminals being directly connected. Mesh networks, as we saw in the previous chapter, require that the nodes be independent of the user's machines.

5.1. Ad hoc networks

An ad hoc network is shown in Figure 5.1.

Contrary to appearances, ad hoc networks date back several decades. They aim to achieve a communication environment that is deployed without any other infrastructure than the mobiles themselves. In other words, mobiles can act as a gateway to enable communication from one mobile to another. Two mobiles that are too far apart to communicate directly can find an intermediate mobile that can act as a relay.

The major difficulty generated by this type of network comes from the very definition of the network topology: how to determine which nodes are neighbors and how to get from one node to another? Two extreme solutions can be compared. The first is that of an ad hoc network in which all nodes can communicate with all others, implying a long range of transmitters. In the second solution, on the other hand, the radio range is as short as possible: in order to communicate between two nodes, it is

Edge Networking,
by Khaldoun Al Agha, Pauline Loygue and Guy Pujolle. © ISTE Ltd 2022.

usually necessary to pass through several intermediate machines. The advantage of the first solution is the security of the transmission since it is possible to go directly from the transmitter to the receiver without depending on intermediate equipment. The network throughput is minimal, as the frequencies cannot be reused. In the second case, if a terminal breaks down or is turned off, the network can be split into two distinct sub-networks, without communication from one to the other. Obviously, in this case, the overall throughput is optimized since there can be high-frequency reuse.

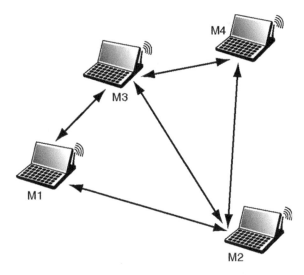

Figure 5.1. *Ad hoc network*

The access techniques are of the same type as in mobile networks. However, because all nodes are mobile, new properties must be brought to the management of user addresses and routing control.

The solution developed for ad hoc networks is based on the IP environment. The mobiles acting as gateways (usually all mobiles) implement a router in their operating systems so that the problems posed are essentially routing problems on the Internet, with mobility being managed by the IP protocol.

The advantages of ad hoc networks are their very simple extensions, their physical coverage and their cost. However, to take full advantage of them, a number of hurdles must be overcome due to the mobility of the nodes, particularly with regard to the quality of service and security.

MANET is the IETF working group concerned with the standardization of ad hoc protocols running over IP. This group has taken the classic Internet protocols and enhanced them to work with mobile routers.

Two main families of protocols have been defined: reactive protocols and proactive protocols :

– Reactive protocols: the terminals do not maintain a routing table but worry about it when a transmission is to be made. In this case, flooding techniques are essentially used to list the mobiles that can participate in the transmission.

– Proactive protocols: mobiles seek to maintain a coherent routing table, even in the absence of communication.

Ad hoc networks are useful in many situations. They can be used to set up networks in a short period of time, for example, in case of an earthquake or for a meeting with a very large number of participants. Another possibility is to extend access to a cell of a wireless network such as Wi-Fi. As shown in Figure 5.2, a terminal outside a cell can connect to another user's machine that is within the cell's coverage area. The latter acts as an intermediate router to access the cell's antenna.

Ad hoc networks pose many problems because of the mobility of all the equipment. The main problem is the routing required to transfer packets from one point to another point of the network. One of the objectives of the MANET group is to propose a solution to this problem. Four major proposals have been made: two of the reactive type and two of the proactive type. Other issues include security, quality of service and mobility management during communication.

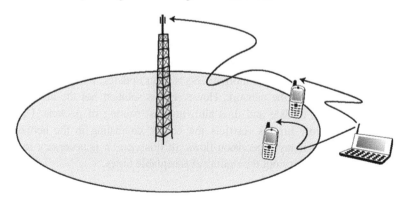

Figure 5.2. *Coverage extension by an ad hoc network*

5.2. Routing

Routing is the most important element of an ad hoc network. Routing software is required in each node of the network to manage the transfer of IP packets. The simplest solution is obviously to have direct routing, such as that shown in Figure 5.3, in which each station in the network can reach another station directly without going through an intermediary. This simplest case corresponds to a small cell, less than 100 meters in diameter, as in an 802.11 network in ad hoc mode.

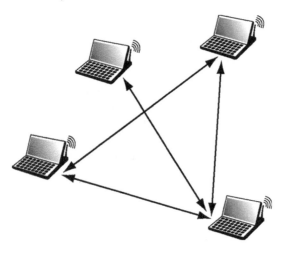

Figure 5.3. *Direct communication between machines in an ad hoc network*

The classic case of routing in an ad hoc network consists of passing through intermediate nodes. The latter must have a routing table capable of directing the packet to the destination. The whole strategy of an ad hoc network consists in optimizing the routing tables with more or less regular updates. If the updates are too regular, this may overload the network. However, this solution has the advantage of keeping the tables up to date and thus allowing fast routing of packets. Updating only when a new flow arrives restricts the charge circulating in the network but relieves the network of many supervision flows. In this case, it is necessary to set up routing tables that can carry out the routing at acceptable times.

Figure 5.4 illustrates the case of an ad hoc network in which, to get from one node to another, it may be necessary to traverse intermediate nodes. Many drawbacks can be found on the way to building the routing table. For example, in signal transmission, the link may not be symmetrical, with one direction of communication being acceptable and the other not. The routing table must take this into account. Since radio signals are sensitive to interference, link asymmetry can also be complicated by possible link fading.

For all of these reasons, network routes must be constantly changed, hence the perennial question debated at the IETF: should routing tables be maintained in the mobile nodes of an ad hoc network? In other words, is it worth maintaining routing tables that change constantly or is it not better to determine the routing table at the last moment?

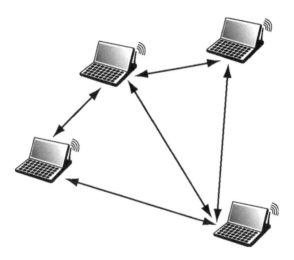

Figure 5.4. *Routing through intermediate nodes*

As explained earlier, reactive protocols work by flooding to determine the best route when a packet stream is ready to be transmitted. Thus, there is no exchange of control packets outside of supervision to determine the path of the stream. The supervision packet that is broadcast to all neighboring nodes is re-broadcast by the neighboring nodes until it reaches the receiver. Depending on the technique chosen, the route determined by the first control packet to reach the destination can be used, or multiple routes can be provided in case of problems with the main route.

Proactive protocols behave completely differently. Control packets are sent out all the time in order to keep the routing table up to date by adding new entries and dropping existing entries. The routing tables are therefore dynamic and vary according to the control packets arriving at the different nodes. One difficulty, in this case, is to compute a routing table that is compatible with the routing tables of the different nodes so that there is no loop.

Another possibility is to find a tradeoff between the two systems. This means regularly calculating routing tables as long as the network is lightly loaded. In this way, the performance of the user flows in transit is not affected too much. When traffic increases, updates are slowed down. This way simplifies the implementation of a reactive routing table when a request reaches the network.

The protocols proposed for standardization by the MANET group are summarized in Table 5.1. Different metrics can be used to calculate the best route:

– The distance vectors give a weight to each link and add the weights to determine the best route which corresponds to the one with the lowest weight.

– Source routing allows the best route to be determined as the one that allows the supervision packet to arrive first at the recipient.

– The link states indicate which links are worth taking and which are not.

Metric	Reactive	Proactive
Distance vector	Ad hoc On-demand Distance Vector (AODV)	Destination Sequence Distance Vector (DSDV)
Source routing	Dynamix Source Routing (DSR)	
Link state		Optimized Link State Routing Protocol (OLSR)

Table 5.1. *Ad hoc protocols*

In conclusion, if the studies of the MANET group are finished concerning the routing, everything or almost everything remains to be done for the quality of service, the safety and the energy consumption. We can just mention Quality of service OLSR (QOLSR), which exists in different versions.

The following lines briefly describe the two main routing protocols in ad hoc networks standardized by the MANET group.

The Optimized Link State Routing (OLSR) is certainly the most used of the ad hoc routing protocols. It is of a proactive type.

To avoid transporting too many supervision packets, OLSR relies on the concept of multipoint relay or MultiPoint Relay (MPR). MPRs are important nodes that have the particularity to be the best relay nodes to reach the whole of the nodes during a flooding process without broadcasting all azimuths. Since the link status is only sent by the MPRs, this reduces the number of supervision messages.

The knowledge of its neighbors is obtained by the Hello messages, which are sent in the broadcast. This makes it possible to determine which neighbors are active and to send the link-state information necessary for the routing algorithm. The Hello message is also used to indicate the MPRs to its neighbors. These Hello messages are only intended for neighboring nodes and cannot be routed to a two-hop destination.

The structure of the Hello package is shown in Figure 5.5.

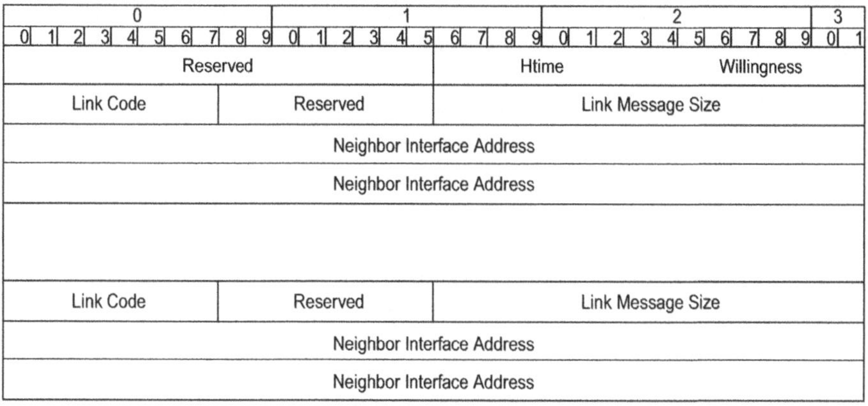

0										1										2										3	
0	1	2	3	4	5	6	7	8	9	0	1	2	3	4	5	6	7	8	9	0	1	2	3	4	5	6	7	8	9	0	1
Reserved																Htime								Willingness							
Link Code								Reserved								Link Message Size															
Neighbor Interface Address																															
Neighbor Interface Address																															
Link Code								Reserved								Link Message Size															
Neighbor Interface Address																															
Neighbor Interface Address																															

Figure 5.5. *Structure of the Hello package*

The Reserved field contains only 0's, the Htime field indicates the time interval between Hello, the Willingness field asks a node to become an MPR and the Link Code field is used to indicate link status information between the sender and the receivers indicated in the "Neighbor Interface Address" list.

The Topology Control (TC) packets are sent only by MPRs, with a flooding process. The information sent indicates the list of all the neighbors who have chosen this node as MPR and allows, by knowing all the MPRs and the state of the links, to deduce the routing table. These messages are flooded on the whole network using the MPR nodes. The structure of the TC packet is illustrated in Figure 5.6.

The Reserved field is always filled with 0. The Advertised Neighbor Sequence Number (ANSN) field carries an integer incremented at each topology change. This trick makes it possible to avoid taking into account information that would be too old. The Advertised Neighbor Main Address fields carry the IP addresses of single-hop nodes.

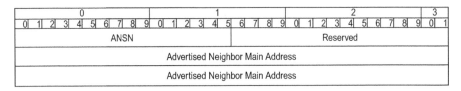

Figure 5.6. *Structure of the TC package*

Multiple Interface Declaration (MID) packets are used when nodes have multiple interfaces, and all available interfaces must be reported.

The MPR selection algorithm is as follows. Using Hello messages, nodes can determine whether they are connected full-duplex to their neighbors. Only symmetric links are considered in the determination of the MPRs. With respect to a given node, a first set is determined, that of its one-hop neighbors, the A set. To determine the MPRs, the Hello messages are rerouted, which allows us to determine the two-hop nodes, which form another well-defined set, the B set. Each node determines the symmetric links to its neighbors. For all nodes in B that have one and only one symmetric link to a node in A, we define that node in A as the MPR and ignore the nodes in B that are connected by that MPR. We repeat the process until there are no more unconnected nodes in B. The MPR nodes are then all determined.

Ad hoc On-demand Distance Vector (AODV) was the first protocol standardized by the MANET group, just before OLSR. It is of the reactive type. This protocol can handle both unicast and multicast routing.

When a packet stream is broadcast by a node, the first action is to determine the route using a flooding technique. To do this, the connection request packet remembers the nodes used during the broadcast. When an intermediate node receives a connection request, it checks that it has not already received such a request. If the response is positive, a message is sent back to the sender to indicate that the route has been abandoned.

The first message that arrives at the recipient determines the route to be taken. The complexity of the route determination process must be simplified as much as possible by avoiding unnecessary broadcasts. To do this, each route request is numbered to avoid duplication and has a Time To Live (TTL) that limits the number of transmissions in the network.

The advantage of AODV is that it does not create traffic when there is no message to transmit. The route determination is quite simple and involves only a few calculi in each node. Obviously, the two major drawbacks are the time required to set up the route and the large amount of traffic generated to set up the routes.

5.3. Mesh networks

Mesh networks (meshed networks) are networks of access points forming a mesh. The clients are connected by a wireless network to the access points of the mesh network, and the access points are connected to each other by wireless links.

The advantage of these networks is that they cover a large geographic area without the need to deploy cables to reach users. For example, on a large campus, access points can be placed on the roofs of different buildings without the network architect having to worry about connecting the access points to an Ethernet-type cable system.

Several possibilities are emerging to realize a mesh network:

– Using the same frequency as the terminals, considering that the access points are treated as terminal machines. The disadvantage is, of course, to use bandwidth taken away from the other end machines. Moreover, care must be taken that the two access points are not too far apart and do not force the transmitter and receiver to lower their speed. This solution is considered the first generation of mesh networks.

– Using different frequencies. For example, a Wi-Fi 802.11b network has three available frequencies, so it is possible to use two communication interfaces with different frequencies. The disadvantage is, of course, that the frequency plan is disrupted, especially if the network is large and has many access points. This solution is part of the second generation of mesh networks.

Also, in the second generation, the mesh network uses a different standard to connect the access points together. For example, a mesh network that connects clients via the 802.11n (Wi-Fi 4) standard can use the IEEE 802.11ac (Wi-Fi 5) standard to interconnect access points.

It is considered that at least four frequencies must be available, three to connect clients and one to interconnect access points. It may be worthwhile to use more frequencies to avoid interference in the interconnecting network of nodes. It is best to have upstream and downstream connections from the same node using different frequencies, but the number of frequencies can become important if the mesh is tight. Typically, 802.11ac (Wi-Fi 5) or 802.11ax (Wi-Fi 6) should be used, which have eight and eleven different frequencies, respectively.

Mesh networks create new challenges to wireless networks, including the following: How do you optimize access point batteries if they are not connected to power? How to optimize routing so as not to disrupt user traffic at access points, especially if they are already saturated? What density of access points should be used? This comes down to the question of access point transmission power.

The advantage of this technology is that it can be easily reconfigured when an access point fails. Clients can connect to another access point, even if it means slightly increasing the power of the access points next to the one that is down.

The main problem comes from routing management. This is handled in access points that are not very powerful machines, and therefore access points that carry a lot of traffic from connected clients should be avoided. Many proposals have been made, first of all, those coming from ad hoc networks.

After reviewing approximately 15 proposals, the IEEE 802.11s working group selected two proposals, SEE-Mesh and Wi-Mesh, which were combined to form a single proposal. This became a standard in April 2007 after many implementation discussions. Access points and stations that have the 802.11s routing algorithm are called Mesh Points (MP). Radio links are used to interconnect them. The default protocol is the Hybrid Wireless Mesh Protocol (HWMP). This hybrid protocol comes from a combination of a protocol from AODV, the Radio Metric-AODV (RM-AODV) and a tree-based algorithm. A second protocol can be used when the MPs accept it: the Radio Aware-OLSR (RA-OLSR) protocol.

The IEEE 802.11s group also defines security solutions for mesh networks. This includes defining mutual authentication of PMs, generating and controlling session keys, enabling data encryption on ad hoc network lines, and detecting attacks. This requires authentication using the IEEE 802.1x protocol. The session keys are managed by a Public Key Infrastructure (PKI). Confidentiality is ensured by the IEEE 802.11i standard.

Inter-cell switching is possible in some mesh networks, allowing for greater mobility of the equipment. This is the case with Green Communications' mesh networks. Moreover, telephony will only become a particular application in these environments. We can therefore expect diversification of handheld terminal stations able to connect to ambient Internet networks available in all busy places, such as the heart of cities, train stations, airports, subways, etc.

The advantage of ad hoc and mesh networks over 3G/4G/5G technologies is that they use frequencies only in very small areas, which allows for high reuse. In addition, the cost of a mesh access point is negligible compared to that of a 3G/4G/5G antenna. Given the explosion of mobile data rates, the gain from ad hoc and mesh networks is enormous. Most mobile network working groups are looking at hybrid solutions to save both energy and spectrum.

Another advantage of mesh networks over a 3G/4G/5G network is the power consumption. A 3G/4G/5G antenna consumes an average of 2,000 W. There are mesh access points that consume less than 20 W. If you replace one 3G/4G/5G cell with a set of thirty mesh points, the overall throughput of the mesh network is much higher, and the power consumption is reduced.

5.4. Participatory networks

Participatory networks come from the combination of mesh technology and Edge technology. The node is, in fact, a Skin data center that can also be classified as an Edge data center whose objective is to process the data coming from the connected devices. The Skin data center can use different technologies supporting virtual application machines, containers or any other similar solution. Participatory networks cannot be too large since all nodes are mobile, and the calculation of routing tables would become prohibitive. The set of nodes forming a participatory network is called a cluster. The Internet of Edges is an interconnection of participatory network clusters.

All of the Skin data centers are grouped together in clusters from a local cloud or Edge Cloud. Data is stored in this Edge Cloud and can be accessed by all clients connected to the cluster. Virtual machines embedded in the system are available to enable the implementation of many distributed services at the edge of the network and, therefore, close to the source of the data and the users.

One of the advantages of Edge technology is, of course, the extremely low latency, which allows the introduction of real-time applications. The Edge Cloud also allows preserving the bandwidth on the networks by favoring the processing of the raw data in the Edge Cloud and the transfer of only the analyzed data to remote servers. The Edge Cloud also brings privacy because the data remains close to the user and does not transit on the infrastructure networks. A final advantage of the Edge Cloud is the reduction of the global energy consumption of the communication networks. The Edge technology reduces the distance traveled by the information bits and limits the use of data center resources.

As in the participatory network environment, nodes can disappear, appear or reappear. The system must be resilient to any form of failure or what can be considered a failure. This requires a fully distributed Internet environment that requires network protocols and applications that are fully distributed and embedded in the nodes.

5.5. Local services

The principle of the participatory Internet is to relocate part of the services from the Cloud to the Edge, close to the users and the source of the data, to reduce latency, optimize throughput, save energy and gain autonomy from the infrastructure networks.

Relocated services are those that allow two people located in close proximity to exchange directly without going through an infrastructure network. Thus, we will find among the basic applications, voice calls, instant messaging and video conferencing services.

The participatory Internet must also allow a user to question his close environment directly thanks to services such as localization, the provision of data from sensors and cameras, but also collaborative applications for exchanging files, publishing information, etc., between users of a participatory network.

These applications can be in a native application or Web services. They are continuously optimized thanks to interference and route control algorithms. Other applications can be added to the open, participatory Internet environment.

The concept of participatory networks is revolutionary because of its ability to adapt to all contexts, mobility, security and agility. It can be deployed or inserted anywhere and in any scenario: open or closed, fixed or mobile environments or a mix of these different possibilities. Its integration into existing systems is simple since there is no need for any external functionality. It is obvious that the scaling up of very large networks poses additional problems that have solutions. However, the primary purpose of participatory networks is to position themselves on tactical bubbles and closed intelligent spaces.

A simple way to use it is to operate in lockdown mode, without any connection to the outside. This solution prevents all external attacks by design. Logical security against cyber-attacks is 100% guaranteed. A gateway can be installed between a participatory Internet network and the external world with an opening policy at times to be determined by precise rules.

Packets traveling through the network are encrypted. Encryption must be enforced even during handovers of clients passing from one node to another, thus providing end-to-end security against eavesdropping.

Participatory networks have been designed to be agnostic to the technology of transmission between nodes so that implementing maps and drivers for specific protocols on various frequencies is not a problem. If the network is a participatory Internet, it uses IP-level routing that leaves a completely open choice for level 2. We are back to the basics of the Internet.

5.6. The digital infrastructure of the Internet of the Edges

A participatory Internet or PI network is built from Edge data centers forming the nodes of the network. These interconnect with each other, with or without a gateway to the Internet. These Edge data centers integrate the Internet protocols, but in a totally distributed way so that the disappearance of one or more nodes does not change the network and its functioning.

Clients are connected to nodes according to the diagram in The disappearance of two nodes results in the diagram in Figure 5.8.

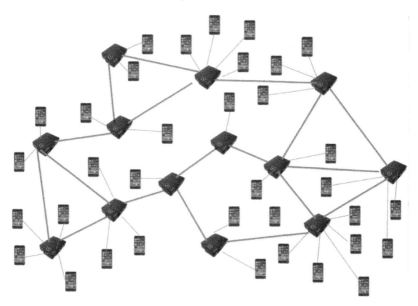

Figure 5.7. *A participatory network. For a color version of this figure, see www.iste.co.uk/alagha/networking.zip*

These networks are mesh if the nodes are different from the users' machines and ad hoc if they are integrated into the users' machines. The nodes connect to each other through direct autonomous connections that can use any type of technology. The most classical case is, of course, Wi-Fi, but it could be a Device-to-Device (D2D) in 5G or Bluetooth or any other wireless technology adapted to the application context. It can also be a fixed network like Ethernet, but in this case, we lose the mobility feature.

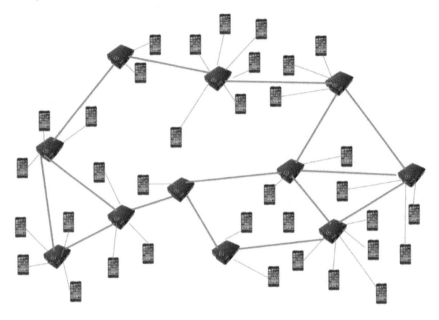

Figure 5.8. *The participatory network in Figure 5.7 after the disappearance of two nodes. For a color version of this figure, see www.iste.co.uk/alagha/networking.zip*

The mesh network can also have its nodes connected to each other by several types of wireless or wired links. For example, nodes and/or end machines can be connected using 4G/5G infrastructure. However, the number of interconnected nodes in a single network cannot exceed about 50 nodes. This network is a participatory Internet if the system is distributed.

These participatory Internet networks can interconnect to form the Internet of Edges. The interconnection is done through the 4G and 5G infrastructure networks. The routing between these networks is done by the 4G or 5G infrastructure. Interconnection involves passing through one or two antennas connected by the 4G or 5G core network.

In summary, nodes can have *n* types of D2D connections simultaneously and an algorithm capable of choosing the best link at any time. This algorithm must be applied from end to end by choosing the best path and taking into account the characteristics of the D2D links. The best path depends, of course, on the criteria that have been chosen, such as the highest throughput, but also the lowest power consumption, the most security, etc.

The clients are connected to the nodes via a second interface, which can be Wi-Fi, Bluetooth, or any other interface that can be implemented in the nodes. So in the most common case, there are two interfaces per node, which usually come from two Wi-Fi interfaces, but anything is possible: separate Wi-Fi on different frequencies, Wi-Fi and Bluetooth, etc. It is even possible to use a single Wi-Fi interface that connects both the nodes to each other and to the clients, but this solution is not recommended for reasons of overall throughput. Of course, there can be several different interfaces in the client devices, which can be objects, machines, human users, etc.

Nodes are either fixed or mobile, or fixed at some times and mobile at others. In the case of mobile endpoints, nodes connect and disconnect based on their neighbors. If a node is too far away from its neighbors, it disconnects without changing the operation of the network. When it gets closer to a neighbor, it connects instantly to its neighbor and, after a short period of time dedicated to updating, participates in the processing of applications integrated into the nodes.

The most commonly used function to connect two devices is based on the maximum throughput between these two devices that may be far apart in the same participatory network. This maximum throughput is often achieved with many short-range links rather than long-range links that greatly decrease throughput.

An Internet of Edges is an interconnection of Edges networks using the TCP/IP protocol. The simplest way to realize an Internet of Edges is to interconnect clusters of participatory networks.

Figure 5.9 shows only one cluster but also an Internet of Edges with large 4G or 5G antennas interconnecting clusters. The cluster is defined as the set of nodes that use the same routing table. Assuming that this figure represents an Internet of Edges, a BGP-like protocol must be used to interconnect the participating networks. Furthermore, Figure 5.9 shows some examples of connections between clients of the Internet of Edges that are more or less distant from each other. To this network of interconnections of the different participatory networks, we add the connections between nodes that themselves ensure the connections of clients and objects that can be supported by various technologies such as Bluetooth, ZigBee, 6LowPAN, Ethernet, etc.

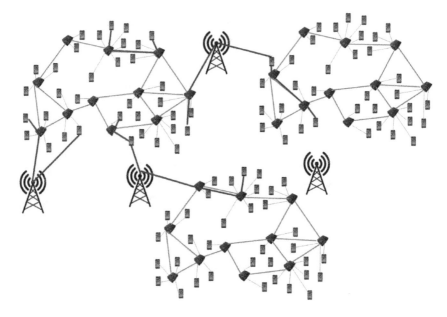

Figure 5.9. *Some examples of connections between devices. For a color version of this figure, see www.iste.co.uk/alagha/networking.zip*

The algorithms that optimize the throughput between two devices can be extremely diverse. For example, if we take the diagram in Figure 5.9 and assume that a node is able to reach another node located two hops away, we immediately notice that the shortest path has a maximum throughput of 1 Mbps, while the path without hopping intermediate nodes promises a maximum throughput of 8 Mbps, that is, with eight times the throughput.

A majority of the routing algorithms used today choose the shortest path and therefore try to skip intermediate nodes, which has a very negative effect on end-to-end throughput. Indeed, the throughput of a connection to a faraway node decreases dramatically as the power decreases with the distance squared. The solution that routes packets from node to node without skipping intermediate nodes gives a much higher throughput. The differences can be enormous, up to a 20-fold increase in throughput or much higher.

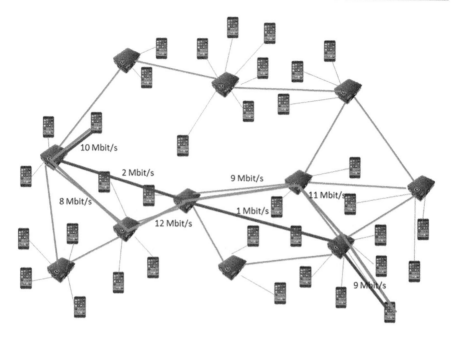

Figure 5.10. *Example of link bitrates. For a color version of this figure, see www.iste.co.uk/alagha/networking.zip*

5.7. Conclusion

Skin data centers today represent only a marginal fraction of the data center world, as centralization is still the order of the day in early 2022. However, a lot of research has been directed for several years toward the distribution of these large centers. Numerous experiments show the feasibility of Skin data center networks that realize uberized networks, that is, that can run without an operator. The nodes of the mesh network can be mobile, connect new nodes on the fly, take care of security by partitioning the networks, be set up almost instantaneously and adapt to their environment. An example concerning vehicular networks will be discussed in Chapter 7, which is dedicated to them. In each vehicle, there will soon be a Skin data center, which is partially the case today with very low power servers and without virtualization management. These servers will be interconnected to realize participatory networks and allow for significant assistance in the automation and the automatic control of the vehicles.

5.8. References

Arafat, M.Y. and Moh, S. (2018). Location-aided delay-tolerant routing protocol in UAV networks for post-disaster operation. *IEEE Access*, 6, 59891–59906.

Arafat, M.Y. and Moh, S. (2019). Routing protocols for unmanned aerial vehicle networks: A survey. *IEEE Access*, 7, 99694–99720.

Barroca, C., Grilo, A., Pereira, P.R. (2018). Improving message delivery in UAV-based delay tolerant networks. *Proceedings of the 16th International Conference on Intelligent Transportation Systems Telecommunications (ITST)*, IEEE, Lisbon.

Chen, J., Mitra, U., Gesbert, D. (2019). Optimal UAV relay placement for single user capacity maximization over terrain with obstacles. *Proceedings of the International Workshop on Signal Processing Advances in Wireless Communications*, IEEE, Cannes.

Gankhuyag, G., Shrestha, A.P., Yoo, S.J. (2017). Robust and reliable predictive routing strategy for flying ad-hoc networks. *IEEE Access*, 5, 643–654.

Gupta, V., Krishnamurthy, S., Faloutsos, M. (2002). Denial of service attacks at the MAC layer in wireless ad hoc networks. *IEEE Military Communication Conference (MILCOM)*, San Diego, CA, 29 November–2 December 2002.

Hong, J. and Zhang, D.H. (2019). TARCS: A topology change aware-based routing protocol choosing scheme of FANETs. *Electronics*, 8, 274.

Hoteit, S., Secci, S., Langar, R., Pujolle, G. (2013). A nucleolus-based approach for resource allocation in OFDMA wireless mesh networks. *IEEE Transactions on Mobile Computing*, 12(11), 2145–2154.

Hu, Y., Perrig, A., Johnson, D. (2002). Ariadne: A secure on-demand routing protocol for ad hoc networks. *ACM Annual International Conference on Mobile Computing and Networking (MOBICOM)*, Association for Computing Machinery, New York.

Johnson, D.B. and Maltz, D.A. (1996). Dynamic source routing in ad hoc wireless networks. *Mobile Computing*, 153–181.

Khatoun, R., Begriche, Y., Khoukhi, L. (2017). A statistical detection mechanism for node misbehaviors in wireless mesh networks (WMNs). *International Journal of Ad hoc and Ubiquitous Computing*, 31, 23.

Kheli, F., Bradai, A., Singh, K., Atri, M. (2018). Localization and energy-efficient data routing for unmanned aerial vehicles: Fuzzy-logic-based approach. *IEEE Communications Magazine*, 56, 129–133.

Kushwaha, V. and Gupta, R. (2019). Delay tolerant networks: Architecture, routing, congestion, and security issues. In *Handbook of Research on Cloud Computing and Big Data Applications in IoT*, Agarwal, D.P., Gupta, B.B. (eds). IGI Global, Hershey, PA.

Lakew, D.S., Sa'ad, U., Dao, N.-N., Na, W., Cho, S. (2020). Routing in flying ad hoc networks: A comprehensive survey. *IEEE Communications Surveys and Tutorials*, 22, 1071–1120.

Le, P.H. and Pujolle, G. (2012). A hybrid interference-aware multi-path routing protocol for mobile ad hoc network. *Computer and Information Sciences*, II, 179–183.

Li, K., Ni, W., Wang, X., Liu, R.P., Kanhere, S.S., Jha, S. (2016). Energy-efficient cooperative relaying for unmanned aerial vehicles. *IEEE Transactions on Mobile Computing*, 15, 1377–1386.

Mamechaoui, S., Didi, F., Pujolle, G. (2013). A survey on energy efficiency for wireless mesh network. *International Journal of Computer Networks and Communications (IJCNC)*, 5(2), 105–124.

Mamechaoui, S., Senouci, S.-M., Didi, F., Pujolle, G. (2015). Energy-efficient management for wireless mesh networks with green routers. *Mobile Networks and Applications Journal (MONET)*, 20(5), 567–582.

Martin, S., Al Agha, K., Pujolle, G. (2012). Traffic-based topology control algorithm for energy savings in multi-hop wireless networks. *Annals of Telecommunications*, 67(3/4), 181–189.

Mohammed, I.Y. (2019). Comparative analysis of proactive and reactive protocols for cluster-based routing algorithms in WSNS. *World Scientific News*, 124(2), 131–142.

Movahedi, Z., Hosseini, Z., Bayan, F., Pujolle, G. (2016). Trust-distortion resistant trust management frameworks on mobile ad hoc networks: A survey. *IEEE Communications Surveys and Tutorials*, 18(2), 1287–1309.

Mukherjee, A., Dey, N., Kumar, R., Panigrahi, B.K., Hassanien, A.E., Tavares, J.M.R.S. (2019). Delay tolerant network assisted flying ad-hoc network scenario: Modeling and analytical perspective. *Wireless Networks*, 25, 2675–2695.

Oubbati, O.S., Atiquzzaman, M., Lorenz, P., Tareque, H., Hossian, S. (2019). Routing in flying ad hoc networks: Survey, constraints, and future challenge perspectives. *IEEE Access*, 7, 81057–81105.

Peng, H., Razi, A., Afghah, F., Ashdown, J.A. (2018). Unified framework for joint mobility prediction and object profiling of drones in UAV networks. *Journal of Communications and Networks*, 20, 434–442.

Sanzgiri, K., Dahill, B., Levine, B.N., Shields, C., Belding-Royer, E.M. (2002). A secure protocol for ad hoc networks. *IEEE International Conference on Network Protocols (ICNP)*, Paris, France, 12–15 November 2002.

Yang, H. and Liu, Z. (2019). An optimization routing protocol for FANETs. *EURASIP Journal on Wireless Communications and Networking*, 2019, 120.

Yaqoob, I., Ahmed, E., Gani, A., Mokhtar, S., Imran, M., Guizani, S. (2016). Mobile ad hoc cloud: A survey. *Wireless Communications and Mobile Computing*, 16(16), 2572–2589.

Yaqoob, I., Ahmed, E., Gani, A., Mokhtar, S., Imran, M. (2017). Heterogeneity-aware task allocation in mobile ad hoc cloud. *IEEE Access*, 5, 1779–1795.

Zapata, M. and Asokan, N. (2002). Securing ad hoc routing protocols. *ACM Workshop on Wireless Security (WiSe)*, 1–10 [Online]. Available at: https://doi.org/10.1145/570681.570682.

6

Applications
of the Internet of Edges

Participatory networks allow the creation of tactical bubbles or intelligent spaces called clusters.

These completely sealed clusters can connect to each other and form the Internet of Edges. The clusters can move, separate or group together. They are connected to each other by fixed, 4G or 5G infrastructure networks.

The interconnection can use VPNs for security reasons. VPN links can be considered as one-hop links to integrate a few isolated nodes into a *cluster*.

We show in Figure 6.1 a possible topology of the Internet of Edges involving three clusters interconnected by an infrastructure network and secured by VPNs.

The Internet of Edges is also ideally suited to networks of vehicles, drones, robots and all things that move, with sufficient node density for the radio to connect the nodes together. Depending on the technology, most often Wi-Fi and 4G in infrastructure mode today and 5G tomorrow, the network can go from small to very large with ranges of several kilometers between nodes using appropriate frequencies and power. The performance achieved depends on the density of the nodes, the radio technology and the transmission powers.

Edge Networking,
by Khaldoun AL AGHA, Pauline LOYGUE and Guy PUJOLLE. © ISTE Ltd 2022.

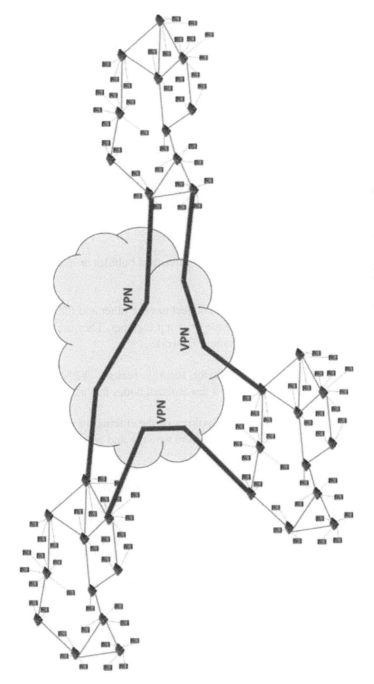

Figure 6.1. *Example of the interconnection of three clusters. For a color version of this figure, see www.iste.co.uk/alagha/networking.zip*

6.1. Civil security and defense applications

Participatory Internet networks are ideally suited for public safety and defense applications that require security, mobility, storage and real-time applications, including voice and video. The networks are made up of resources from the users and, more specifically, from the nodes brought by each participant. Applications must continue to run regardless of which nodes disappear or appear in the infrastructure. Clusters are made up of several dozen nodes and can grow to as many as 50 nodes.

A public safety example is the surveillance of a stadium full of spectators. Each security agent carries a node that together form a network. In case of an emergency, agents can communicate with each other using instant messaging and stream real-time video of events happening in the stadium. Depending on their location, they belong to a cluster, and the interconnection of these clusters forms an Internet of Edges. Each cluster can elect a cluster leader through a distributed consensus mechanism. Cluster leaders are connected via VPNs to ensure security and allow communications from any point in the stadium to any other point.

Another example is a group of firefighters intervening in a fire inside a building. They can similarly create a network and use voice and video applications. The network itself can be linked to a remote site (e.g. for a command) via an infrastructure network. It is also possible, rather than having a single cluster, to create multiple clusters to which the command staff could connect simultaneously thanks to the Internet of Edges network.

Examples of defense applications are numerous, starting with tactical bubbles, for which participatory networks are perfectly adapted. Indeed, the distributed environment that characterizes them provides very strong resilience to the system. The autonomous feature of participatory networks with regard to the Internet's servers is also a strong asset to protect tactical bubbles. The virtual machines that will be added over time will contain more and more artificial intelligence making tactical bubbles particularly efficient. As in the case of a fire, multiple tactical bubbles can be linked together.

Also, in the context of national defense, each ship in the naval force can be a tactical bubble, and multiple ships could be interconnected. There are different ways to design these secure interconnections and achieve their interworking.

6.2. Applications of the Internet of Things

Many objects are introduced into knowledge-based control systems to realize more intelligent clusters, for example, in a smart building or smart city. These objects connect to the Edge data centers, using the connection technologies available in the network. The cluster nodes collect the data streams coming from the objects and analyze them to feed either directly to the cluster applications or marketplaces that will sell some of these streams to other applications.

The Internet of Things (IoT) started with the idea of connecting to the Internet all wireless and wired sensors deployed at home, in the office and everywhere in daily life. One of the major sensors is Radio-Frequency Identification (RFID), or electronic tags. The IoT makes it possible to connect everything that is connectable, from large objects to smart dust. The concept is simple and challenging because objects are generally not sophisticated enough to manage communications and processing related to applications.

A sensor network is defined as a set of sensors connected to each other, each sensor is equipped with a network interface. Sensor networks are a new generation of networks with specific properties that do not fit into the framework of classical architectures. However, the arrival of the IoT has changed the vision of sensor networks. Sensor networks framework may continue to be a closed set, or it can open up to the Internet.

The miniaturization of sensors poses problems for communication and energy resources. The sensor must be intelligent enough to gather the required information and transmit it appropriately. In addition, the sensor processor should not be used too intensively in order to save energy. It should therefore incorporate reactive rather than cognitive elements. Finally, to ensure good throughput, the range of the network interface must necessarily be small, about 10 m. The implementation of a sensor network, therefore, poses problems with routing, error control and power management.

A particular type of sensor comes from what is known as smart dust. This dust is almost invisible and has radio equipment in addition to the treatments linked to the internal sensor. We can consider that these intelligent dusts will have a picocenter able to carry out some basic functions. The functions can eventually be modified thanks to virtualization supported by the electronic dust. Numerous use cases are already underway or planned in the coming years in the fields of health, defense, transportation, etc.

From a communication point of view, the TCP/IP protocols environment needs capacity that small sensors could not provide. Indeed, the Internet protocols generate a very important overhead for microcontrollers whose goal is just to send/receive information and not participate in the network operations. The solutions that have been derived from field networks, or real-time industrial networks, offer a better compromise between efficiency and energy consumption. As sensors can be arranged in hundreds per square meter, IPv6 addressing seems a good solution to manage addresses. However, the IPv6 environment requires a certain amount of computing capacity, and the implementation of a TCP/IP or even UDP/IP protocol stack in sensors is often impossible.

For the moment, security and quality of service issues are less considered than consumption ones. In any case, an important field of research is open to making sensor networks efficient and resilient.

The main radio standards are ZigBee, WiBree and 6LowPAN. WiBree is a very low-power technology with a range of 10 m and a bitrate of 1 Mbps. This solution was developed by Nokia to compete with both ZigBee and Bluetooth. WiBree was integrated with Bluetooth in 2009 to give a product called Bluetooth Low Energy (BLE). The IPv6 over Low power Wireless Personal Area Networks (6LowPAN) come from a working group of the IETF. The objective is to allow the continuity of the IP on low-power machines with limited energy resources. The use of the IPv6 standard in order to obtain a very large number of addresses for massive sensor networks poses a problem. Indeed, the 16 bytes occupied by the sender's address, added to the 16 bytes of the receiver's address, plus the mandatory fields lead to a bad use of the radio link to transport the supervision information. This can become a real problem because of the low energy resource available to the sensor. ZigBee, on the contrary, limits the length of its frame to 127 bytes, which can also cause problems if a large amount of information is to be transported from a sensor.

Sensor networks are ad hoc networks, and they need a routing protocol. Using a protocol like IEEE 802.11s, combined with IPv6 addresses, would be catastrophic to the battery life of the sensors. For this reason, current proposals are much simpler with protocols like 6LowPAN Ad hoc Routing Protocol (LOAD), a simplification of AODV, Dynamic MANET On-demand for 6LowPAN (DyMO-Low), a simplification of DyMO, the Hierarchical Routing over 6LowPAN (MANET Hi-Low), which includes hierarchical addressing. These different protocols come from IETF proposals and thus from the standardization of ad hoc networks, but they do not take into account all the options.

Another important feature of sensor network protocols is service discovery, which should allow the network to be started up in an automatic way. The IETF also plays an important role in this field by proposing several solutions, including one oriented towards sensors: LowPAN Neighbor Discovery Extension. This protocol is a reduction of the Neighbor Discovery standard concerning all energy-consuming elements such as broadcast communications and multicast communications management.

Smart dust is a particular sensor network whose goal is to develop sensors in nanotechnology and to link them by an ad hoc type network. The smart dust fits in a space smaller than a cubic millimeter, hence its name dust. In this dust are all the components necessary to build a communicating computer: a processor, memory, radio, battery, etc.

The main problem remains to save energy during the execution of the sensor functions. In particular, the network communications must lead to very low energy consumption. The University of Berkeley has thus designed an operating system and specific protocols named TinyOS and Tiny Protocol. TinyOS was written in a simplified C language, called nesC, which is a kind of programming language designed to optimize memory usage.

6.3. The tactile Internet

The tactile Internet can be defined as a network environment that allows remote access to manipulate, execute and control real or virtual objects in real-time by humans or machines. An IEEE working group has been defined to determine and standardize this new environment: IEEE P1918.1. The 5G technology is one of the great solutions to introduce this tactile Internet thanks to its extremely low latency of 1 ms and high reliability. Essential functions such as security, trust and identification must also be added in order to realize tactile Internet applications.

The tactile Internet must deliver not only content but also skills remotely. This requires ultra-reliable and ultra-responsive network connectivity that can provide the reliability and latency necessary for real-time physical interactions. Technically, the tactile Internet involves the implementation of a communication infrastructure that combines low latency, determinism, high availability, resilience and reliability with a high level of security. These requirements will not necessarily have to be met simultaneously for all applications but will have to be met for the so-called critical applications and partially met for many non-critical applications. In order to meet these stringent requirements, the tactile Internet will have to be combined with Cloud Computing; since the interaction time must be extremely short, the control and processing data centers must be located very close to the user, which we have called Edge Computing. If we refer to the previous chapters, this corresponds to MEC, Fog or Skin Computing.

The tactile Internet will also have to be associated with virtual or augmented reality for sensory and haptic controls in order to be able to process commands with millisecond reaction times. When these conditions are met, the tactile Internet is also capable of handling real-time critical applications (e.g. in industrial manufacturing), transportation control and anomaly detection (e.g. in healthcare) and non-critical applications (e.g. gaming or educational software) simultaneously. To better understand the way the tactile Internet operates, we have to examine the classes of applications concerned by the tactile Internet. We give some examples of applications in the following areas:

– Industry 4.0: the traditional manufacturing industry is undergoing a massive digital transition. The control of industrial equipment, such as robots or smart sensors, falls into this category, where real-time and remote control are paramount. The upcoming industrial revolution (Industry 4.0) is based on automated systems that can be activated in real-time. This revolution involves many important changes in manufacturing, engineering, use of new materials, supply chain and life cycle management. These smart factories must be particularly flexible and self-organizing. Services and applications must be combined with platforms that enable the automation of the environment, which will also be used for communication between people, objects and systems. The latency requirements for the different applications ranging from several tens of milliseconds for mechanical systems to a few milliseconds for Machine to Machine (M2M), and 1 ms for electrical devices. The value of the response time for the control cycles of fast-moving devices can reach values well below 1 ms. Finally, some very sensitive subsystems require a very low latency that is counted in a few tenths of milliseconds.

– The automotive sector: fully autonomous or automated driving should completely change traffic behavior. By detecting distances between automated vehicles and identifying potentially dangerous situations, the autonomous driving system, represented by a set of virtual machines located in a data center, is expected to significantly reduce traffic jams and accidents. The time required to avoid a collision between two vehicles following each other is less than 10 ms. If two-way data exchange for autonomous driving maneuvers is considered, millisecond latency will likely be required.

– eHealth: with the help of advanced telediagnostic tools, medical expertise can be made available anywhere and anytime, regardless of the location of the doctor. This application comes with strict requirements regarding reliability, availability, performance and security. Specific applications such as telemedicine may require less performance than remote surgery. In the latter case, latency, image quality, availability and security are critical parameters that require acute control. Furthermore, precise remote medical treatment can only be achieved with tactile feedback, which is also possible if the human-machine interaction (HMI) takes place in real-time. In eHealth applications for the tactile Internet, end-to-end latency of a few milliseconds is required, as well as extremely high reliable connection and data transmission.

Figure 6.2 describes some complementary applications of the tactile Internet in terms of latency and throughput. These include massive real-time gaming, multi-user video conferencing, real-time virtual reality, remote office work, etc.

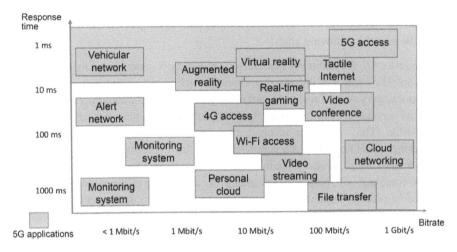

Figure 6.2. *Some 5G-specific applications. For a color version of this figure, see www.iste.co.uk/alagha/networking.zip*

The features required to realize a tactile Internet are numerous: in particular, we have seen the importance of low latency and high reliability. The main network for the tactile Internet should be the 5G network.

However, it is quite possible to realize a tactile Internet with a terrestrial network as long as the required performances are met.

A 5G-driven communication architecture, consisting of the radio interface to connect the client, the radio access network (RAN) and the core network (CN), meets the requirements for realizing a tactile Internet. As shown in Figure 6.3, the end-to-end architecture for the tactile Internet is divided into three distinct domains: the master domain, the network domain and the controlled domain. The master domain consists of a human or an automated machine operating a system via the system interface. This interface contains a control system that converts the operator's input into a tactile Internet input using various coding techniques. If the control device is a haptic device, it allows a human to touch, feel, manipulate or control objects in real or virtual environments. The control device primarily drives the operation of the controlled domain. In the case of a networked control system, the master domain that contains the operator has a controller that drives the sensors and actuators in the network. The controlled domain consists of an object that can be a robot, a machine tool or any other more or less complex machine. This object is directly controlled by the master domain via various control signals to interact with the remote environment. In the case of remote operation with haptic feedback, energy is exchanged between the operator and the controlled domains forming a global control loop.

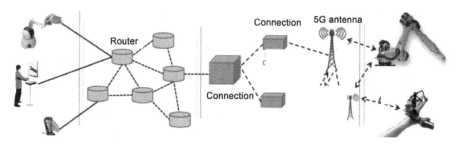

Figure 6.3. *Architecture of the tactile Internet. For a color version of this figure, see www.iste.co.uk/alagha/networking.zip*

The networks provide the basic support absolutely necessary for the communication between the operator, the machine or the human and the real or virtual object controlled remotely. This network must have all the necessary resources to provide high-quality communication with very low latency, thus, meeting the real-time requirement for the control of a remote object. Carrier-grade networks provide these properties and, more particularly, 5G networks. The carrier-grade indicates networks with very high availability, quality of service and a system to monitor this quality. In order to realize a tactile network, whether it is via 5G or a carrier-grade network, it is necessary to meet the following properties:

– Highly reactive network connectivity: this property is particularly important for systems with haptic interactions or for critical communications, for example, M2M communication for real-time control and automation of dynamic processes in areas such as industrial automation, manufacturing of complex objects, remote surgery, or process control by voice or touch;

– Reliability and availability of carrier-grade access: network connectivity must be ultra-reliable, which is a requirement of the tactile Internet. However, the reliability requirement is very specific to the application process and can vary greatly depending on the desired outcome.

– The possibility of managing multiple accesses: the use of several networks simultaneously is important to increase the reliability and availability of the network. This also represents a solution to reduce latency thanks to controllers capable of choosing the optimal network at any time, both for its latency and for the security of communications. The controller must be equipped with sufficient intelligence to make choices in real-time, directing the traffic to the network that has the performance required for the application to run smoothly. Artificial intelligence techniques should play a crucial role in the realization of the tactile Internet;

– Proactive allocation of resources to achieve the required Quality of Service (QoS): resource control has a direct impact on throughput, latency, reliability, QoS and protocol layer performance. In order to achieve very tight latency, resources must be prioritized for mission-critical applications on the tactile Internet. In addition, when applications need to coexist, whether they are haptic, voice-controlled, sight-controlled or machine-controlled, networks require high intelligence to achieve flexible resource control and be able to provide certain functionality on demand. In particular, for 5G, which is one of the main networks used for the tactile Internet, radio frequency allocation is an important task. The access network (the RAN) must also provide the necessary quality of service. RAN virtualization technologies can go the right way but also lengthen response times if the architecture in place does not meet real-time needs;

– Feedback loop control: feedback loops to react on systems that deviate from the custom operation of an application are necessary to maintain the desired quality of service. The tactile Internet requires such feedback loops when signals are exchanged bi-directionally over the network to allow remote control of real or virtual objects and systems;

– A highly reactive core network to accommodate the quality of service required by the tactile Internet: the network design can help significantly reduce latency in the core network. SDN techniques that provide tight control over resources and allocate those resources centrally, through a controller, are ideally suited to the tactile Internet. Function virtualization with NFV is also a very good way to achieve the necessary reliability, availability and security. In the context of the 5G core network, slicing is perfectly adapted to the tactile Internet by customizing a slice with all the functionalities required by the applications;

– A global conception of the end-to-end network: indeed, the tactile Internet supports end-to-end applications and therefore requires that the sum of the networks traversed is always capable of providing the necessary quality of service. Each sub-network may have the necessary resources to provide the necessary QoS for the tactile Internet, but their combination may not provide the performance required for tactile Internet applications to run in real-time, have the right security or reach the availability of a carrier-grade network. It is therefore important to design and size all the technology components involved, such as the LAN, access network and core network, and to consider the response time, throughput, security and availability of the whole. If the end-to-end network is 5G, the overall review requires proper sizing of the radio access, RAN and core network, which can be easier, especially if the whole thing is orchestrated, controlled and managed by the same system.

6.4. Telecom applications

The participatory Internet introduces natural extensions to operator networks. In Figure 6.4, we have represented the possible extensions through network technologies of the Internet of Edges.

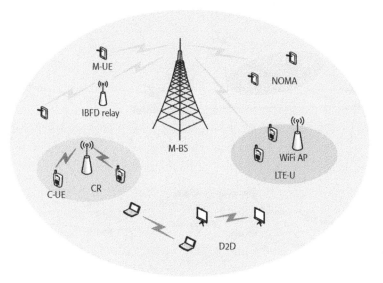

Figure 6.4. *Extensions of the participatory Internet. For a color version of this figure, see www.iste.co.uk/alagha/networking.zip*

Participatory Internet can take over locations without coverage where only one of the nodes needs to be able to connect to the main antenna, and communications can flow from node to node until they reach the antenna. This solution is also excellent for supporting areas with limited coverage and bitrate. Interconnection with the more traditional operator networks is done through simple gateways since both networks use the same IP. For example, in a tunnel without coverage or a white spot in the middle of a city, coverage can be provided by a set of participatory nodes located in vehicles or deployed for a more or less long period of time.

In-Band Full-Duplex (IBFD) relays allow communication between the main antenna and the relay; the relay can be a node of the participatory Internet. This solution again allows a simple extension of the antenna's coverage via relay antennas. This solution does not require any civil work.

A participatory Internet can also be deployed in an isolated town with, for example, satellite access to serve the whole village without having to do civil works. It can also be used in drone networks to cover overcrowded areas, such as large traffic jams in rural areas poorly equipped with relay antennas.

More globally, the Internet of Edges can bring together many objects, terminals and machines on the same network while being autonomous from the Internet. An example is shown in Figure 6.5.

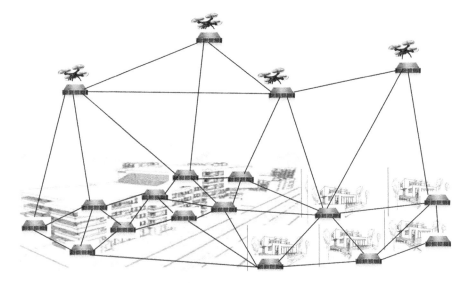

Figure 6.5. *An Internet of Edges infrastructure*

6.5. Industry 4.0

The Industry 4.0 concept brings a new production method that integrates physical machines, control software and management methods such as Enterprise Resource Planning (ERP). Figure 6.6 shows the progression of industrial technology toward digitalization.

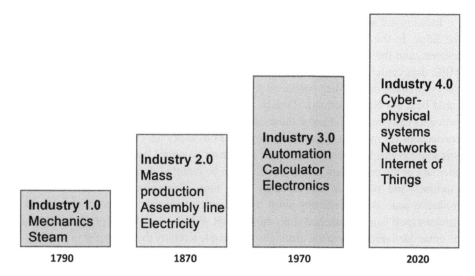

Figure 6.6. *Generations of industrial manufacturing. For a color version of this figure, see www.iste.co.uk/alagha/networking.zip*

The structure of the participatory Internet applies directly to Industry 4.0 environments. Edge data centers are fixed or mobile and can follow assembly lines or machine tools. Security is inherently provided by the properties of the participatory Internet.

The different architectures that could be opposed are introduced in Figure 6.7.

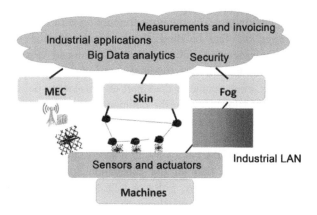

Figure 6.7. *Solutions for moving to Industry 4.0. For a color version of this figure, see www.iste.co.uk/alagha/networking.zip*

Industry 4.0 solutions take the same path as most services with the three levels of the Edge. In the first case, the machine tools are connected directly through a 5G antenna, and the virtual machines that drive the system are in the telecom operators' MEC data center. In the second case, the solution comes from the Fog vision with the on-premise data center connected to the machine tools by an industrial LAN that could be a 5G NR-U network. Finally, the third way is represented by participatory networks carrying the industrial processes in the mesh network nodes with Wi-Fi-type connections for machine tools. The advantage is obviously the extremely low latency of this solution thanks to the proximity of the sensor's control process and actuator. An anomaly in the production line or a hazard can be reported directly to the neighboring machines and people in an extremely short time. This solution also provides high resilience and excellent security since the network connecting the processes with the machine tools can be detached from the Internet. Finally, a participatory network can be embedded directly into the machines and people to enjoy these benefits in mobility.

6.6. The smart city

The smart city is a new paradigm that uses IoT technologies combined with networks and services to make the urban environment capable of providing multiple applications with good quality of service to its inhabitants while reducing operating costs. It is difficult to define exactly the intelligence expected by citizens. Nevertheless, six criteria are used to define the smart city: smart economy, smart mobility, smart environment, smart citizens, smart lifestyle and smart administration. The characteristics can be grouped in completely different ways. Instead, let us try to describe a few major development paths for the smart city by looking at the different levels of infrastructure.

Let us start with the lowest level: the infrastructure layer of the intelligent city. In the infrastructure layer, we find buildings, businesses, residential houses, streets, transportation, stores, gardens and other vertical environments that are supposed to work with elements outside their own perimeter. All these vertical infrastructures, conceived today in silos, must change in the smart city project to be rethought in the framework of a global vision allowing the definition and commercialization of new advanced services. Behind this infrastructure lie the many networks and equipment that must facilitate their interoperability. These include wired access networks such as fiber optic or data subscriber line (DSL) at a very high speed like very high-speed digital subscriber line (VDSL). We find all the connection solutions through wireless networks, such as 5G, Wi-Fi, SigFox, LoRa or LTE-M and specific interfaces with many objects using networks such as Bluetooth or Zigbee, but also through any other solution that allows obtaining speeds ranging from the highest to the lowest. The services offered by these networks are also very diversified, ranging from the health management of the inhabitants to the automatic reading of counters and mobility management. Figure 6.8 summarizes the infrastructure of the smart city.

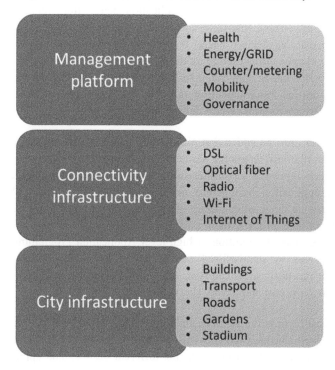

Figure 6.8. *The smart city infrastructure. For a color version of this figure, see www.iste.co.uk/alagha/networking.zip*

As far as end machines are concerned, many sensors will feed the smart city data centers. A city's sensors come from multiple suppliers, use a vast array of interfaces, etc. They are the most important pieces of the smart city puzzle. Sensors collect a large amount of data and allow the acquisition of vital statistics that, in turn, ensure the proper functioning of the city. Thus, networks of sensors, cameras, wireless devices and data centers are the key infrastructure providing services in the fastest and most efficient way possible. There are many sensors in a smart city with different purposes, integrated and managed by different stakeholders. These sensors include mobile sensors, wearable sensors, weather sensors, pollution sensors, metering and transportation management sensors, traffic and security cameras, sensors for parking space management, lighting, metering, waste management, etc.

Behind the infrastructure layer are the interfaces to realize the communications between this infrastructure layer and the smart city services. Interfaces materialize between the infrastructure and many application actors from public and private services of the city. These interfaces come from telecom operators, standards groups and governmental legislators. There is a need to focus on creating a secure, standardized and open infrastructure model for service delivery. These interfaces must be designed by combining application software, standards and infrastructure gateways and using a unified communication protocol and data semantics to establish a common open framework for service delivery and management.

Then, a layer must be added that plays the role of the platform that provides the services. This platform supports services adapted to the smart city and smart buildings, which represent a considerable amount of work. This puzzle requires a vision of the application architecture and a solution to secure and scale the interspaces with a wide range of connectivity options. This requires software to manage devices, collect and process their data, display results, automate functions and provide new services. In addition, a high-level Application Programming Interface (API) with access to standardized data must be available so that application developers or vertical silos can use the infrastructure to deliver value-added applications at a low cost and in very short timeframes.

The topmost layer is the services and applications layer. Through this layer and all the other layers, the provision of real-time information about urban environments and vertical silos provides useful sets for different services and applications. It is obvious that the number of application areas is very large. Among other examples, we can mention:

– real-time travel information, essential for applications, allows people to plan their trips by public transport or private vehicle. The user can get real-time information about the next bus or train;

– parking information that is accessible to allow drivers to quickly find available spaces;

– information on air quality, traffic and many other values that allow you to react to thresholds being exceeded.

Access to this data represents an opportunity for developers to create new applications. In this way, stakeholders can access a wide range of online services through information portals, citizen services, business applications and tourist services, all based on a common infrastructure and a Big Data of city information.

Smart cities offer new services that should make them more attractive. In addition, many gains are expected in different areas, the most important of which are the following:

– economies of scale through cost optimization and better engagement of the city's residents;

– benefits to citizens through improved healthcare, lifestyle and transportation efficiency;

– economic expansion opportunities for businesses but also for public services;

– spectacular growth opportunities for companies that will follow these new smart city technologies.

All Edge network architectures will be mobilized in the smart city domain (MEC for operator networks, Fog for enterprises, Skin networks for proximity uses, participatory networks for mobility and the Internet of Edges for scaling up) in order to guarantee the speed of information processing, data sovereignty and the resilience of smart city functions.

6.7. Conclusion

The Internet of Edges offers a new vision of the network world through its low latency, resilience and security by design. Even if this solution is still underdeveloped due to the power of the large Web industrialists who manage the world from very large central machines, its arrival is only a matter of time, which will allow us to return from centralization to distribution and put back at the center the paradigms that made the success of the Internet. In this chapter, we have noted the advantages of this solution for distributed systems.

6.8. References

Fox, R. and Hao, W. (2017). *Internet Infrastructure: Networking, Web Services, and Cloud Computing*. CRC Press, Boca Raton.

Hassan, N., Gillani, S., Ahmed, E., Yaqoob, I., Imran, M. (2018). The role of edge computing in Internet of Things. *IEEE Communications Magazine*, 99, 1–6.

Wang, P., Yao, C., Zheng, Z., Sun, G., Song, L. (2017). Joint task assignment, transmission and computing resource allocation in multi-layer mobile edge computing systems. *IEEE Internet of Things Journal*, 99, 1–1.

Wang, T., Zhang, G., Liu, A., Bhuiyan, M.Z.A., Jin, Q. (2019). A secure IoT service architecture with an efficient balance dynamics based on cloud and edge computing. *IEEE Internet of Things Journal*, 6(3), 4831–4843.

7

Vehicular Networks

Vehicular networks form an environment that is developing very rapidly. The transition to reality is near and will become a reality with the autonomy of vehicles that will need to interconnect to talk to each other and make decisions together. In fact, three types of vehicular networks will be overlaid: the control network, which allows the automation of driving, the passenger data network knowing that the driver himself will become a passenger and finally, the manufacturers' network whose objective is to follow the life cycle of the vehicle, to carry out maintenance and to make repairs, sometimes while driving, following a failure analysis.

7.1. Communication techniques for vehicular networks

Vehicular networks are a great example of participatory networks since all components are mobile and independent. The system must be formed by autonomous vehicles that are able to take care of themselves if they find themselves alone. However, if the vehicle is connected, the automation processes are much more efficient, and the vehicles will be able to move much faster. An example of a vehicular network is described in Figure 7.1.

In fact, three vehicular networks are overlapped but do not require the same quality of service. The first is the real-time control network, which can be seen as the control plane but which only supports the automation processes of the vehicles themselves and not the services associated with the data plane. The second network is the data plane, which represents the packets that carry user information, often to the Internet to reach an application server. Finally, the third network is that of the vehicle manufacturers who wish to maintain the vehicles in real-time and provide applications related to the road environment.

Edge Networking,
by Khaldoun AL AGHA, Pauline LOYGUE and Guy PUJOLLE. © ISTE Ltd 2022.

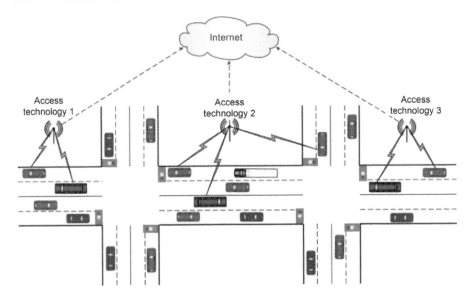

Figure 7.1. *A vehicular network. For a color version of this figure, see www.iste.co.uk/alagha/networking.zip*

The debate to choose the components of these vehicular networks is great because the market is huge. Numerous solutions are being developed, sometimes complementary and sometimes competing. Globally, we can say that three solutions are confronting each other for the vehicle interconnection part. The first is the use of networks connecting vehicles directly without using a large antenna. This solution is illustrated in Figure 7.2.

The second solution comes from 5G, thanks to its mission-critical property, which has the possibility to have latency times of the order of 1 ms. This solution requires the data to pass through the antenna to access a server or, if there is no large antenna available, 5G allows direct communication between vehicles. Figure 7.3 illustrates this second type of network, which corresponds to 5G.

The third solution is direct communication between vehicles thanks to light beams that obviously do not penetrate obstacles. This technology is generally called Visible Light Communication (VLC) with products like Li-Fi. Figure 7.4 illustrates this last solution.

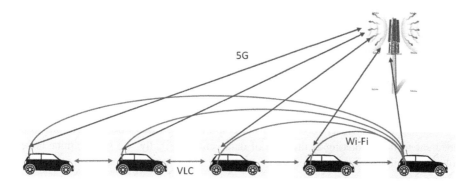

Figure 7.2. *Communication between vehicles: V2V. For a color version of this figure, see www.iste.co.uk/alagha/networking.zip*

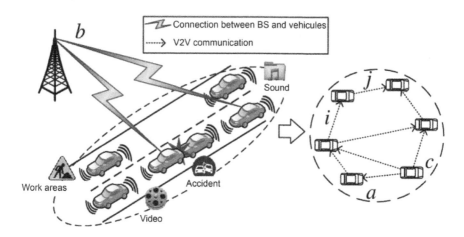

Figure 7.3. *V2V in the context of 5G. For a color version of this figure, see www.iste.co.uk/alagha/networking.zip*

Figure 7.4. *Communication by light between two vehicles. For a color version of this figure, see www.iste.co.uk/alagha/networking.zip*

Another major difference between these three solutions is where the control data is processed. In the case of vehicle-to-vehicle communications via Wi-Fi, the control is done in servers located in the vehicles, which can be called Skin data centers. For 5G techniques, the control is carried out in the MEC data center. Finally, when communications are carried out by light, the control is carried out directly from the server to the control server.

We will take a closer look at the three solutions we described above, but in a different form by looking at the type of data centers. Finally, we will examine these solutions for the three types of service: control, data and maintenance.

7.2. Vehicular Ad hoc NETworks

Vehicular Ad hoc NETwork (VANET) is a network concept from the so-called Intelligent Transportation Systems (ITS). As shown in Figure 7.5, vehicles communicate with each other through inter-vehicle links or Vehicle-to-Vehicle (V2V), or with equipment located along the roads via equipment-to-vehicle communication, or Roadside-to-Vehicle communication (RVC). These vehicular networks will contribute to safer and more efficient roads in the future by providing timely information to drivers and interested authorities.

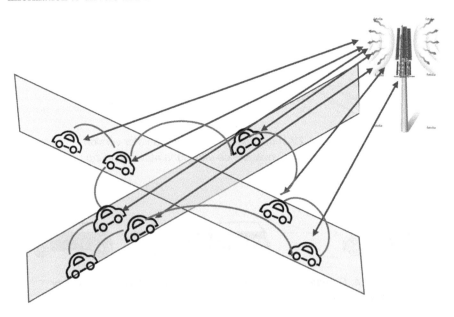

Figure 7.5. *An example of a VANET network. For a color version of this figure, see www.iste.co.uk/alagha/networking.zip*

Many applications have been developed in the context of the road network, such as reporting a problem on the road. A crashed car can automatically transmit a warning signal to the vehicles following or approaching the accident. Green lights can be synchronized as a vehicle approaches. Engine self-diagnostics can, after connection to a Cloud, cause a warning to be sent to the driver indicating the problem and the associated diagnosis. VANETs are, in this case, quite similar to MANETs but with the particularity of having fixed clients such as traffic lights or traffic signs. A characteristic of VANET networks, compared to MANET networks, is the greater simplicity of mobility patterns related to roads and railroads that usually determine the direction in which the user is traveling.

Another case is a vehicle carrying many passengers, be it a bus, a plane or a boat. Specific applications have been developed for this type of transport, such as multiplayer games or video sharing applications.

7.3. Connected and intelligent vehicles

A connected vehicle is described in Figure 7.6. It contains a server that will quickly enable virtualization and become a small-scale Skin data center. Objects and user machines are connected to this data center. The Skin data centers are interconnected by hybrid techniques, which can be, of course, Wi-Fi but also 4G or 5G and visible light communication (VLC). The interconnection of these boxes forms the participatory network. There is no master server since the vehicles can move away and disconnect as soon as they are too far from each other. It is necessary that vehicles that are approaching each other can automatically and quickly interconnect. The processes that manage the control must be distributed throughout the boxes.

Radar and lidar

Skin data center

Figure 7.6. *An intelligent vehicle*

In the state of standardization of these automated driving systems, vehicles move in cohorts, that is, train equivalents, in which vehicles can move from one train to another. This solution is quite simple to implement on a highway. Such a control scheme is described in Figure 7.7.

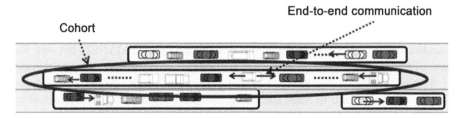

Figure 7.7. *Vehicles in cohorts. For a color version of this figure, see www.iste.co.uk/alagha/networking.zip*

The most important vehicle is the leader of the cohort, followed by the other vehicles. The braking of the leader should cause the braking of all the following vehicles with each time a delay of 1 ms so that about 50 vehicles in a cohort produce a propagation delay from vehicle to the vehicle of 50 ms, which is still very low compared to the reaction time of the foot during human braking which requires about 500 ms. Obviously, if the cohort is under 5G coverage, the reaction time will be much shorter since the signal will go directly from the antenna to the last vehicle without passing through intermediaries.

The network of a cohort can perfectly be a participatory network where each vehicle has a connection box. The cohorts form a cluster, and the interconnection of these clusters gives rise to an Internet of Edges where all the functions are distributed.

7.4. The MEC and the VEC

Figure 7.8 describes the case of a vehicular network using 5G technology for control.

The vehicles are all under the coverage of 5G antennas that are attached to MEC data centers. The processes managing the automatic driving are located in the MEC data centers, with latency times of one millisecond to access them.

Figure 7.9 represents an intermediate case where some vehicles are under cover, and others are out of cover.

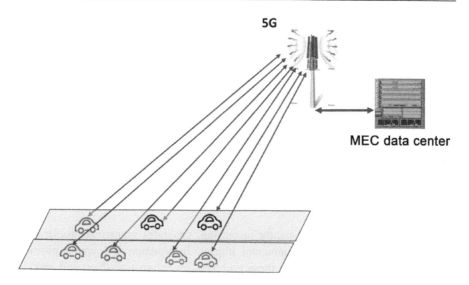

Figure 7.8. *The MEC. For a color version of this figure, see www.iste.co.uk/alagha/networking.zip*

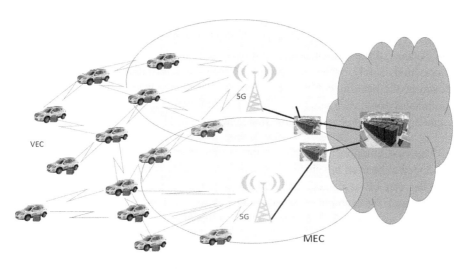

Figure 7.9. *The MEC and the VEC. For a color version of this figure, see www.iste.co.uk/alagha/networking.zip*

In Figure 7.9, we have two MEC data centers that each manage a 5G antenna. Vehicles that are within the coverage of the 5G antenna communicate via the 5G antenna. Vehicles that are not within the 5G coverage can be connected to the 5G antenna via a participatory network. In this case, the Skin data center we saw in the previous section becomes a Vehicular Edge Computing (VEC). The VEC boxes are interconnected by a participatory network allowing to fetch the automatic driving processes either locally or in the MEC data center.

The third case that we will find later concerns isolated groups of vehicles that are not under cover. In this case, the participatory network is the solution to interconnect them.

7.5. Intelligent transport systems (ITS)-G5

Road traffic, which is constantly increasing, generates numerous problems of management, safety and environmental impact. Information and communication technologies provide solutions to these problems by automating them and making vehicles autonomous. Intelligent transport systems (ITS) cover a wide variety of solutions for vehicle-to-vehicle communication. These solutions are intended to increase travel safety, minimize environmental impact, improve traffic management and, more generally, optimize travel.

Driver assistance for autonomous vehicles helps them maintain a regulated speed and distance, drive in their lane, avoid overtaking in dangerous situations and cross intersections safely, which has positive effects on safety and traffic management. However, the benefits could be even greater if vehicles were able to communicate continuously with each other or with the road infrastructure. We will first look at the important technical elements in the first generation of ITS.

The first component of automation comes from the radar technology that is developed to be used in vehicles to smooth traffic and avoid accidents. Several types of radar can be explained, including long-range radars that operate at 77 GHz and are used, for example, in speed control between following vehicles. This allows a vehicle to maintain a constant cruising distance from the vehicle in front. Short-range radars are used to manage anti-collision systems operating at 24 and 79 GHz. In the event that a collision is unavoidable, the vehicle has time to prepare for the collision by braking, of course, but also by activating protective equipment such as airbags to minimize injuries to passengers and others. A band has been allocated on 79 GHz to implement this radar service.

In recent years, research on intelligent vehicles has focused on cooperative ITS (C-ITS) in which vehicles communicate with each other and/or with the infrastructure. A C-ITS can significantly increase the quality and reliability of information available in the vehicles, their location and the road environment. A C-ITS enhances existing services and creates new ones for road users, bringing significant social and economic benefits, increased transportation efficiency and improved safety.

The technology used to enable vehicles to communicate with each other comes from the IEEE 802.11p standard, which is an approved amendment to the IEEE 802.11 standard, aimed at adding wireless access for vehicular environments (WAVE) defining an in-vehicle communication system. It defines the enhancements to the 802.11 standards (the working group that defines Wi-Fi standards) required to support ITS applications. This includes data exchange between high-speed vehicles and between vehicles and roadside infrastructure, known as vehicle-to-infrastructure (V2I), in the ITS band, licensed at 5.9 GHz (5.85-5.925 GHz). IEEE 1609 is the standard that applies to the upper layer based on IEEE 802.11p. It is also the basis for a European standard for vehicular communication known as ETSI ITS-G5.

The IEEE 802.11p standard uses the Enhanced Distributed Channel Access (EDCA) medium access control (MAC) channel access method, which is an enhanced version of the Distributed Coordination Function (DCF) that is the core solution for Wi-Fi, defined by the 802.11 group. The EDCA method uses Carrier Sense Multiple Access (CSMA) with Collision Avoidance (CSMA/CA), which means that a node that wants to transmit must first detect if the medium is free or not. If it is free during the Arbitration Inter-Frame Space (AIFS) time, it defers the transmission by drawing a random time. The random time determination procedure works as follows:

– The node draws a random value uniformly on the interval [0, CW + 1] where the initial value contention window (CW) is equal to CWmin.

– The size of the CW doubles each time the transmission attempt fails until the CW value is equal to CWmax. If the backoff value is 0, the sender immediately sends its packet. To guarantee the transfer of urgent messages with high security, the 802.11p protocol uses priorities corresponding to different access classes (AC). There are four classes of data traffic with different priorities: Background traffic (BK or AC0), Best Effort traffic (BE or AC1), Video traffic (VI or AC2) and Voice traffic (VO or AC3). Different AIFS (time to transmit) and CW are chosen for the different access classes. This algorithm, quite similar to those of other Wi-Fi networks, allows, at a very low cost, to obtain a good quality of service for priority clients and a lower quality of service for non-priority data. The parameters are shown in Tables 7.1 and 7.2.

AC	CWmin	CWmax
Background (AC_BK)	aCWmin	aCWmax
Best Effort (AC_BE)	aCWmin	aCWmax
Video (AC_VI)	(aCWmin+1)/2-1	aCWmin
Voice (AC_VO)	(aCWmin+1)/4-1	(aCWmin+1)/2-1

Table 7.1. *Priority classes*

For a typical value of CWmin = 15 and CWmax = 1023, we obtain the following values.

AC	CWmin	CWmax	AIFSN	Max TXOP
Background (AC_BK)	15	1 023	7	0
Best Effort (AC_BE)	15	1 023	3	0
Video (AC_VI)	7	15	2	3.008 ms
Voice (AC_VO)	3	7	2	1.504 ms
Legacy DCF	15	1 023	2	0

Table 7.2. *Default values for EDCA parameters*

Table 7.3 gives the transfer rates, modulation, code rate and finally, the number of bits transmitted on an OFDM symbol.

In conclusion, ITS-G5 is the most advanced of all the proposed techniques for interconnecting vehicles and building a vehicular network. Many experiments to evaluate its performance have been conducted in the real environment. This solution is perfectly suited to support inter-vehicle communications and represents a simple method to implement with a relatively low cost. The only drawback of this solution is that it is limited to the control part because of the Wi-Fi channel used, which has very limited bandwidth. The CSMA/CA solution can also be criticized for being somewhat random because if the number of vehicles is large, strong interference can significantly affect performance.

Bit rate (Mbps)	Type of modulation	Rate of coding	Bit rate per OFDM symbol	Number of bits per OFDM symbol
3	BPSK	1/2	24	48
4 and 5	BPSK	3/4	36	48
6	QPSK	1/2	48	96
9	QPSK	3/4	72	96
12	16-QAM	1/2	96	192
18	16-QAM	3/4	144	192
24	64-QAM	2/3	192	288
27	64-QAM	3/4	216	288

Table 7.3. *Baud rate, modulation scheme and code rate in 802.11p*

7.6. 5G V2X

The standardization of 5G is almost complete. The first phase represented by release 15 was completed in 2018, and the second phase ended in 2020. Both phases are important for vehicle control. Indeed, the first phase normalized the radio part and the second phase the critical missions. The latency retained in this second phase of standardization is one millisecond, which is a perfectly acceptable time for vehicle control. The reaction time of the foot of an individual to brake is higher than 100 ms, it is considered that the reaction times taking into account the latency and the calculations of control carried out in a server must be lower than 100 ms.

For more than 15 years, the ITS has defined a spectrum band, harmonized worldwide in the 5.9 GHz band, dedicated to vehicle traffic safety applications. The IEEE 802.11p standard has been chosen as we have just seen for the communication system providing active safety functions. During the last 15 years, authorities, industry and road operators have succeeded in deploying this common communication infrastructure using this standard, but on a relatively small scale. An alternative comes from a rather similar technique, this time based on the standardization carried out by 3GPP for mobile networks, proposing direct communication between vehicles. This alternative to traditional IEEE 802.11p communication can combine the strengths of cellular connectivity based on V2N communication with the strengths of direct V2V communication. In the automotive industry, since cellular connectivity is required for various other controls, standardized direct communication can be established in parallel with the deployment of cellular connectivity.

The V2V or V2I are appropriate solutions to manage safety elements in the vehicle domain. Many manufacturers have already implemented many use cases of these technologies by adding intelligent sensors in the vehicle and collecting information during V2N. We will now describe some examples in this area.

A first example is a collision warning based on sensor information from vehicles, pedestrians or the infrastructure, indicating the position and speed of vehicles that may be involved in the collision. A second example is the detection of a dangerous location from a back-office, such as the detection of a strong deceleration of a vehicle during emergency braking, reported by sensors from different vehicles. If a safety function relies on data from other vehicles and needs to provide active safety, the network latency must be strongly limited to a maximum time of 100 ms. Without this upper bound, the information must be transmitted directly between vehicles, to or from the road infrastructure or to or from pedestrians. A third example is given by V2I. For example, a traffic light transmits to vehicles when the light is about to turn green. Another example comes from a construction vehicle transmitting information about speed limits around the construction site or about the dangers linked to the work in progress.

The new term used in the 5G world to describe communications in the vehicular environment is Cellular-V2X (C-V2X). The basic V2X mode includes two communication modes: Mode 3 and Mode 4. In Mode 3, the cellular network allocates and manages the radio resources used by the vehicles for their communications. The signaling goes through the eNodeB or through the MEC data center that virtualizes the eNodeB. In mode 4, the vehicles autonomously select the radio resources to perform direct V2V communications, directly from one vehicle to another. Mode 4 uses scheduling for congestion control, which allows priority packets to be routed first and given the required quality of service. V2X communications in Mode 4 can operate without cell coverage, going directly from one vehicle to another if they are close enough to each other to be within their respective coverage areas. Mode 4 is considered the basic mode of V2V, as traffic safety applications cannot depend on the availability of radio coverage. These control applications must be able to run without coverage outside of the antennas in the vehicles.

In the event that a cellular connection cannot be established, direct communication via the PC5 interface (the name of the interface from one vehicle to another vehicle) must work to maintain communication. This requirement arises because vehicles may not be covered by a radio cell associated with an eNodeB, or vehicles may be using their V2N connectivity from the Uu interface for other services. The ecosystem-based on the PC5 interface must therefore be able to function at all times, regardless of the mobile operator network to which the connected vehicle belongs. In addition to all the technical reasons, direct communication is a matter of trust because, unlike a telecom operator, no third party is involved in establishing the communication. If a vehicle cannot trust the information transmitted via PC5 communication, the system cannot work. The security systems for direct communication are largely supported by the C-V2X standard. All security and data privacy rules are defined in the C-V2X direct communication standard in the same way as they are specified in the IEEE 802.11p standard. On the other hand, these security rules benefit from V2N functionalities for operational purposes such as distribution, calculation, storage, certificate renewal and revocation lists. This is why C-V2X emphasizes direct PC5 communication with different service classes:

– Different types of user equipment are involved in C-V2X (vehicles, pedestrian areas, roadside infrastructure).

– Different network providers, including lack of network coverage.

– Different components of the safety management system establish a level of trust between the entities of the system.

In 2015, 3GPP specified V2X functionality to support LTE-based V2X services in release 14. V2X covers both V2V and V2I specifications. The first infrastructure connection specifications were made in September 2016. Additional enhancements to support new V2X operational scenarios were added in release 14, which was finalized in June 2017.

V2V communications are based on device-to-device (D2D) communications defined in the Proximity Services (ProSe) framework, which is defined in Releases 12 and 13. As part of these ProSe services, a new D2D interface, called PC5, which we have already discussed in the previous section, was introduced to support the use case of inter-vehicle communications, in particular, to define the enhancements needed to support V2X requirements for inter-vehicle communication. Improvements have been made to handle high vehicle speeds (Doppler shift/frequency shift, etc.) up to 500 km/h, synchronization outside of eNodeB coverage, better resource allocation, congestion control for high traffic load and traffic management for V2X services. Two modes of operation for LTE-V V2V communications V2V communications have been introduced in release 14: the first one corresponds to communication via 5G and the second one corresponds to a communication on the PC5 interface (V2V) from peer to peer.

The Uu interface corresponding to V2N represents the case where communication is implemented via an eNodeB. 5G V2V communication over the PC5 interface is supported via two modes: managed mode (PC5 mode 3), which operates when communication between vehicles is scheduled by the network and unmanaged mode (PC5 mode 4), which operates when vehicles communicate independently of the network. PC5 mode 4 and interference management are supported by distributed algorithms between vehicles, while PC5 mode 3 scheduling and interference management are managed via the base station (eNodeB) by control signaling using the Uu interface. The deployment scenarios, supported by one or more operators, benefit from the additional advantages of using Uu-based connectivity with broadcast services.

C-V2X involves V2N/V2N2V/V2I/V2N2P connectivity based on an interface called Uu with V2V/V2I/V2P connectivity based on PC5 (reference point of a direct vehicle-to-vehicle connection). We will mainly examine the advantages of the PC5 technology for V2X regarding the way to deploy it. In addition, this technology takes into account all aspects of V2N, which must be present in the PC5 direct connection in order to achieve a fully controlled connectivity. Operationally, the PC5 interface can be established for the following communications:

– vehicle to vehicle (V2V);

– vehicle to infrastructure (V2I);

– between a vehicle and road users, whether pedestrians, cyclists or other road users (V2P).

From a physical layer perspective, signals are transmitted using LTE technology. LTE defines an elementary resource by a frequency band of 15 kHz, taking a time of 0.5 ms. These elementary resources are grouped into elementary blocks of data to be transmitted consisting of 12 bands of 15 kHz following the technique used in OFDM. An elementary block in LTE, therefore, uses a spectrum of $\times 12$ 15 kHz = 180 kHz. It is called Resource Block (RB) and covers all 12 bands of 15 kHz.

In LTE-V (LTE-Vehicle), the frame lasts 10 ms. It is divided into 10 subframes of 1 ms duration. Each subframe is divided into two slots of 0.5 ms. A slot, therefore, lasts 0.5 ms, during which seven symbols are transmitted per OFDM band. Since there are 12 subbands, this gives a total of 84 symbols that are transmitted every 0.5 ms. In V2X, the slot is not divided into two parts, so for a slot of 1 ms 168 symbols are transmitted. A symbol can transmit from 1 bit to 6 bits depending on the chosen modulation (QPSK at 16 QAM in V2X, but this can go up to 128 QAM in the classic LTE framework).

The data is transmitted in Transport Blocks (TB) via Physical Sidelink Shared Channels (PSSCH). Control information is transmitted in Sidelink Control Information (SCI) messages, also called SA (Scheduling Assignment), on PSCCH. A TB contains a complete packet and may occupy one or more subchannels. This packet can be a beacon or a Cooperative Awareness Message (CAM), or any other event-driven message. Each TB has an SCI value associated with it, and both must always be transmitted in the same subframe. The SCI occupies two RBs and includes information such as the MCD (Modulation and Coding Scheme) used to transmit the TB, the RBs occupied by the TB and the resource reservation interval for the semi-persistent scheduling scheme. This interval refers to the periodicity used by the vehicles to transmit their packets (in multiples of 100 ms). Because the SCI information is critical, the SCI must be correctly received to receive and decode the TB. Figure 7.10 shows an example with three C-V2X subchannels. The figure differentiates between the RBs used for TB and SCI transmissions.

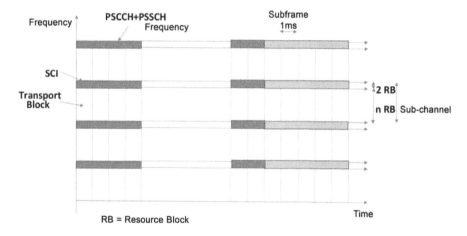

Figure 7.10. *An example of frames and subframes of a C-V2X communication. Comparison of 5G and Wi-Fi 802.11bd solutions. For a color version of this figure, see www.iste.co.uk/alagha/networking.zip*

In parallel with preparations for the mass deployment of first-generation V2X deployment using 802.11p Wi-Fi and C-V2X, the development of next-generation technologies continues. New specifications have been developed: next-generation Dedicated Short-Range Communications (DSRC) (IEEE 802.11bd) and the NR-V2X specified in release 16. The new specifications open up new possibilities. We introduce some of them below:

– The bandwidth is much higher: the messages transmit information about the objects detected by the vehicle's sensors, which greatly expands the content of the first-generation messages that simply reported the status of the vehicle. The new specification can support the significant increase in bandwidth by effectively enabling 20 MHz in 802.11bd and 40 MHz in NR-V2X. In addition, higher 256-QAM modulation is supported for 802.11bd and NR-V2X.

– Reliable operation: NR-V2X introduces group-casts for increased reliability using a new feedback channel (PSFCH). The group-cast request is useful for cooperative driving where one vehicle needs to be sure that messages have been received by the other vehicle. The 802.11bd standard introduces blind retransmission, similar to a concept already existing in LTE-V2X.

– Robustness at higher speeds: 802.11bd and NR-V2X are designed to operate at a relative speed of 500 km/h between two vehicles. Both solutions gain robustness at higher speeds by adding midambles in 802.11bd and DMRS as well as in the NR-V2X box.

– Communication range is increased: 802.11bd and NR-V2X use the LDPC error correction scheme and OFDM modulation. In addition, 802.11bd adds an additional range mode using dual-carrier modulation (DCM), similar to LTE-V2X's operation on narrow channels.

– Configuration flexibility: NR-V2X expands the number of possible configurations and includes subcarrier spacing to support short distances.

– Broadcast support: the NR-V2X adds support for diffusion, already supported by 802.11p. The 802.11bd further expands access capability by adding MIMO to double the speed between two vehicles.

Although 802.11bd can coexist on the same channel as 802.11p, the applicability of 802.11bd in the first generation is questionable since a single vehicle using 802.11p in the neighborhood would force all vehicles using 802.11bd to downgrade to 802.11p operation. Therefore, 802.11bd is not expected to come to market until second-generation services are introduced everywhere as a replacement for the first generation. The NR-V2X design goal supports the compatibility of both generations. The first generation would continue to be supported in parallel with the second generation.

7.7. The VLC

Light is another means of communication that is very useful in vehicular networks: between two cars following each other, there is no obstacle that would stop the light. On the other hand, the communication can only be done from vehicle to vehicle, and the vehicular network is realized by point-to-point links, which must be relayed by equipment located in the vehicles. In this section, we will look at the characteristics of these networks, which are called VLC, of which one of the major products is the Li-Fi.

Li-Fi is a wireless communication technology based on the use of visible light, with a wavelength between 460 and 670 THz. The principle of Li-Fi is based on the coding and sending of data by amplitude modulation of light according to a well-standardized protocol. The protocol layers of Li-Fi are adapted to wireless communications up to ten meters, which is an acceptable limit for communication between two vehicles.

The data are coded to allow a crossing of the optical channel, which is far from perfect. The signal in electrical form is converted into a light signal by means of an electronic circuit that allows the light intensity of the LEDs to vary according to the data to be transmitted. The modulation used is an intensity modulation where the logical 0 and 1 are transmitted according to the Manchester coding. The emitted light propagates in the environment and undergoes deformations for various reasons, such as weather conditions. This environment and the associated distortions are grouped under the term optical channel.

Li-Fi is a wireless technology that uses a protocol very similar to the 802.11 group, but it uses light instead of radiofrequency. Visible and invisible light uses a much larger bandwidth than radio frequencies, which obviously results in much higher throughput. Specifically, the Li-Fi has followed the IEEE 802.15.7 standard, which has been modified to take into account the latest advances in the field of optical wireless communications. In particular, the standard now incorporates modulation methods with optical orthogonal frequency division multiplexing (O-OFDM). The IEEE 802.15.7 also defines the physical layer (PHY) and the MAC layer. The standard defines data rates that allow audio, video and multimedia services to be carried out without problems. It takes into account the mobility of the optical transmission, its compatibility with the artificial lighting present in the infrastructures and the interferences that the ambient lighting can generate. The standard defines three PHY layers with different data rates:

– The PHY 1 is designed for outdoor applications and operates from 11.67 to 267.6 Kbps.

– The PHY 2 layer allows to reach data rates ranging from 1.25 to 96 Mbps.

– The PHY 3 is used for many emission sources with a particular modulation method called Color Shift Keying (CSK). PHY 3 can offer data rates ranging from 12 to 96 Mbps.

The recognized modulation formats for PHY 1 and PHY 2 use On-Off Keying (OOK) and Viable Pulse Position Modulation (VPPM). The Manchester coding used for PHY 1 and PHY 2 layers includes the clock in the transmitted data by representing a logical 0 with an OOK symbol "01" and a logical 1 with an OOK symbol "10", all with a continuous component. The continuous component avoids the extinction of the light in the case of an extended series of logical 0s.

7.8. Conclusion

Vehicular networks are expanding rapidly. Automated driving at somewhat higher speeds requires coordination that can only be achieved by connecting vehicles to each other. As the market is extremely important, the industry is preparing for a battle to impose its standard. The first propositions come from the G5 standard using IEEE 802.11p, and many tests have already been carried out showing the efficiency of this method. However, this solution can see its speeds drop in bad conditions, especially with interference from different antennas. 5G, which is a much younger technology and not yet fully mature, is coming in full force with classic techniques from the world of telecom operators. This solution is seen as a potential winner because of its less random nature. In addition, the 5G world has standardized a mode 4, which allows for direct vehicle-to-vehicle communication without an eNodeB cell.

7.9. References

Abbas, N., Zhang, Y., Taherkordi, A., Skeie, T. (2018). Mobile edge computing: A survey. *IEEE Internet of Things Journal*, 5(1), 450–465.

Baron, B., Campista, M., Spathis, P., Costa, L.H.M.K., Amorim, M.D., Duarte, O.C.M.B., Pujolle, G., Viniotis, Y. (2016). Virtualizing vehicular node re-sources: Feasibility study of virtual machine migration. *Vehicular Communications*, 4(C), 39–46.

Chen, M., Li, W., Hao, Y., Qian, Y., Humar, I. (2018). Edge cognitive computing-based smart health care system. *Future Generation Computer Systems*, 86, 403–411.

Cui, J., Wei, L., Zhang, J., Xu, Y., Zhong, H. (2018). An efficient message-authentication scheme based on edge computing for vehicular ad hoc networks. *IEEE Transactions on Intelligent Transportation Systems*, 20, 1621–1632.

Gupta, S. and Chakareski, J. (2020). Lifetime maximization in mobile edge computing networks. *IEEE Transactions on Vehicular Technology*, 69(3), 3310–3321.

Hatoum, A., Langar, R., Aitsaadi, N., Boutaba, R., Pujolle, G. (2014). Cluster-based resource management in OFDMA femtocell networks with QoS guarantees. *IEEE Transactions on Vehicular Technology*, 63(5), 2378–2391.

Kozik, R., Choras, M., Ficco, M., Palmieri, F. (2018). A scalable distributed machine learning approach for attack detection in edge computing environments. *Journal of Parallel and Distributed Computing*, 119, 18–26.

Li, X., Dang, Y., Aazam, M., Peng, X., Chen, T., Chen, C. (2020). Energy efficient computation offloading in vehicular edge cloud computing. *IEEE Access*, 8(37), 632–644.

Monteiro, T., Pellenz, M.E., Penna, M.C., Enembreck, F., Souza, R.D., Pujolle, G. (2012). Channel allocation algorithms for WLANs using distributed optimization. *International Journal of Electronics and Communications*, 66(6), 480–490.

Movahedi, Z., Ayari, M., Langar, R., Pujolle, G. (2012). A survey of autonomic network architectures and evaluation criteria. *IEEE Communications Surveys and Tutorials*, 14(2), 491–513.

Pace, P., Aloi, G., Gravina, R., Caliciuri, G., Fortino, G., Liotta, A. (2019). An edge-based architecture to support efficient applications for healthcare industry 4.0. *IEEE Transactions on Industrial Informatics*, 15(1), 481–489.

Rodrigues, J. (2018). *Advances in Delay-tolerant Networks (DTNs): Architecture and Enhanced Performance*. Woodhead Publishing, Sawston.

Sethom, K. and Pujolle, G. (2018). Spectrum mobility management in cognitive two-tier networks. *International Journal of Network Management*, 28(3), e2019.

Sharma, A. (2020). Mission Swachhta: Mobile application based on mobile cloud computing. *10th International Conference on Cloud Computing, Data Science Engineering (Confluence)*, Noida, India, 29–31 January 2020.

Wang, S., Zhao, Y., Huang, L., Xu, J., Hsu, C.-H. (2017). Qos prediction for service recommendations in mobile edge computing. *Journal of Parallel and Distributed Computing*, 1–11, 127, Issue C, May 2019, 134–144 [Online]. Available at: https://doi.org/10.1016/j.jpdc.2017.09.014.

Wu, Y. and Hu, F. (2017). *Big Data and Computational Intelligence in Networking*. CRC Press, Boca Raton.

Yao, D., Yu, C., Yang, L.T., Jin, H. (2019). Using crowdsourcing to provide QoS for mobile cloud computing. *IEEE Transactions on Cloud Computing*, 7(2), 344–356.

Zhang, Z., Zhang, W., Tseng, F. (2019). Satellite mobile edge computing: Improving QoS of high-speed satellite-terrestrial networks using edge computing techniques. *IEEE Network*, 33(1), 70–76.

Zhang, J., Guo, H., Liu, J., Zhang, Y. (2020). Task offloading in vehicular edge computing networks: A load-balancing solution. *IEEE Transactions on Vehicular Technology*, 69(2), 2092–2104.

Zhao, Z., Min, G., Gao, W., Wu, Y., Duan, H., Ni, Q. (2018). Deploying edge computing nodes for large-scale IoT: A diversity aware approach. *IEEE Internet of Things Journal*, 5(5), 3606–3614.

8

Virtualization of the Internet of Edges

8.1. Network virtualization

Virtualization is not a new technique since it was introduced in the first mainframe computers to share memory via the pagination system. The trick was to bring memory pages from the hard disk back into memory just before the processor needed them. Subsequently, a number of mechanisms were implemented with this solution so that the user would have the impression that the necessary services were located on a nearby machine when, in fact, they were on a remote machine.

Server virtualization has been a huge success in consolidating multiple servers on a single machine. The user has the impression of having his own server when, in fact, he is only sharing a machine. Network virtualization is based on the same principle: several virtual networks share the same physical infrastructure.

Network virtualization was initiated by an American project called Global Environment for Network Innovations (GENI), in which Intel intended to build a router composed only of its hardware part without any network operating system, the control part is located remotely. The control software vendors could implement their system on a more powerful machine a few miles away or even much further. Figure 8.1 shows the virtualization of three physical routers that become software in a data center of varying sizes. The advantage of this solution is that the size of the router depends on the load to be handled. At night, the virtual router can be very small and, during the day, very powerful. The difficulty is not to spend too much energy

Edge Networking,
by Khaldoun Al Agha, Pauline Loygue and Guy Pujolle. © ISTE Ltd 2022.

compared to hardware routers which require less energy thanks to the hardware components which accelerate the processing. To do this, it is necessary to urbanize the virtual machines in the data centers by grouping them on the same physical machine as soon as necessary to make good use of the processor and to distribute the virtual machines on different servers as soon as greater power is required.

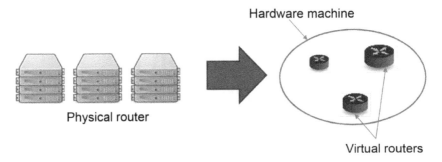

Figure 8.1. *Three virtual routers. For a color version of this figure, see www.iste.co.uk/alagha/networking.zip*

The advantages of this technology are agility, flexibility and versatility, while the disadvantage comes from the decrease in performance and, therefore, the use of more powerful machines, even much more powerful, which consume much more energy. It is therefore absolutely necessary to be very careful with the placement of virtual machines and to do excellent urbanization to succeed in not spending more energy than with physical machines.

A virtual router is a logical instance of a physical router, and several virtual routers can run simultaneously on the same physical machine or on a generic machine (commodity) with the necessary I/O to perform the same functions as the physical router.

We get the ability to deploy multiple virtual networks that can run on the same physical network, which is a digital infrastructure in this case with antennas, fiber and data centers. A virtual network is the re-grouping of a set of compatible virtual nodes (routers or switches). The virtual nodes use physical fiber links to interconnect.

Such an environment is represented in Figure 8.2, in which four networks co-exist on the same digital infrastructure containing data centers composed of servers. These data centers, as we have seen, are more or less large.

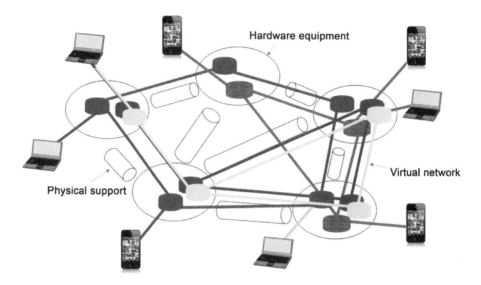

Figure 8.2. *Network virtualization. For a color version of this figure, see www.iste.co.uk/alagha/networking.zip*

A virtual network consists of virtual nodes that use the same communication protocols. Each virtual network can use completely different protocols, for example, an IPv4 virtual network, an IPv6 virtual network, an MultiProtocol Label Switching (MPLS) virtual network, etc. In other words, it is possible to build a virtual network for each application with the best possible protocols, which is called slicing.

In all cases, the resources must be completely isolated. This provides a high level of security by preventing an attack from spreading from one network to another. If one of the virtual routers fails, it does not affect the others. If, of course, a physical node fails, all the virtual nodes will also fail.

8.2. Virtualization on the Edge

The virtual machines on the Edge are found in the data centers that are in the three tiers that have been defined in this book: the Multi-access Edge Computing (MEC), the Fog and the Skin. In the MEC, we find all the virtual machines of the infrastructure and the applications. This ranges from signal processing to the most diverse applications, including routers, switches and, more generally, the most diverse nodes and boxes.

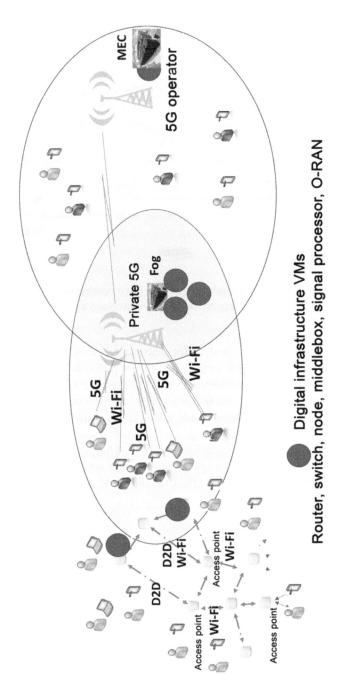

Figure 8.3. *Virtual machines in the Edge's digital infrastructure. For a color version of this figure, see www.iste.co.uk/alagha/networking.zip*

In terms of Fog, which corresponds to companies, the virtual machines are those that one meets in the companies and, more specifically, in the local networks. There are the servers with the business applications, but also the virtual machines linked to the company's networks such as the authentication server, Domain Name Service (DNS) management, the company's gateway router, accelerators, etc.

Finally, at the skin level, virtual machines are going mobile with small data centers following users, vehicles and soon all mobile equipment. The virtual machines are always those supported by the physical infrastructure that provides functions such as signal processing, digital infrastructure applications that can be linked to private 5G or Wi-Fi, infrastructure services such as urbanization algorithms, functions providing intelligence, security or resilience and finally, the functions provided by the virtual machines of the application services. Figure 8.3 gives some locations of these virtual machines on the Edge.

These various Edge networks should gradually, from 2020, become Software Defined Networking (SDN) networks. Indeed, the specifications of 5G and slicing in mobile networks require that control is done automatically by using SDN controllers. This indicates virtual nodes that no longer have to take care of the control, which is done automatically via the controller. The standardized signaling protocol that carries the controls is OpenFlow, which was specified as part of the Open Network Foundation (ONF).

OpenFlow is a signaling system corresponding to the southern interface, that is, the interface between the controller and the SDN nodes of the network. OpenFlow provides a solution not only for setting up production networks but also for building experimental networks that are completely isolated from production networks. The OpenFlow interface, initiated by Stanford University, aims to create networks with an automatic node configuration system. The underlying idea is the separation of control and data planes. Therefore, different virtual machines perform the frame and packet transfer functions (data plane), and others perform the network control functions (control plane). The transfer of frames and packets takes place via a flow table that represents the data plane, while the control plane is centralized around a controller. This controller is able to use different functions to control the virtual network. An example of OpenFlow control is shown in Figure 8.4.

The OpenFlow protocol defines the communication between the forwarding nodes and the network controller. It establishes a secure channel between each node and the controller by using a secure channel to monitor and configure the forwarding nodes. Each time a new frame reaches an SDN forwarding node, and there is no previously configured path, the control information in the frame or packet header is passed to the controller in an OpenFlow frame. The controller determines a path for the corresponding flow since it has almost perfect knowledge of the network and regularly sends it the status of all nodes. The controller can also select an action to be performed on the flow, such as changing the priority, destroying one or more packets, performing specific processing to regulate the flow or copying the packet to send it to several nodes in a multicast mode.

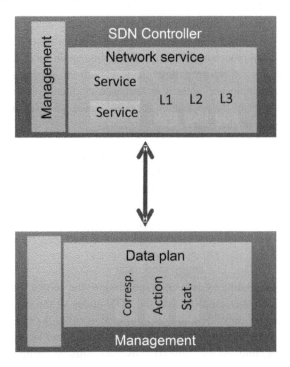

Figure 8.4. *OpenFlow signaling. For a color version of this figure, see www.iste.co.uk/alagha/networking.zip*

The transmission of packets in the data plane using OpenFlow is carried out; thanks to the set of flow tables. The OpenFlow frame consists of a header field, counters and indications of actions to be performed on frames or packets. The header field forms a structure composed of twelve tuples, as shown in Figure 8.5. These tuples completely specify a flow by defining the characteristics from level 1 (port number) to level 4 (message address), passing through the MAC address and the IP address at levels 2 and 3. This 12-tuple structure gives great flexibility to frame or packet transfers, as a flow can be routed to the IP destination address or switched to a reference. The SDN can be a conventional TCP/IP network, using the TCP port, IP address, MAC address, port number, or the frame can be switched over a path defined by a sequence of references entered in the flow tables of the individual SDNs. OpenFlow forwarding nodes are most commonly switches that work at Layer 2. However, it is possible to do routing with OpenFlow, but to optimize the network operation, it would be necessary to send a routing table to each node when each new flow arrives. One of OpenFlow's future goals is to build routing tables programmatically to increase the control possibilities for any type of network.

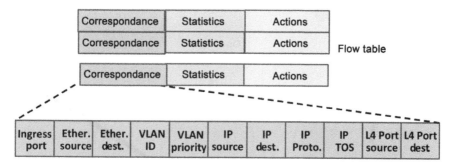

Figure 8.5. *The OpenFlow frame. For a color version of this figure, see www.iste.co.uk/alagha/networking.zip*

OpenFlow configures nodes by adding rows to the flow tables to allow switching or possibly routing of frames or packets. The 12-tuple description uniquely identifies the flow. This first field of the header is followed by counters that carry information about the state of the nodes, which allows them to be monitored and to have an up-to-date view of the network. The counters carry information such as the number of bytes transmitted per time slot, the state of the buffers in the nodes and anything else that can give the controller a near-perfect view of the state of the network. The last field of the OpenFlow frame describes the actions to be taken in the network nodes. These actions form a set of instructions that are applied to each frame or packet of a specific flow crossing the SDN nodes. These actions include not only switching a frame or routing a packet but also changing header fields such as virtual LANs (VLANs) or source and destination addresses.

The controller is a central network element located in the MEC, Fog or Skin data center. It communicates with all nodes to configure flow tables. The controller provides the control functions for the active networks. The controller also retrieves a lot of information through the north interface that connects it to client applications.

SDNs work with any controller that supports the OpenFlow protocol. In this case, each control plane consists of a set of functions implemented by the controller.

Therefore, an SDN network has a control plane driven by functions running on the controller, which can be located in a data center but also on a physical machine, as shown in Figure 8.6.

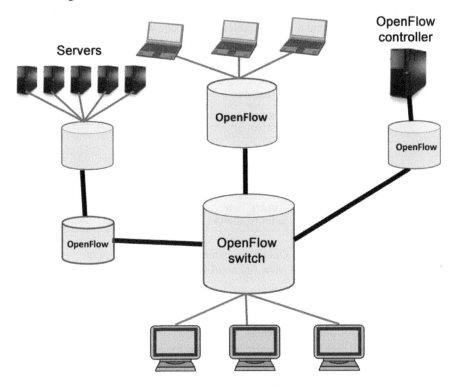

Figure 8.6. *A physical OpenFlow controller. For a color version of this figure, see www.iste.co.uk/alagha/networking.zip*

The choice between physical and virtual depends on the context. In general, a controller is a virtual machine, but for security reasons, it can very well be implemented on a physical machine to avoid jumping attacks from one virtual machine to another.

With a single controller, it is possible to create several virtual networks corresponding to different slicing techniques and applications. Each virtual network has its own flow table. The controller can allocate resources to the different networks. However, if a problem occurs in the network, it can negatively affect the controller's operation, thus affecting all other virtual networks. It is therefore preferable that each virtual network has its own controller, that is, its own data plan and control plan.

It should be noted that the controller in the first products only took care of the configuration of the flow tables but that many functions were added later to manage security, reliability, availability or mobility functions. For example, the security of an enterprise around its Fog data center may require the implementation of many mini-firewalls associated with each physical server. In this case, the controller acts as a central firewall coordinating the security rules between all the devices that are equipped with mini-firewalls.

Another example comes from Wi-Fi access points. Today, Wi-Fi controllers of different brands are incompatible because the functions associated with Wi-Fi are not distributed in the same way between the Wi-Fi box and the controller. By using OpenFlow-enabled access points, that is, the existence of a function managing the OpenFlow protocol in the box, it would be immediate to control Wi-Fi access points of different brands from the same controller. This would give an enterprise a much wider choice of equipment that could be integrated into the enterprise network. In particular, as soon as a new standard is released with new products, it is possible to include them in the corporate network if they are compatible with OpenFlow.

8.3. Using virtual networks on the Edge

Several types of uses can be realized with network virtualization:

– Slicing on the MEC network of a 5G operator. Slices are virtual networks, and for example, each company can be connected to the MEC data center by a specific network taking into account the characteristics of the business applications. The operator can also decide to have only one slice for a given application, and the different users using this application will be connected to the same virtual network. The number of virtual networks can be increased tenfold by assigning a virtual network to each user and each application. Scaling up could be a problem, although it is one of the solutions considered for 6G.

– Several virtual networks within the same company. This solution makes it possible to create a virtual network for telephony, one for remote monitoring, another for videoconferencing within the company, etc. This slicing solution is strongly studied to allow a very good quality of service and strong security to all the applications of a company.

– In the context of Skin Networking with mobile data centers that follow the users, it is also quite conceivable to set up many virtual networks. The major problem is that the controller becomes mobile in one of the data centers in the environment. This means that controller election functions must be added as soon as the node that hosts the controller disappears. SDN is not the best solution for controlling these mobile networks. It is better to have a distribution of functions across all the nodes or to have a completely distributed controller across all the nodes in the Skin network, which is almost the same thing.

Another growing use of virtualization schemes is the migration of virtual machines from one data center to another to optimize a number of criteria such as, obviously, performance, but also energy consumption, availability, resiliency, etc. Virtual resources can be migrated from one server to another to optimize their use. Virtual resources can be migrated from one server to another to optimize their use. The migration can be done within the same data center but also from one data center to another. For example, a virtual machine installed in a 5G operator's MEC can be migrated to the Skin network to satisfy latency or immediate availability constraints, but also for security reasons by disconnecting the Skin network from the Internet after recovering the virtual machines that will allow the desired services to continue to be provided without any external connection.

Another application, which is quite common today, concerns customers moving around the Internet who want to have access to resources from anywhere. To link resources to the mobile user, it is possible to create an environment adapted to this communication with networks and mobile virtual machines.

Finally, virtualization is an ideal technology for testing new protocols and architectures without shutting down operational networks. It is quite simple to create a new virtual network using OpenFlow or any other southern interface. In this case, isolation is an essential property to avoid attacks from a new, perhaps less secure virtual network to another.

8.3.1. *Isolation*

Isolation is a fundamental principle of virtualization: a virtual network cannot have a connection with another virtual network; otherwise, the whole virtual network will collapse as soon as one of them is attacked.

The first simple and very efficient solution consists in partitioning the resources between the different networks. In this case, there would be nothing to gain in terms of resource multiplexing because the unused resources at the time t cannot be reallocated to other virtual networks. We need to find a solution to partition resources and ensure that unused resources can benefit other networks.

This property can be achieved by using several specific solutions. The simplest way is to have nodes with as many queues as there are virtual networks. In each queue, the virtual networks grant credits according to the resources allocated to the node for each virtual network. Each network uses one credit to send a frame. When a virtual network runs out of credit, the node can no longer transmit frames. If at some point, all queues are empty, a reallocation of credits is made to all queues. However, this can lead to a deadlock situation, where some queues have no credits, and other queues have credits but no packets to serve. To avoid this problem, blocked queues can create negative credits and continue to transmit. When the sum of positive and negative credits becomes zero, the system is reset by providing positive credits to all nodes. From this example, a queue can be allowed to serve multiple packets as soon as the queue has available credits.

8.3.2. *Extending network virtualization*

Virtualization technology was first applied to routers and is certainly one of the most interesting applications for a virtual machine. However, many other hardware devices can also be virtualized. As an example, we can virtualize Wi-Fi controllers. This is used to manage Wi-Fi access points from a virtual machine located in a data center away from the local network. The associated access points can have their own protocol stack.

A firewall can also be virtualized. To access an enterprise, packets are routed to a general virtual firewall which, in turn, can redirect the flow to a virtual firewall dedicated to a specific application. Virtual firewalls can be given the power to perform deep frame inspection to detect even the most subtle attacks.

The access points themselves can be virtualized, as we saw in the previous section. Each virtual access point has its own management and control software. Virtual access points can be independent of each other even if they are located in the same infrastructure. It is also possible to virtualize NodeB, eNodeB, gNodeB, HeNB, etc. This makes it possible to share antennas between different operators.

Overall, any resource can be virtualized, with the exception of sensors that require a hardware element to measure a value, physical antennas and transceivers that transmit or receive electrical or light signals. Therefore, a virtual sensor can be defined as software associated with a physical sensor to perform calculations from the measured values. This software can be modified, hence the name virtual sensor. The digital infrastructures of the 2020s can be seen as the virtualization of all physical machines and, more explicitly, of all functions contained in physical machines. A large number of network devices can be virtualized, as shown in Figure 8.7.

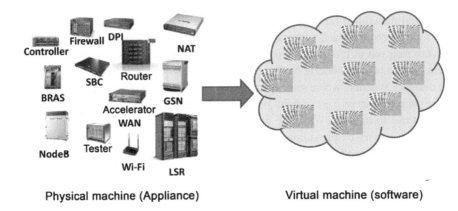

Figure 8.7. *Network device virtualization. For a color version
of this figure, see www.iste.co.uk/alagha/networking.zip*

In this figure, the functions correspond to a wide variety of protocol stacks adapted to different problems such as optimization of energy consumption, security, quality of service, network availability, etc. Each virtual network can use its own protocol stack and modify the protocol stack whenever necessary, for example, when a problem such as an almost empty battery or a distributed denial-of-service (DDoS) attack is discovered. Each virtual network can use its own protocol stack and modify the protocol stack as soon as necessary, for example, when a problem such as an almost empty battery or a DDoS attack is discovered.

Virtualization of physical or radio links is not possible as such. However, it is possible to replace a physical link with a virtual link integrated into a digital infrastructure as soon as the customer cannot see the difference due to identical performance. Wi-Fi can also be virtualized, as we have seen by putting all the processing functions encapsulated in the box in a data center more or less far from the Wi-Fi antenna. Here again, the performance of the virtualized system must be identical to that of a non-shared infrastructure. For Wi-Fi access points, this will be the case for very high capacity Wi-Fi technologies such as IEEE 802.11ax (Wi-Fi 6), where the throughput is such that its partitioning between several virtual access points does not lead to any slowdown for the customers.

Finally, virtualization is an important technique that allows new technologies to be introduced effortlessly as virtual private networks. Thus, it is possible to test a network running a new architecture without any risk.

Virtualization is also a long-term solution for introducing next-generation networks such as Post-IP proposals that integrate non-IP protocols. Once the network architecture of the future is perfectly defined, this new architecture can be gradually implemented worldwide through virtualization.

8.4. Mobile Edge Computing

Mobile Edge Computing (MEC) can correspond to several quite different structures. The first one concerns mobile telecommunication operators with virtual machines attached to users that follow their server. The objective is to continue to offer the same quality of service to the customer, even when he is on the move, as when he is stationary at the office or home. In this case, the virtual machines migrate from one MEC data center to another MEC data center as soon as the customer changes the antenna during a handover. Virtual machines become mobile, but the term roaming should be used to indicate that they are fixed between migrations.

A second completely different case is where the data center is mobile and follows the client, allowing the virtual machines to also follow the client. This technology has already been seen in the general context of Skin networks. The data center is a small but very powerful box with a large amount of memory. In the long term, the data center will be integrated into the smartphone or will be a pocketable device.

Software and application providers can serve the new ecosystem by developing and bringing to market innovative and revolutionary new services and applications that are fully distributed and can leverage information about the capabilities of the Skin network and the characteristics of the available radio network. The application space in these small data centers is open to all: application service providers, infrastructure service software and digital infrastructure software. The use of open standards and APIs, as well as the use of microservice or function-based programming models, relevant toolchain and software development kits, are key pillars to encourage and accelerate the development of new disruptive applications or the adaptation of existing services and applications to the mobile environment.

8.4.1. Examples of MEC applications

We will describe different use cases using Mobile Edge Computing as seen by 5G operators. IT offers a new ecosystem and value chain and the opportunity for all players within it to collaborate and develop new business models. Mobile network operators can rapidly deploy new services for consumer and enterprise segments, which can help them grow their service portfolio. Adding new revenue streams through the marketing of innovative services is a way to improve the bottom line while increasing the end user's Quality of Experience (QoE). In addition, these new applications can take into account the local context in which they operate, thereby opening up new categories of services and enriching the offering to users. The setting of relevant functions close to the user not only offers performance and security benefits but also reduces the volume of signaling to the core network and could also reduce the OPEX of operators compared to hosting all functions in the core network.

8.4.2. Geolocation

Figure 8.8 describes an example of a use case for tracking the location of terminal equipment such as a smartphone or a multimedia object. This use case allows for real-time geolocation of a device based on measurements made in the network and controlled by an application hosted on the MEC server. The server uses a geolocation algorithm, for example, triangulation. This provides an efficient and scalable solution with local processing and triggers based on predefined events. This system allows companies to set up geolocation services on a subscription basis, for example, of an object in a store, of a person through his smartphone in an area where GPS coverage is not available or of an infant with a connected watch, for example.

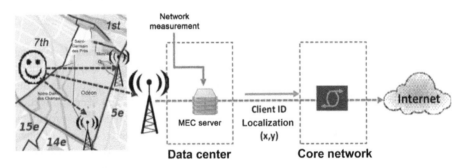

Figure 8.8. *Example of geolocation managed by the MEC data center. For a color version of this figure, see www.iste.co.uk/alagha/networking.zip*

8.4.3. Augmented reality

An augmented reality application on a smartphone or tablet overlays the augmented reality content on the objects viewed on the device's screen (as shown in Figure 8.9). Applications on the MEC server can provide local object tracking and caching of augmented reality content. The solution minimizes round-trip time and maximizes throughput for optimal quality of experience. It can be used to deliver consumer or business propositions, such as tourist information, sports event information, advertisements, etc.

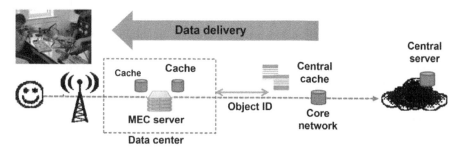

Figure 8.9. *Example of an augmented reality application on the MEC. For a color version of this figure, see www.iste.co.uk/alagha/networking.zip*

8.4.4. *Video analytics*

Figure 8.10 describes a distributed video analytics solution that provides a mobile, efficient and scalable solution using an LTE connection from the MEC data center. The video management application transcodes and stores the video streams captured from the cameras over the radio uplink. The video analytics application processes the video data to detect and notify specific events, for example, a moving object, abandoned luggage, a count of the number of people on a train platform, etc. The application sends low-bitrate video metadata to the MEC operations and management data center for local database searches to retrieve control elements associated with the video. Applications can range from surveillance to public safety to smart city applications to tracking an object in a hospital.

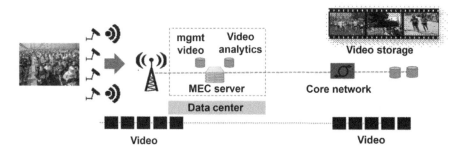

Figure 8.10. *Example of video analytics. For a color version of this figure, see www.iste.co.uk/alagha/networking.zip*

8.4.5. *Content optimization*

In this example, the application exports accurate cell and subscriber air interface information (cell load and link quality) to the MEC data center to optimize the content to be carried. This solution enables dynamic content optimization, improving QoE, network efficiency and enabling new service and revenue opportunities. Dynamic content optimization improves video delivery by reducing the amount of information to be transmitted, shortening start-up time and improving video quality. Figure 8.11 shows an example of content optimization. The concept also allows for improvements through additional algorithms such as Big Data analysis or machine learning software. The applications concern content delivery and throughput increase for subscriber content.

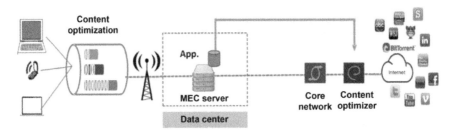

Figure 8.11. *Example of content optimization. For a color version of this figure, see www.iste.co.uk/alagha/networking.zip*

8.4.6. *Content cache and DNS cache*

Distributed data caching technology (as shown in Figure 8.12) can provide transport savings and improved quality of service. Caching content in the MEC data center stores has the potential to reduce backhaul capacity requirements by up to 35%. Similarly, caching DNS resolutions, that is, matches between IP addresses and domain names, in the MEC data center can reduce web page download times by up to 20%.

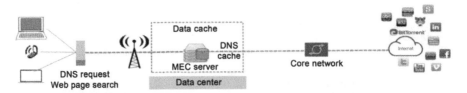

Figure 8.12. *Example of a data cache system and DNS resolution. For a color version of this figure, see www.iste.co.uk/alagha/networking.zip*

8.4.7. *Performance optimization*

Optimizing the performance of the connected clients in a cell, based on the applications running on each device, in real-time, greatly improves the efficiency of the network and thus the user experience (see Figure 8.13). This optimization can reduce the video throughput and increase the throughput for user navigation. Latency can also be significantly reduced. The solution can also provide independent metrics on application performance (video, telephony, browsing throughput and latency) for improved network management and reporting. The optimization functions are located in the MEC data center servers and therefore have very low latency to be able to optimize in real-time.

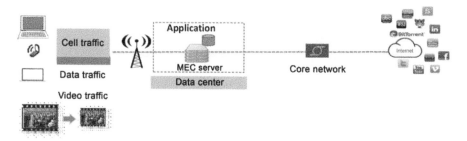

Figure 8.13. *Example of performance optimization. For a color version of this figure, see www.iste.co.uk/alagha/networking.zip*

8.4.8. *Positioning of MEC servers*

The MEC data center must be at a relatively short distance from the end device to ensure a very short latency time of the order of 1 ms. A distance of a few kilometers seems to be the right value. Some third-party equipment considers that up to 50 km, the latency time is acceptable. Indeed, the propagation time on an optical fiber remains relatively negligible since it is less than 200 µs for a distance of 50 km.

Figure 8.14 provides an overview of the different positioning options for the MEC data center.

The first possible position would be to place the server in the user's connection equipment, that is, in the HNB (Home NodeB). This case does not correspond to the vision of 5G operators who prefer to group several antennas on the same data center. In the HNB case, the MEC server is small and replaces the Wi-Fi broadband router or the Home Gateway or the Internet Box. This is a Skin Networking solution with potential data center mobility.

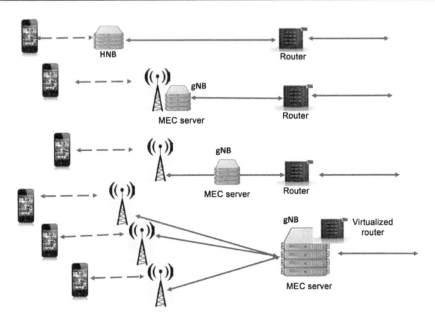

Figure 8.14. *Different placements of the MEC data center. For a color version of this figure, see www.iste.co.uk/alagha/networking.zip*

The second case proposes a location very close to the antenna, on the mast or at the foot of the antenna mast. The data center is dedicated to a single antenna. Several possibilities are offered to the operators, like right next to the antenna or directly at the antenna. These solutions are acceptable if the antennas are very scattered in very sparsely populated areas. On the other hand, in densely populated areas, to take advantage of multiplexing, several antennas must be grouped together for a single data center. This latter possibility should be widely used by mobile operators using large MEC servers. Furthermore, these MEC data centers can themselves be interconnected to optimize the use of resources when some data centers are saturated.

The management of MEC servers is crucial for mobile operators. Much of the cost of implementation and maintenance is at this level. Figure 8.15 describes a MEC server architecture and management. The server consists of three layers.

The first is the hardware that supports the software environment. Included in this hardware is a virtualization hypervisor or containers that can support virtual machines. These virtual machines provide the various services required by the MEC data center. A first management system corresponds to this layer. This system must support the entire hardware infrastructure and the virtualization layer.

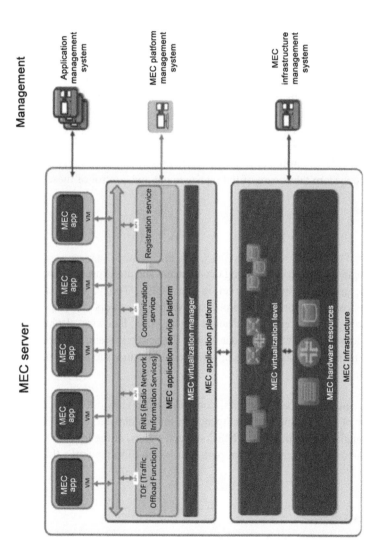

Figure 8.15. *Architecture of a MEC server. For a color version of this figure, see www.iste.co.uk/alagha/networking.zip*

The second part concerns the application platform for the MEC server. This platform supports all the applications needed to operate the communications of the users to the core network or between them if its users are connected to the same MEC server. The platform operates access network control functions (RAN), forwarding schemes, attachment structures, traffic control algorithms, call management systems and, more generally, all the services required by the clients. This MEC server layer is managed by a system that deals exclusively with this platform.

The last part of the MEC server is the virtual machines themselves. These virtual machines support the functions described above. They can be available all the time, but they can also migrate to other servers and MEC data centers to group virtual machines with the objective of spending less energy, offloading servers approaching saturation, or tracking clients handing off to another cell. Virtual machine migration plays an important role in optimizing energy consumption and improving resource utilization. A third system takes care of the management and control of these virtual machines.

8.5. Conclusion

MEC technologies are undergoing strong development and are expected to occupy a large part of the mobile network market in the 2020s. Today, there is much discussion about the data stored and processed in MEC servers. Indeed, mobile operators are strongly pushing for enhanced intelligence functions deployed as infrastructure services directly in the MEC data center. These services aim to process data more efficiently and make it more valuable, which could be an issue for the personal nature of user data.

The network equipment manufacturers, contrary to the views of the operators, are more in favor of distributing the intelligence in intermediate equipment located between the terminal equipment and the MEC servers, that is, at the level of the Fog data centers, but above all on the terminal part, that is, the Skin networks that serve the users.

8.6. References

Belabed, B., Secci, S., Pujolle, G., Medhi, D. (2015). Striking a balance between traffic engineering and virtual bridging in virtual machine placement. *IEEE Transactions on Network and Service Management*, 12(2), 202–216.

Ben Jemaa, F., Pujolle, G., Pariente, M. (2016). Cloudlet- and NFV-based carrier Wi-Fi architecture for a wider range of services. *Annals of Telecommunications*, 71(11/12), 617–624.

Bourguiba, M., Haddadou, K., El Korbi, I., Pujolle, G. (2014). Improving network I/O virtualization for cloud computing. *IEEE Transactions on Parallel and Distributed Systems*, 25(3), 673–681.

Bourguiba, M., Haddadou, K., Pujolle, G. (2016). Packet aggregation-based network I/O virtualization for cloud computing. *Computer Communications*, 35(3), 309–319.

Chayapathi, R. and Hassan, S.F. (2016). *Network Functions Virtualization (NFV) with a Touch of SDN*. Addison-Wesley, New York.

Chen, W., Wang, D., Li, K. (2019). Multi-user multi-task computation offloading in green mobile edge cloud computing. *IEEE Transactions on Services Computing*, 12, 726–738.

Gray, K. and Nadeau, T.D. (2016). *Network Function Virtualization*. Morgan Kaufmann, Burlington.

He, Y., Ren, J., Yu, G., Cai, Y. (2019). D2D communications meet mobile edge computing for enhanced computation capacity in cellular networks. *IEEE Transactions on Wireless Communications*, 18(3), 1750–1763.

Liu, H., Cao, L., Pei, T., Deng, Q., Zhu, J. (2020). A fast algorithm for energy-saving offloading with reliability and latency requirements in multi-access edge computing. *IEEE Access*, 8, 151–161.

Mao, Y., You, C., Zhang, J., Huang, K., Letaief, K.B. (2017). A survey on mobile edge computing: The communication perspective. *IEEE Communications Surveys Tutorials*, 19(4), 2322–2358.

Mattos, D., Duarte, O., Pujolle, G. (2018). A lightweight protocol for consistent policy update on software-defined networking with multiple controllers. *Journal of Network and Computer Applications*, 122, 77–87.

Moraes, I., Mattos, D., Ferraz, L., Campista, M., Rubinstein, M., Costa, L., Dias de Amorim, M., Velloso, P., Duarte, O., Pujolle, G. (2014). FITS: A flexible virtual network testbed architecture. *Computer Networks*, 63(4), 221–237.

Moura, J. and Hutchison, D. (2019). Game theory for multi-access edge computing: Survey, use cases, and future trends. *IEEE Communications Surveys Tutorials*, 21(1), 260–288.

Park, J., Samarakoon, S., Bennis, G., Debbah, M. (2019). Wireless network intelligence at the edge. *Proc. IEEE*, 107, 2204–2239.

Pham, Q., Fang, F., Ha, V.N., Piran, M.J., Le, M., Le, L.B., Hwang, W., Ding, Z.A. (2020). Survey of multi-access edge computing in 5G and beyond: Fundamentals, technology integration, and state-of-the-art. *IEEE Access*, 8, 116974–117017.

Porambagea, P., Okwuibe, J., Liyanage, M., Ylianttila, M., Taleb, T. (2018). Survey on multi-access edge computing for Internet of Things realization. *IEEE Communications Surveys and Tutorials*, 20, 2961–2991.

Satyanarayanan, M., Bahl, P., Caceres, R., Davies, N. (2009). The case for VM-based cloudlets in mobile computing. *IEEE Pervasive Computing*, 8(4), 14–23.

Stallings, W. (2015). *Foundations of Modern Networking: SDN, NFV, QoE, IoT, and Cloud.* Addison-Wesley, New York.

Tang, F., Kawamoto, Y., Kato, N., Liu, J. (2020). Future intelligent and secure vehicular network toward 6G: Machine-learning approaches. *Proceedings of the IEEE*, 108, 292–307.

Xu, X., Zhang, X., Liu, X., Jiang, J., Qi, L., Bhuiyan, M.Z. (2021). Adaptive computation offloading with EDGE for 5G-envisioned Internet of connected vehicles. *IEEE Transactions on Intelligent Transportation Systems*, 22(8), 5213—5222.

Zhu, Y., Hu, Y., Schmeink, A. (2019). Delay minimization offloading for interdependent tasks in energy-aware cooperative MEC networks. *IEEE Wireless Communications and Networking Conference (WCNC)*, 15, 1–6.

9

Security

Security is crucial for today's networks and will be even more so in the future. With the Internet, it is necessary to constantly invent new processes that guarantee the non-disclosure of many elements, such as location, the names of those who are authenticated, the semantics of messages, private life information, etc. Among the different solutions that can be considered, we will detail three: the use of a Cloud of security, the use of secure elements and the arrival of blockchain. The first one is a new paradigm that is becoming more and more widespread, the second solution has been used for a long time but is being renewed with eSIM and iSIM and the third one is spreading rapidly for certification and traceability.

9.1. Cloud of security on the Edge

The security of the network world is a paradigm that has no simple solution apart from improvements to the already large number of existing algorithms to respond to new attacks. However, this chapter discusses a new solution in the world of security: the Cloud of security, that is, a Cloud whose objective is to secure information and networks in the world of operators, businesses and the general public. An initial diagram of a Cloud of security is shown in Figure 9.1. The Cloud of security contains numerous virtual security machines such as authentication servers, authorization servers, identity management servers, but also firewalls and, more precisely, specialized firewalls corresponding to particular applications. We can also find secure element servers that can contain thousands of SIM, eSIM and iSIM cards or Hardware Security Module (HSM).

Let's describe three examples of servers found in the Cloud of security. First is a Deep Packet Inspection (DPI). The objective of a DPI is to determine the

Edge Networking,
by Khaldoun AL AGHA, Pauline LOYGUE and Guy PUJOLLE. © ISTE Ltd 2022.

applications transported in the flows passing through a network. To do this, DPI listens to a stream and looks for application signatures which, in general, can be found by examining the grammar of an application. Every application on the Internet has its own signature. The DPI examines the sequence of bits and determines the signatures. The advantage of this solution over examining the port number is that it checks all the binary elements in transit, not just the frame and packet headers. Indeed, attackers encapsulate their attack in messages of known type that pass through conventional firewalls without any problem. However, finding signatures in a high-speed stream is particularly complex and requires very high-capacity, and therefore expensive, hardware.

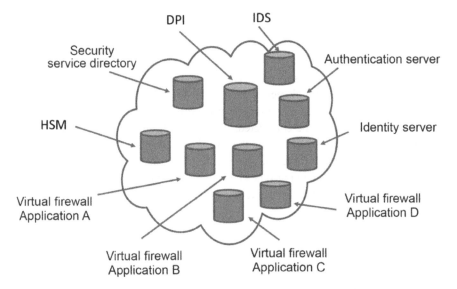

Figure 9.1. *A Cloud of security. For a color version of this figure, see www.iste.co.uk/alagha/networking.zip*

By moving the function of examining the binary elements of a stream to find signatures to a cloud, the cost of a DPI can be greatly reduced. The stream recognition function is therefore moved to a remote data center. The cost is often that of transporting the stream to the data center. Several solutions have emerged on the market depending on the requirements. For example, only the header parts of the messages can be transmitted, which drastically reduces the number of streams to be examined, but with the risk of missing the encapsulated binary elements.

The second example is firewalls. Today, firewalls take the form of physical boxes located between the company's network and the access networks to the operator. The power of these boxes is generally limited for cost reasons. The Cloud fundamentally changes this vision by virtualizing these boxes and moving them to data centers, thus bringing many advantages. The first advantage is to have virtual firewalls specialized by the application instead of having a monolithic firewall. We also add a DPI thanks to the data center's power, without any throughput limitation. Thanks to the DPI, the firewall detects the nature of the application flows and sends them to the corresponding virtual firewalls.

The firewall has a processing capacity that allows it to verify all the details of the flow. We also add artificial intelligence with automatic learning techniques to recognize attacks after having let dangerous packets through without realizing it due to lack of learning. Figure 9.2 describes a firewall of the 2020s with its various components.

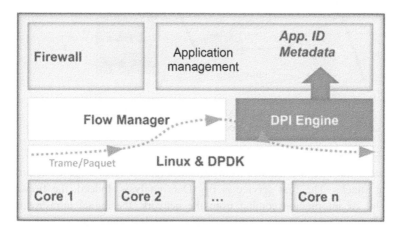

Figure 9.2. *A firewall for the 2020s. For a color version of this figure, see www.iste.co.uk/alagha/networking.zip*

In short, a firewall with not a lot of power and handling all the flows simultaneously is replaced by a set of very powerful and specialized firewalls. A disadvantage could come from the flows that have to be sent to the specialized firewalls, and that must then return to the enterprise while having the possible advantage of being able to hide the firewalls to avoid denial of service attacks. This problem is practically eliminated in Edge Computing structures since the firewall can be placed on one of three levels: MEC, Fog and Skin. In the first case, the data has to go up to the MEC data center, and the filtering is a service provided by the 5G operators. In the second case, companies deploy their own firewalls, and this solution should be the majority in the 2020s. Finally, in the third case, the customer himself takes care of his firewall, but for this, he might need help to set the security rules properly. Again, intelligence services could automate the security rules and automate the security of the users, but this is more for the second part of the 2020s. Figure 9.3 describes some of the topologies adopted by firewalls in the context of Edge Networking.

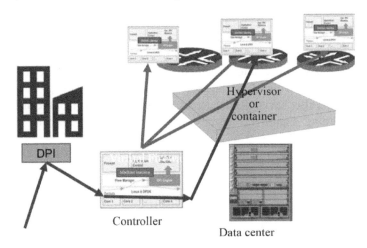

Figure 9.3. *Some topologies for firewalls on the Edge. For a color version of this figure, see www.iste.co.uk/alagha/networking.zip*

Firewalls can also use features from infrastructure services to go even further in detecting attacks. The first service is Big Data analysis. Indeed, the firewall can store a lot of information coming from the network, the digital infrastructure, the connected objects and the users themselves. The analysis of Big Data, made up of all this knowledge, can perfectly characterize suspicious behaviors that will be scrupulously followed to determine if the anomalies have a high probability of leading to an attack. These behavioral analyses can detect data leakage from company employees or attack behavior from external customers. In addition, Big Data analysis can lead to the refusal to perform an action when correlation results between knowledge stored in the data center demonstrate the dangerousness of the action under examination. We describe this environment in Figure 9.4.

The third example of a Cloud of security concerns a secure element server which, as we will see in this chapter, allows secure access to sensitive services such as mobile payment. These servers can gather thousands or even millions of secure elements such as smart cards that can be reached through secure channels that require strong trust services.

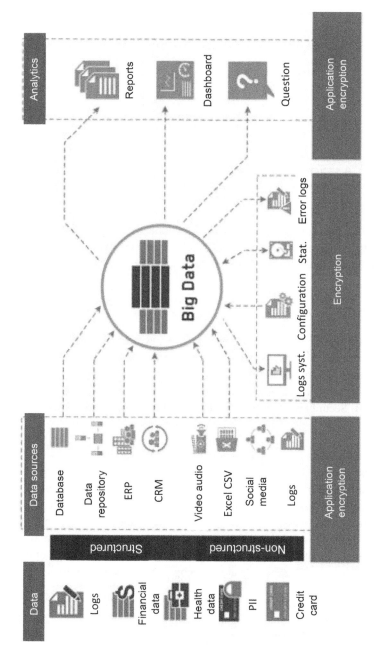

Figure 9.4. *Big Data Analytics-based security environments. For a color version of this figure, see www.iste.co.uk/alagha/networking.zip*

Figure 9.5. *A secure element server in a Cloud of security (©EtherTrust).*
For a color version of this figure, see www.iste.co.uk/alagha/networking.zip

We could also mention putting them in the Cloud of security, authentication servers, identity management servers, encryption servers (but these have the particularity of having to be very close to the user), intrusion detection servers, etc.

9.2. Secure element

This paragraph deals with a new generation that has been slowly implemented over the last few years. This new generation uses secure elements as a basis. Indeed, high security cannot be satisfied simply with software that can always be broken by a memory dump, a good knowledge of the location of the keys and a very high computing power. Secure elements come in different forms, but the most classic today is the smart card.

The protection of the smart card is mainly provided by the operating system. The physical addressing mode for data access is only available after the card has been personalized and handed over to the user. The data is accessed through a logical file structure secured by access control mechanisms. The smart card is widely used in mobile networks (SIM cards) or through the implementation of public key infrastructures (PKI). This technology has enabled operators to operate their networks while greatly limiting the number of frauds, thereby ensuring financial profitability. It is also the legal basis for electronic signatures recognized by many countries.

The Extensible Authentication Protocol (EAP) smart card directly processes the EAP protocol in the secure chip. The main applications are EAP-SIM and EAP-TLS. The advantages of an EAP-TLS protocol running in a smart card are numerous. First of all, the authentication is independent of a software vendor, for example, Microsoft.

In addition, the security provided is much better than with the EAP-TLS protocol implemented in software by the processor of a personal computer since it is always possible for spyware introduced into the PC to capture the keys. The advantage of the smart card is that all the calculations are done on the card. Moreover, only an encrypted stream leaves the smart card. The secret keys never leave the card.

The main functions found in smart card environments are as follows:

– Multiple identity management. The cardholder can use several wireless networks. Each of them requires an authentication triplet, EAP-ID (value delivered in the EAP-RESPONSE.IDENTITY message), EAP-Type (type of authentication protocol supported by the network) and cryptographic credentials, that is, the set of keys or parameters used by a particular protocol (EAP-SIM, EAP-TLS, MS-CHAP-V2, etc.). Each triplet is identified by a name (the identity), which can be interpreted in many ways (SSID, user account name, mnemonic, etc.).

– Assignment of identity to the card. The identity of the card is a function of the visited network. The card can have several identities internally and adapt to the network to which the terminal and the smart card are connected.

– EAP message processing. Because the smart card has a processor and memories, it can execute code and process received EAP messages and send messages in response.

– Calculation of the unicast key. At the end of the authentication session, the EAP tunnel can be used to transmit various information, such as keys or profiles. It is possible to transmit a session key, for example, and make it available to the terminal wishing to access the wireless network resources.

Figure 9.6 shows an authentication procedure between an authentication server and an EAP smart card. The primitive flow passes through the PC software, that is, first the EAP software, which only transitions the EAP packets to the RADIUS server on the one hand and to the smart card, on the other hand, then the operating system of the machine, which takes care of the interface to the smart card, and finally the IEEE 802.11 interface of the wireless link.

For additional security, smart cards can also be inserted on the server-side so that the EAP-TLS algorithm of the authentication server also runs in the smart card. With the new smart cards, which can store up to 1 GB, it is possible to store the logs required for traceability. Obviously, the more customers there are, the more smart cards are needed.

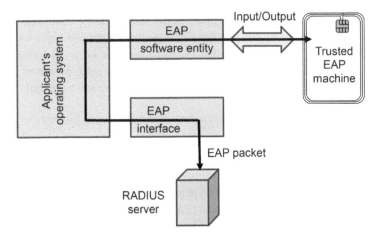

Figure 9.6. *EAP smart card authentication procedure. For a color version of this figure, see www.iste.co.uk/alagha/networking.zip*

The eSIM or embedded SIM card is a secure element that is much smaller than a traditional SIM card. This embedded card, which we discussed earlier in this book, is only there to manage client profiles, and the real card is virtualized to run the algorithms either in the terminal itself or in a remote data center. Figure 9.7 describes how an eSIM card works. The profiles are located in the card itself but also remotely through a secure connection between the card and the remote server that supports the virtual card. There can be as many profiles as there are functions to be secured, such as access to different payment cards and door locks for the home, vehicle or company. It is even possible to search for specific profiles remotely to perform a secure action that has not been provided for in the existing profiles. This instant subscription to a profile obviously has a more or less high cost depending on the service provided.

These eSIMs can be found in smartphones, of course, but their primary interest is in objects, especially small objects that do not have room for a conventional SIM card. The security management is then managed remotely.

The eSIM card has several advantages for the customer. He can easily change the operator by using many profiles. This embedded card can therefore play the role of several SIM cards from different operators. The major disadvantage is that if the object has no power, the card is useless. It cannot be removed and replaced with another object. However, a complex procedure allows replacing the object with a new one with a new eSIM programmed to take over the actions of the previous object.

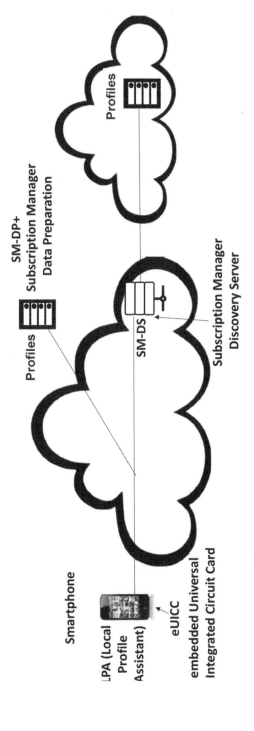

Figure 9.7. *Location of the profiles on an eSIM card. For a color version of this figure, see www.iste.co.uk/alagha/networking.zip*

The iSIM is a new form factor for a smart card. It is miniaturization of a SIM card or eSIM card that is integrated into the SoC of a machine. The surface is in the order of 1 mm^2 and soon even less.

Its principle is to integrate an eSIM card to miniaturize it. This eSIM card must be combined with an equally miniaturized modem and placed on the platform that houses the processor, memory and various components of the System on a Chip (SoC). This solution has many advantages, the first of which is a significant gain in space in the terminal equipment, especially small objects. The reduction of the manufacturing cost is a second advantage. Another advantage is the difficulty of attacking this dust-sized component. iSIMs will be particularly appreciated for security in the Internet of Things. Finally, it is possible to integrate a large number of iSIMs associated with a processor to secure, for example, virtual machines running on a server.

We show in Figure 9.8 the decrease in the size of the SIM cards.

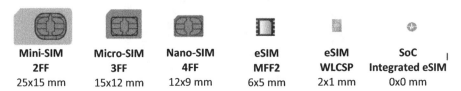

Mini-SIM	Micro-SIM	Nano-SIM	eSIM	eSIM	SoC
2FF	3FF	4FF	MFF2	WLCSP	Integrated eSIM
25x15 mm	15x12 mm	12x9 mm	6x5 mm	2x1 mm	0x0 mm

Figure 9.8. *Evolution of SIM card size. For a color version of this figure, see www.iste.co.uk/alagha/networking.zip*

9.2.1. *Security based on secure elements*

The virtualization solution of the secure card can be seen in a completely different way: for example, through a set of hardware cards deported in a Cloud of security or through the use of an HSM server that has the same level of security as a smart card, but in the form of a server with very strong security.

One of the paradigms of the new generation of security is to put a secure element associated with each element to be defended, be it an individual, an object, a virtual machine or any other object. To connect to the Internet, you must first authenticate yourself with your secure element. Before going further into the processes of securing access, let's take a look at the different solutions to bring security to an Edge environment and to next-generation digital infrastructure. Data centers form the backbone of these new digital infrastructures and can carry software functions such as Trusted Execution Environment (TEE).

9.2.2. *The TEE*

Figure 9.9 shows the three major cases possible with software-based security, hardware-based security and intermediate security, referring to the TEE. As we have seen, software-based security is not expensive, but it is usually not very high level. It is often possible for a very good attacker to recover a copy and to be able to retrieve a certain number of keys. That's why we try to associate a hardware element. The other end of the security hierarchy is to always have a hardware element to hide keys or important security elements that even allow performing algorithms inside the safe. The TEE is an intermediary between the client and the terminal processor that has been commercialized on the market for several years.

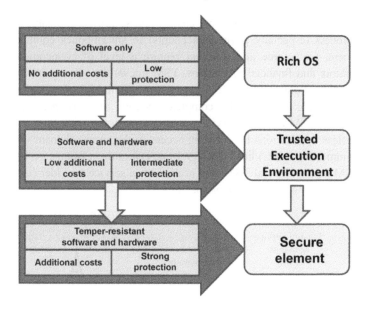

Figure 9.9. *The different security solutions. For a color version of this figure, see www.iste.co.uk/alagha/networking.zip*

The TEE is a secure area that resides in the main processor of a smartphone, tablet, server or any other fixed or mobile device. This secure area ensures that sensitive data is stored, processed and protected in a trusted environment. The characteristic of the TEE is to offer a secure execution of software known as "trusted applications", which provides end-to-end security by enforcing data protection, confidentiality, integrity and access rights. Smartphone manufacturers or chip makers have developed versions of this technology and included them in their devices as part of their proprietary solutions. Application developers are therefore faced with the complexity of creating and securely evaluating different versions of each application in order to comply with the set of specifications and security levels established by each individual proprietary solution. The first solution for using the TEE is to attach a local security element such as a smart card, which is found on many mobile terminals. The smart card is used to house the secure part of the applications. The difficulty is to put several independent applications and be able to modify them, remove them and add new ones with strong security. For this purpose, the Trusted Service Manager (TSM) solution has been developed, and we briefly detail it in the following section.

9.2.3. *The trusted service manager*

A TSM is a neutral third party that ensures the security of the entire application download process (especially payment accounts) in smartphones equipped with a secure element. Commerce and payment require a level of cooperation between mobile operators and financial institutions. TSM knows the security mechanisms of both banks and cell phones, bridging the gap between multiple financial institutions and operators while ensuring the complete security of consumers' credit card information. The TSM allows a service provider to remotely distribute and manage their contactless applications by enabling access to the secure element via the Near Field Communication (NFC) link. Figure 9.10 describes the relationships between the different TSM actors. Several TSMs are needed for a service provider (issuer), such as a bank, when they support different operators.

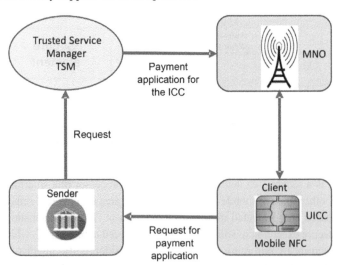

Figure 9.10. *Relationships between TSM participants. For a color version of this figure, see www.iste.co.uk/alagha/networking.zip*

Security features are essential for NFC services to ensure that security-critical applications are protected and that the same security standards are met for debit and credit cards. However, it's not enough to simply build a security device into the smartphone. Specific functions manage the secure allocation of memory so that the areas of different service providers are separated from each other. In addition, new secure services (applications and associated cards) must be able to be implemented on-demand without a third party having access to the PIN code or other sensitive information.

9.2.4. *The Cloud-based security solution*

A non-TSM solution has been provided by several companies, including Google and EtherTrust. This solution consists of offshoring the security devices to servers that can be controlled by the service providers (banks, various companies, etc.) or by a Cloud of security providers with a secure SIM or HSM. In this solution, all the defects of the current TSM implementation are removed. However, a new constraint replaces the TSM defaults, and the mobile equipment must always be connected. This solution is shown in Figure 9.11.

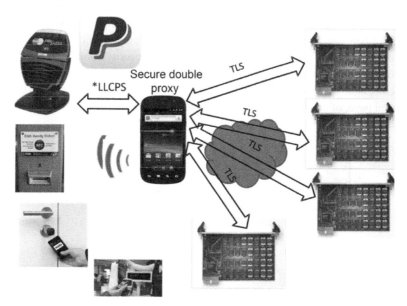

Figure 9.11. *The solution without TSM. For a color version of this figure, see www.iste.co.uk/alagha/networking.zip*

The connection is no longer made with the security device in the smartphone but with the security devices that are in the secure card grids. There are as many security devices as there are applications to be accessed by a user. Forwarding: applets or program modifications are made directly in the security devices that are either in the NFC service provider or in a security device provider. This system is scalable since a user can have as many security devices as needed and, therefore, as many secure domains as NFC applications. All the difficulties due to the sharing of the security device do not exist anymore.

9.2.5. *Solutions for security*

We have described two opposing solutions to achieve very high security: the local solution with a secure element in the terminal or connected directly to the terminal and the delocalized solution based on virtualized secure elements.

Figure 9.12 describes the first solution in which a locally secure element must be available. This secure element can be the SIM card of a telecom operator, it can be an eSIM soldered on the processor by the supplier that manufactured the terminal or it can still be a secure element embedded in an SD card and inserted in the reader of the mobile terminal, and it can still be a secure external element communicating with the mobile through an NFC interface. These different solutions were strongly developed between 2010 and 2015 since it was practically the only high-security solution available in a standard way or almost. The equipment manufacturers who were able to make a sufficient place for themselves on the market of smartphones, tablets and portable equipment have, of course, chosen this solution. The secure element is a smart card or an embedded secure element, usually from the company NXP.

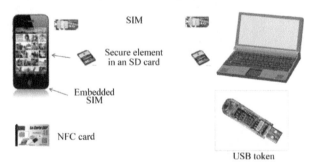

Figure 9.12. *Securing with a local secure element. For a color version of this figure, see www.iste.co.uk/alagha/networking.zip*

This solution is simple to implement with the advantage of being able to carry out secure communications but with the disadvantage of a strong limitation of the number of applications that can be embedded in a secure element and the difficulty of configuring the secure element when adding a new service.

The second major solution is the virtual card or remote smartcard if you want strong security by using a secure element. In particular, NFC communications allow the smartphone or tablet to be directly connected to the secure external element, as described in Figure 9.13.

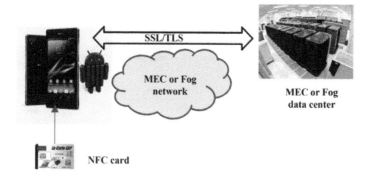

Figure 9.13. *Securing with secure external elements. For a color version of this figure, see www.iste.co.uk/alagha/networking.zip*

In Edge Networking, the Cloud of security is usually located in the operators' MEC data center. But it is entirely possible to use a Cloud of security that is itself virtualized in an enterprise's Fog data center. This allows the company to keep control of its security, provided, of course, that the data center itself is highly protected from external access.

Before describing this security solution in more detail and giving examples of how it works with typical applications, let us look at how the trusted communication between the mobile terminal and, for example, an Internet merchant takes place. This relationship is described in Figure 9.14.

The communication takes place between the mobile terminal and the secure element located in the Cloud of security. This communication takes place after opening a secure tunnel using the Secure Sockets Layer/Transport Layer Security (SSL/TLS) protocol. As soon as this communication is set up, the secure element connects with the merchant, always through a secure channel that opens between the secure element and the merchant site. Purchases can be made in complete security. Once the purchase has been made, the hand is returned to the mobile terminal, which can retrieve the music or video purchased or any other type of purchase. The secure element can be found in a Cloud of secure elements but also in an HSM that plays the same role, provided that the customer has confidence in this equipment. This is why secure element clouds are still the most likely to develop because the secure elements, which can be smart cards, can be owned by the user, and the user has a high level of trust in this system.

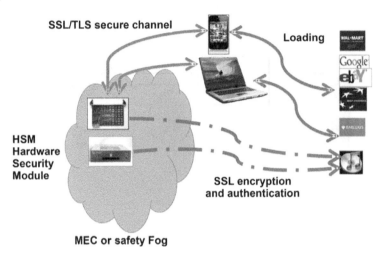

Figure 9.14. *Securing a Cloud of secure elements. For a color version of this figure, see www.iste.co.uk/alagha/networking.zip*

The first advantage of this virtualized or decentralized smart card solution comes from the possibility of assigning to a single user, not just one smart card or profile but as many as the user needs. The customer can have several banks, several key managers and several security service providers. A telecom operator can enter this market very easily by setting up its own secure element server in its MEC data center. A company can perfectly introduce this solution in its Fog data center. This architecture is illustrated in Figure 9.15.

To be complete, the environment must have its own management system for secure elements. The Global Platform consortium provides a simple solution for this by adding an administration center that can itself be virtualized. Figure 9.16 describes the complete environment with its administration server.

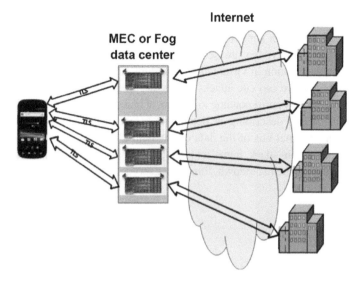

Figure 9.15. *Advantages of the eSIM solution. For a color version of this figure, see www.iste.co.uk/alagha/networking.zip*

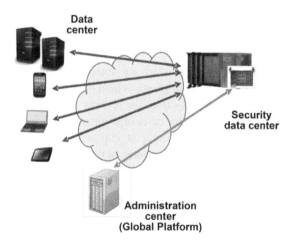

Figure 9.16. *Security architecture by secure external elements. For a color version of this figure, see www.iste.co.uk/alagha/networking.zip*

Many security services can be built on the model described above using a Cloud of security. We have already seen virtual firewalls and virtual DPIs. For the Secure Element Cloud, we can mention the management of virtual machine identities and the management of hotel, car or house keys, and more generally, all the keys that one might need to protect something. Figure 9.17 symbolizes the securing of virtual machines. In fact, today, we are seeing more and more attacks coming from the clouds, such as the creation of virtual attack machines that can be external or internal. In the internal case, we can cite attacks by forging in a virtual attack machine all the frames in a random way corresponding to a protocol based, for example, on the Requests for Comments (RFC) describing in detail this protocol. These random frames are then sent on the internal bus of the data center with a very high probability that one of these frames is an attack frame and brings down one or several servers, which themselves, following their shutdown, force other servers to shut down.

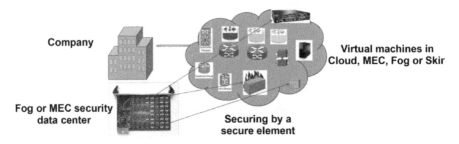

Figure 9.17. *Securing virtual machines. For a color version of this figure, see www.iste.co.uk/alagha/networking.zip*

Another application is mobile keys, which are stored in a secure data center and can be used to open a door when the smartphone is held up to the lock to be opened. The communication is established directly from the security data center to the NFC lock. Of course, it is necessary to provide for cases of communication failure, such as when the connection to the security data center is impossible when the smartphone is presented to the lock. The key can then be stored in the TEE of the mobile device for a limited time.

Purchasing and banking applications are also part of the services that can be rendered by this eSIM virtual smart card solution. One type of transaction is described in Figure 9.18. The transaction takes place between the NFC reader of the merchant site and the user's secure element, which in this figure is a smart card in a Cloud of security. As in the case of the mobile key, the mobile only serves as a modem to enable the transaction between the two ends and set up the necessary secure channels. This solution is sufficient for limited-cost purchases. For larger transactions, additional communications with the service provider and the bank itself must be added.

Figure 9.18. *Securing an electronic payment. For a color version of this figure, see www.iste.co.uk/alagha/networking.zip*

In conclusion in this section, we have seen a new approach to security through the use of secure elements. This approach forms one of the key solutions for security in the world of telecommunications and the Internet. After having introduced the techniques based on secure elements, we have described the potential for innovation brought by the security Fog or MEC.

Service providers and operators can choose between two approaches: local with a secure element in the mobile device or remote with a secure element in the Cloud of security. The choice is usually dictated by whether or not a secure element is available on the mobile device.

9.3. Blockchain

Blockchain is a tool for certification and traceability. This technology can be used in particular in network environments. It was initially developed for cryptocurrencies such as Bitcoin, but there are many other applications for network environments to certify transactions representing various actions. For example, it is possible to verify the identity of virtual machines to prevent identity theft.

Blockchain is a database technology that uses an immutable register, that is, one that cannot be changed. In this register, transactions are recorded and, once recorded, cannot be changed. Anyone can consult this register and all exchanges, present and past, without a trusted third party. The system works directly in a user-to-user mode. Being completely distributed, the database cannot be tampered with and the verification of operations can be done in the nodes that manage the chain, called miners. However, some attacks are possible if an attacker manages to control a majority of the nodes, or even more than two-thirds in some cases.

The transactions encapsulated in the chain are collected in blocks, the last block being correlated to the previous one by the hash value of the previous block. All transactions in a new block are validated by the miners. If the block is valid, it is time-stamped and added permanently to the chain. The transactions it contains are then visible throughout the network and can easily be verified by anyone who wants to. If the calculations are complex to perform (they are hash calculations), their verification is very simple. Once added to the chain, a block cannot be modified or deleted, which guarantees the authenticity and security of the whole.

As shown in Figure 9.19, each block in the chain consists of several transactions, a checksum (hash) used as an identifier and a checksum from the previous block (except for the first block in the chain, called the genesis block). A consensus method is chosen to determine the miner within the chain who will have the task of encrypting the block. Many consensus methods have been proposed, such as Proof-of-Work (PoW) or Proof-of-Stake (PoS).

Figure 9.19. *Functioning of a blockchain*

9.3.1. *Blockchain consensus*

Blockchain is a system based on trust. The system arrives, after some fairly complex calculations, at a consensus that can no longer be questioned. The method to reach this consensus can be the PoW, the PoS or other solutions that are proposed in the literature. The first method uses complex work to prove that the miner has succeeded in finding the right hash value of the block, and the second takes into account the value of the assets of each mining node. Indeed, the more a node is involved in the process, the less interest it has in having the system stop. The other solutions are often linked to the property of the nodes doing the mining.

The protocol associated with the PoS uses a cryptographic calculation requiring a significant computing power provided by the miners. This process cannot be broken, except over periods of several thousand years. The miners are entities whose role is to feed the network with computing power in order to allow the updating of the decentralized ledger. For this update, the miners must be able to find a rather complex hash. The first one to do this becomes the leader who manages the new block and wins a reward in bitcoins. It takes about fifteen minutes on extremely powerful machines to find a solution to the problem.

Competition exists between miners to become the leader and take over the transactions of a block, allowing the power available on the network to grow. Anyone can use their computing power to mine. However, the more miners there are, the more difficult it is to achieve consensus. Thus, the protocol becomes almost unbreakable as soon as the competition is strong between the nodes of the network, that is, no group of miners becomes the majority.

9.3.2. *Blockchain in Edge Computing*

We will examine more specifically the case of a blockchain in the Edge and, more precisely, for Skin Networking. Indeed, for MEC or Fog, usual blockchains can be used since connections are known from the user to the data center and vice versa. But in a mobile environment, connections between nodes fluctuate and can give rise to disconnections and reconnections. We define the partition problem as the set of problems that must be solved when a network splits into several subnets (split) and when several sub-networks meet to form a new network (merge). These changes in the network configuration occur because of the mobility of the nodes. But the algorithm that we will define can also be applied in the case where the partition of a network is decided by an operator for management purposes. Splits and merges can affect both distributed consensus algorithms and distributed databases that are managed by the nodes in the network. We will first describe how a consensus algorithm designed to manage the consistency of a distributed log is affected. Then, we will show why the consensus algorithm provides a good solution by supporting splits and merges.

In mobile networks, partitions are primarily caused by the mobility of nodes. The faster the nodes move, the more the network topology can change. The mobility pattern can also impact the overall performance of the implemented distributed system. In the proposal described here, we consider a mobility behavior in which nodes are clustered around a set of leaders. Some individual nodes can also move independently to join and leave groups freely. Each group, built around a leader, forms a connected subnetwork. From this situation, mobility can result in the following configuration changes:

– Merge: several subnetworks meet, as the distance between the leaders of several groups is reduced. The result is a larger network composed of the nodes that formed the original subnetworks. In this situation, the consensus algorithm must deal with a situation where multiple leaders may be active at the same time. First, the algorithm must be able to adapt its leader election process to the new network configuration. Second, a synchronization procedure may have to be performed to maintain the consistency of the local copies of the distributed database (the registry). However, a lot of precautions must be taken because the work to be done on the data structure used for the registry to be managed (chained list, indexed tables, relational tables, directed graph, etc.) can be considered as simultaneous updates that are often complex to perform. The context of the top-level application must also be taken into account.

– Split: a network is partitioned into several subnets as the distance between nodes increases. In this case, just after the split, most of the new subnets do not have a leader to schedule registry updates. Therefore, the consensus algorithm must also be able to adapt to the new configuration of each subnet. Since subnets cannot physically communicate, the algorithm must primarily adapt the leader election procedure so that subnets that do not have a leader can elect one and so that those that do have a leader can update the list of reachable nodes. The consistency of the registry does not need to be maintained, as each group may consider that unreachable nodes (nodes in other groups) have had problems and have disappeared. However, knowing that a merge may occur in the future, precautions must be taken to prevent updates to some critical data in the registry.

– Arbitrary: an arbitrary change is a change in the network configuration that is not exactly a split or a merge. It can be a new node added to the network, a node removed from the network, or a set of nodes moving from one subnet to another. In such cases, the procedures used to handle a division or a merge cannot be used alone, as each case may require a specific solution. However, we can use this theory to define any arbitrary configuration change as a split followed by a merge.

In each of these three types of changes that can alter a network configuration, we have seen that the consensus algorithm must adapt to the new configuration in order to continue electing leaders. By this, we mean that the algorithm must update its parameters according to this configuration. For example, a voting-based consensus algorithm such as Raft must be able to update its majority parameter to the size of the subnet it is currently running on. In the case of a stochastic algorithm such as the proof-of-work in Bitcoin, this could be as difficult as a cryptographic puzzle that the nodes have to solve. In fact, all the nodes need is a way to detect that a change has occurred and what the new configuration is.

To take into account all the difficulties mentioned above, the blockgraph is today the only available solution. Similar to the blockchain, a blockgraph starts with a genesis block (the first block in the chain). Each block is made up of transactions propagated from other nodes. Most of the fields we present in this data structure are also present in a traditional blockchain. However, the following fields are necessary for the proper functioning of the blockgraph:

– Group ID: this refers to the group identifier, which is the output of a hash function computed by the group management system having the identifiers of all nodes belonging to the same network partition as input.

– Parent hash list: this is a list of hashes of the parent blocks of a block. As the system evolves, the blockgraph adapts to a structure that accounts for splits and merges caused by node mobility. When a split occurs, nodes in the same network partition form a group in which they continue to evolve the blockgraph. In this case, when a new block is operated, this new block will be labeled with the group ID calculated by the management system and will refer to the last common block among all network partitions before the split. Once the block is created, it is propagated to all nodes in the group. At this point, each group has created a branch in the global blockgraph structure. In contrast, when a merge occurs, the group resulting from the merging of all network partitions involved in the merge will create a block in which the references of all previous blocks of the former groups are specified; such a block is called a merge block.

We define the terminology used for the blockgraph structure as follows:

– Genesis block: the starting block of the graph and the ancestor of all blocks. It is used as a root to identify the blocks attached to the same application;

– Branch: a chain of blocks in the blockgraph structure where each block has the same group identifier as its identifier;

– Merge block: a block of transactions that can refer to several previous blocks. It is the result of a merger of several network partitions;

– Childless block: a block in the blockgraph structure that is not referenced by any other block in the system. In other words, it is the last committed branch block in the blockgraph. When the network is partitioned, each group in the partitioned network will continue to maintain its version of the register that is actually a branch of the blockgraph data structure. Since the groups are independent of each other, each branch will evolve differently, and, therefore, data consistency is only relevant among the group members in that particular state. However, when a merge occurs, it is important to unify all branches involved in the merge into one so that the historical data of all branches is guaranteed and thus safeguards the properties of immutability and transparency.

The blockgraph system must be broken down into three different subsystems necessary for the proper functioning of the overall system. To do this, we must define the subsystems as follows:

– Consensus: the consensus algorithm is responsible for providing an appropriate leader for the protocol to propose new blocks to be added to the blockgraph. It must also be able to adapt to changes in network topology during operation.

– Block management: this is the protocol in charge of managing the local data structure of the blockgraph. This includes creating and validating blocks, ensuring partial block order, recovering missing blocks and managing a node's pending transaction list.

– Group management: this is the module responsible for detecting changes in the network topology and determining the nature of these changes so that they can be passed on to consensus and block management. It is also responsible for creating groups.

We now have all the elements of the blockgraph to implement it on a Skin network with mobile nodes. It is thus quite possible to certify events on mobile networks.

9.4. Conclusion

The world of security is vast, and this chapter only shows a very partial view of network security on the Edge. It focused on the new generation of Edge data centers, especially Clouds or Security Edges. This solution has advantages and disadvantages, but it is positioned on new ground, that of a simplified entry into the market and easily customizable in relation to the objective to secure. The future will tell us how much of the market it will capture. Another solution that is beginning to be deployed comes from blockchain, which offers certification and traceability without a central point. In particular, a specific version, blockgraph, adapts to the endpoint mesh network.

9.5. References

Belotti, M., Kirati, S., Secci, S. (2018). Bitcoin pool-hopping detection. *4th IEEE International Forum on Research and Technologies for Society and Industry*, IEEE RTSI, Palermo, Italy.

Belotti M., Bozic N., Pujolle G., Secci S. (2019). A vademecum on blockchain technologies: When, which and how. *IEEE Transactions on Surveys and Tutorials*, 21(4), 3796–3838.

Borisov, N., Goldberg, I., Wagner, D. (2002). Intercepting mobile communications: The insecurity of 802.11. *ACM Annual International Conference on Mobile Computing and Networking (MOBICOM)*, Atlanta, GA.

Bozic, N., Pujolle, G., Secci, S. (2016). A tutorial on blockchain and applications to secure network control-planes. *3rd Smart Cloud Networks & Systems (SCNS)*, Dubai, United Arab Emirates.

Bozic, N., Pujolle, G., Secci, S. (2017). Securing virtual machine orchestration with blockchains. *1st Cyber Security in Networking Conference (CSNet)*, IEEE, Rio de Janeiro, Brazil.

Bragadeesh, S. and Arumugam, U. (2019). *A Conceptual Framework for Security and Privacy in Edge Computing*. Springer, Berlin, Germany.

Caprolu, M., Di Pietro, R., Lombardi, F., Raponi, S. (2019). Edge computing perspectives: Architectures, technologies, and open security issues. *IEEE International Conference on Edge Computing (EDGE)*, IEEE, Milan, Italy.

Chwan-Hwa, J. and Irwin, J.D. (2017). *Introduction to Computer Networks and Cybersecurity*. CRC Press, Boca Raton, FL.

Du, M., Wang, K., Xia, Z., Zhang, Y. (2020). Differential privacy preserving of training model in wireless big data with edge computing. *IEEE Transactions on Big Data*, 6(2), 283–295.

Fajjari, I., Aitsaadi, N., Dab, B., Pujolle, G. (2016). Novel adaptive virtual network embedding algorithm for Cloud's private backbone network. *Computer Communications*, 84(C), 12–24.

Gai, K., Wu, Y., Zhu, L., Xu, L., Zhang, Y. (2019). Permissioned blockchain and edge computing empowered privacy-preserving smart grid networks. *IEEE Internet of Things Journal*, 6(5), 7992–8004.

Goransson, P. and Black, C. (2016). *Software-Defined Networks: A Comprehensive Approach*. Morgan Kaufmann, Burlington, VT.

He, D., Chan, S., Guizani, M. (2018). Security in the internet of things supported by mobile edge computing. *IEEE Communications Magazine*, 56(8), 56–61.

Hu, Y., Perrig, A., Johnson, D. (2003). Packet leashes: A defense against wormhole attacks in wireless networks. *IEEE Annual Conference on Computer Communications (INFOCOM)*, IEEE, San Francisco, CA.

Ibrahim, M.H. (2016). Octopus: An edge-fog mutual authentication scheme. *IJ Network Security*, 18(6), 1089–1101.

Kang, A., Yu, R., Huang, X., Wu, M., Maharjan, S., Xie, S., Zhang, Y. (2019). Blockchain for secure and efficient data sharing in vehicular edge computing and networks. *IEEE Internet of Things Journal*, 6(3), 4660–4670.

Khan, W.Z., Aalsalem, M.Y., Khan, M.K., Arshad, Q. (2016). Enabling consumer trust upon acceptance of IoT technologies through security and privacy model. In *Advanced Multimedia and Ubiquitous Engineering*, Park, J.J., Jin, H., Jeong, Y.-S., Khan, M.K. (eds). Springer, Berlin, Germany.

Khan, W.Z., Aalsalem, M.Y., Khan, M.K., Arshad, Q. (2019a). Data and privacy: Getting consumers to trust products enabled by the Internet of Things. *IEEE Consumer Electronics Magazine*, 8(2), 35–38.

Khan, W.Z., Ahmed, E., Hakak, S., Yaqoob, I., Ahmed, A. (2019b). Edge computing: A survey. *Future Generation Computer Systems*, 97, 219–235.

Khatoun, R. and Zeadally, S. (2017). Cybersecurity and privacy solutions in smart cities. *IEEE Communications Magazine*, 55(3), 51–59.

Lamport, L., Shostak, R., Pease, M. (1982). The byzantine general problem. *ACM Transactions on Programming Languages and Systems (TOPLAS)*, 4(3), 382–401.

Laube, A., Martin, S., Al Agha, K. (2019). A solution to the split & merge problem for blockchain-based applications in ad hoc networks. *International Conference on Performance Evaluation and Modeling in Wired and Wireless Networks*, 1–6.

Li, Q., Meng, S., Zhang, S., Hou, J., Qi, L. (2019a). Complex attack linkage decision-making in edge computing networks. *IEEE Access*, 7, 12058–12072.

Li, X., Liu, S., Wu, F., Kumari, S., Rodrigues, J.J.P.C. (2019b). Privacy preserving data aggregation scheme for mobile edge computing assisted IoT applications. *IEEE Internet of Things Journal*, 6(3), 4755–4763.

Liu, M., Yu, F.R., Teng, Y., Leung, V.C., Song, M. (2019). Distributed resource allocation in blockchain-based video streaming systems with mobile edge computing. *IEEE Transactions on Wireless Communications*, 18(1), 695–708.

Lopez, M.A., Mattos, D.M.F., Duarte, O.C.M.B., Pujolle, G. (2019). A fast unsupervised preprocessing method for network monitoring. *Annals of Telecommunications*, 74(3/4), 139–155.

Ma, L., Liu, X., Pei, Q., Xiang, Y. (2019). Privacy-preserving reputation management for edge computing enhanced mobile crowdsensing. *IEEE Transactions on Services Computing*, 12(5), 786–799.

Mosenia, A. and Jha, N.K. (2017). A comprehensive study of security of internet-of-things. *IEEE Transactions on Emerging Topics in Computing*, 5(4), 586–602.

Nakamoto, S. (2008). Bitcoin: A peer-to-peer electronic cash system [Online]. Available at: http://www.bitcoin.org/bitcoin.pdf.

Nakkar, M., Al Tawy, R., Youssef, A. (2021). Lightweight broadcast authentication protocol for edge-based applications. *IEEE Internet of Things Journal*, 7(12), 11766–11777.

Ni, J., Lin, X., Shen, X.S. (2019). Toward edge-assisted internet of things: From security and efficiency perspectives. *IEEE Network*, 33(2), 50–57.

Nogueira, M., da Silva, H., Santos, A., Pujolle, G. (2012). A security management architecture for supporting routing services on WANETs. *IEEE Transactions on Network and Service Management*, 9(2), 156–168.

Onieva, J.A., Rios, R., Roman, R., Lopez, J. (2019). Edge-assisted vehicular networks security. *IEEE Internet of Things Journal*, 6(5), 8038–8045.

Rathore, S., Kwon, B.W., Park, J.H. (2019). BlockSecIoTNet: Blockchain-based decentralized security architecture for IoT network. *Journal of Network and Computer Applications*, 143, 167–177.

Roman, R., Lopez, J., Mambo, M. (2018). Mobile edge computing, fog *et al.*: A survey and analysis of security threats and challenges. *Future Generation Computer Systems*, 78, 680–698.

Salah, K., Rehman, M.H.U., Nizamuddin, N., Al-Fuqaha, A. (2019). Blockchain for AI: Review and open research challenges. *IEEE Access*, 7, 10127–10149.

Schneider, F. (1990). Implementing fault-tolerant services using the state machine approach: A tutorial. *ACM Comput.*, 22(4), 299–319.

Stiti, O., Braham, O., Pujolle, G. (2014). Creation of virtual Wi-Fi access point and secured Wi-Fi pairing, through NFC. *International Journal of Communication Networks, and System Sciences*, 7(6), 175–180.

Torres, J., Nogueira, M., Pujolle, G. (2013). A survey on identity management for the future network. *IEEE Communications Surveys and Tutorials*, 15(2), 787–802.

Wang, T., Zhang, G., Liu, A., Bhuiyan, M.Z.A., Jin, Q. (2019). A secure IoT service architecture with an efficient balance dynamics based on cloud and edge computing. *IEEE Internet of Things Journal*, 6(3), 4831–4843.

Wang, B., Li, M., Jin, X., Guo, C. (2020a). A reliable IoT edge computing trust management mechanism for smart cities. *IEEE Access*, 8, 46373–46399.

Wang, J., Wu, L., Choo, K., He, D.R. (2020b). Blockchain-based anonymous authentication with key management for smart grid edge computing infrastructure. *IEEE Transactions on Industrial Informatics*, 16(3), 1984–1992.

White, R. and Banks, E. (2018). *Computer Networking Problems and Solutions: An Innovative Approach to Building Resilient, Modern Networks*. Addison-Wesley, New York.

Xiao, L., Ding, Y., Jiang, D., Huang, J., Wang, D., Li, J., Poor, H.V. (2020). A reinforcement learning and blockchain-based trust mechanism for edge networks. *IEEE Transactions on Communications*, 68(9), 5460–5470.

Yang, Y., Wu, L., Yin, G., Li, L., Zhao, H. (2017). A survey on security and privacy issues in internet-of-things. *IEEE Internet of Things Journal*, 4(5), 1250–1258.

Yang, J., Lu, Z., Wu, J. (2018). Smart-toy-edge-computing-oriented data exchange based on blockchain. *Journal of Systems Architecture*, 87, 36–48.

Yang, R., Yu, F.R., Si, P., Yang, Z., Zhang, Y. (2019). Integrated blockchain and edge computing systems: A survey, some research issues and challenges. *IEEE Communications Surveys Tutorials*, 21(2), 1508–1532.

Yuan, J. and Li, X. (2018). A reliable and lightweight trust computing mechanism for IoT Edge devices based on multi-source feedback information fusion. *IEEE Access*, 6, 23626–23638.

Zhang, H., Hao, J., Li, X. (2020). A method for deploying distributed denial of service attack defense strategies on edge servers using reinforcement learning. *IEEE Access*, 8, 78482–78491.

10

The Example of Green Communications

Today, it is common to use a smartwatch and a mobile application to ask for information about your heartbeat, sleep quality, stress level, etc. When the associated IoT services are hosted on clouds located in California, this requires information to travel to California and back to you to provide an answer. This long travel raises concerns about privacy, energy consumption, security and sovereignty of your data. Lengthy data travel introduces very high latency for critical applications such as connected surgery or safety in a connected vehicle.

Moving IoT services to the edge of the Internet network near the end device to keep local data local seems like common sense. The Edge offers significant advantages in terms of throughput, personal or sensitive data control and reduced power consumption of the Internet and data centers. But the Edge is limited to local coverage. Non-local, mobile and large-scale IoT projects such as autonomous transportation, smart cities, utilities, telemedicine, manufacturing automation, etc., still need to use Internet and cloud resources.

Green Communications innovates and creates the equivalent of a large cloud at the edge by federating multiple mobile Edges via secure tunnels without a central Cloud. These collaborative Edge Clouds form an Internet of Edges (IoE) where IoT data is processed locally and travels among Edges for greater data correlation. In this way, the IoE of Green Communications brings large-scale edge services to the Internet of Things in motion, massive IoT and other IoT applications in constrained environments.

Green Communications is an innovative company specialized in low power networks and distributed systems. The company is strongly committed to developing new network solutions to meet the challenges of the Internet: mobility, saturation and its energy footprint. Therefore, we have created Green PI, a new generation of autonomous participatory networks with embedded services, after a technology transfer from the top French universities (Sorbonne University and Paris Saclay) and the French National Centre for Scientific Research (CNRS). Green PI products have gained the trust of leading companies in the defense, civil security, IoT, telecommunications and public Internet sectors to provide resilient communication services in mobile and/or resource-constrained environments.

10.1. The Green PI solution

Green PI federates smart devices, smartphones and servers located at the network edge to create a cloud distributed near users, an edge cloud. The Edge Cloud provides users and devices with low-latency, highly resilient and secure services that can operate autonomously from a centralized cloud as well as interact with it. Green PI also federates multiple edge clouds operating at multiple locations to create an IoE with greater scale and data correlation capabilities.

10.2. The Edge Cloud

Figure 10.1 illustrates Edge Cloud infrastructure. Sensors and devices connect to IoT platforms via various wireless network interfaces (Wi-Fi, Bluetooth, Ethernet, 4G, etc.). The same platform also connects various machines that process the information from sensors. These machines contain the intelligence to process data locally in order to optimize the various processes of the IoT system. The owner of the Edge Cloud can view and manage it via a local web page.

The scale of the Edge Cloud depends on the following parameters:

– The communication infrastructure can be extended by deploying additional IoT platforms. Thus, to provide wider coverage and connect a larger number of smart devices. These platforms are mobile, plug and play and connect via robust mesh communications to form a participatory Internet.

– The edge machines that contain the applications and the system's intelligence depend on the computing power needed for the various processes. You can use one powerful machine or several smaller ones. The Edge machines can be specific to each connected object for security reasons or for processing compacity. This distribution can also be done through the virtualization of several machines on a single physical edge server.

To ensure a smooth transition to the central cloud, the Edge Cloud enables VPN tunnels to be created with machines located in the centralized cloud for backups or to synchronize with global intelligence in the cloud.

10.3. The IoE

Edge-based intelligence (on the Edge Cloud) makes sense when you address the isolation constraint. Indeed, the major shortcoming of any Edge solution is that it is isolated and confined where it is installed. Our solution allows connecting Edge Clouds operating at multiple locations to extend their reach and thus create an IoE.

Imagine two hospitals with two interconnected edge clouds. A doctor located at hospital A could interact with machines or patients at hospital B as if they were next door, directly, without any data being processed or stored in a centralized cloud.

Thus, the IoE solution proposes to connect two or *n* different sites via secure tunnels (VPN) and then ensure that the machines of the two or *n* sites hear and see each other as if they were together at the same location. IoE synchronizes its edges without the need for a central machine in the cloud. Figure 10.2 shows three remote sites synchronized with each other via secure tunnels. The solution also offers the possibility to synchronize edges with a cloud for a smooth transition from the cloud to the edge. Imagine an industrial company divided into multiple sites, each equipped with an edge cloud and sensors that regularly send reports to a digital log that company personnel log into to inquire about the status of these objects. As soon as the synchronization between the company's edge clouds takes place, the log automatically displays sensor information from all sites without requiring any configuration.

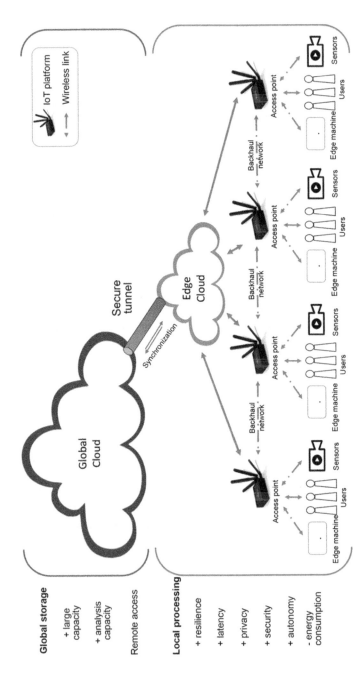

Figure 10.1. *Edge Cloud's IoT Platform. For a color version of this figure, see www.iste.co.uk/alagha/networking.zip*

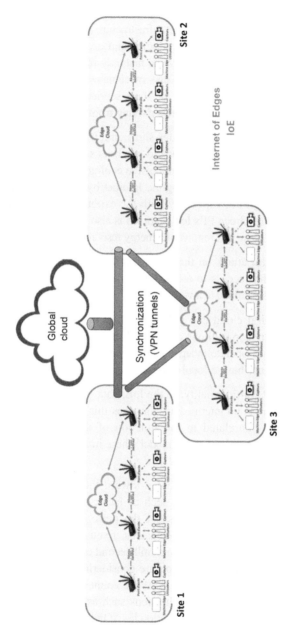

Figure 10.2. *Internet of Edges platform. For a color version of this figure, see www.iste.co.uk/alagha/networking.zip*

This infrastructure has many advantages for the processing of connected objects:

– Mobility: all the components of the Internet of the Edges can move. The IoT platforms that create the participatory Internet infrastructure are in an embedded format, equipped with Wi-Fi and Bluetooth technologies and are preconfigured to form a mesh network of platforms that automatically and instantly reconfigure themselves if the platforms move. Connected objects and Edge machines can also move within the infrastructure without being disconnected, or their services interrupted, as the IoT platforms support handovers (connected objects moving from one platform to another).

– A low carbon footprint: the IoE creates short circuits between objects and their intelligence. Data only travels a short distance to reach its servers in the Edge Cloud. Today's centralized clouds represent an impressive ecological cost with information traveling thousands of miles. Deglobalizing the Internet by bringing servers closer to their objects is becoming a must, especially with the exponential growth of the IoT. The power consumption of Green PI's IoT platform is also optimized. The platform is low power and can run on clean and renewable energy resources.

– Security: a successful attack on the cloud has dramatic consequences because once inside, the hacker has access to a lot of information. If an attack on the Edge Cloud succeeds, it remains confined to a very small site compared to the global Cloud.

– Resilience: the central cloud is a point of failure in the system. If a problem occurs in the cloud, it can stop millions or even billions of connected objects. On the other hand, the edge clouds operate independently, each in its own area. A failure in one Edge Cloud would only have a local impact.

– Data protection and confidentiality: in the IoE, data goes directly from the object to its edge machine. There is no intermediary that sees this information pass through and uses it for purposes unrelated to the function of the connected object. Data protection is very difficult to achieve with a model where information is processed in a central server located far away in the cloud.

– Latency: the IoT is increasingly oriented toward the automation of industrial tasks that require extremely low latency, such as factory automation or connected driving. This very low latency, regardless of the performance of the technology used, can only be guaranteed over short distances. Even if you go at the speed of light (physically the fastest), a latency of one millisecond can only be achieved over a distance of less than 300 km (150 km if you are considering a round trip). No cloud today can guarantee that it is within 150 km of the connected objects. Milliseconds are a requirement for mission-critical applications such as robot-assisted surgery, the autonomous vehicle and the automated production line. On the Edge Cloud, this latency is possible.

– Simplicity and openness: breaking down a centralized global architecture into smaller components makes it easy to customize the configuration of the IoE using specific edge machines.

In summary, the short circuit remains a major asset that should dominate the communication of the future with the objective of scaling up the Internet of Things and its commercial applications.

10.4. The IoE platform

Green Communications offers an open platform for managing connected objects (IoT) with a focus on:

– data processing at the edge of the network;

– the flexibility and openness of the solution, which will allow all types of objects and edge machines to be connected and will offer the possibility of working autonomously or in interaction with a centralized cloud;

– security with the use of a blockchain system to certify communications on this distributed system;

– scaling by providing connection and synchronization with other platforms in multiple geographic locations.

Figure 10.3 shows the software stack of Green PI's IoE platform. These stacks consist of several horizontal and transverse layers. The green layers are provided by Green PI. The blue ones are left to the platform user who can install the software best suited to his applications:

– Diversified connectivity: this is a level of abstraction of connectivity that allows to integrate any type of communication interface to connect various objects. Green PI's IoT platform offers Wi-Fi, Bluetooth, Ethernet and 4G connections.

– Device management: this is the management layer for connected objects and edge machines. This layer offers the necessary tools to control the objects, create a profile for them, display their profile, display their characteristics, access their content, allow updates, etc.

– Edge management: this is the heart of the IoE system where we can establish a set of edges to form a kind of virtual Cloud composed of its different Edges. This layer allows us to create these tunnels and apply the necessary routing and configuration protocols to merge the different physical edges to form a single logic.

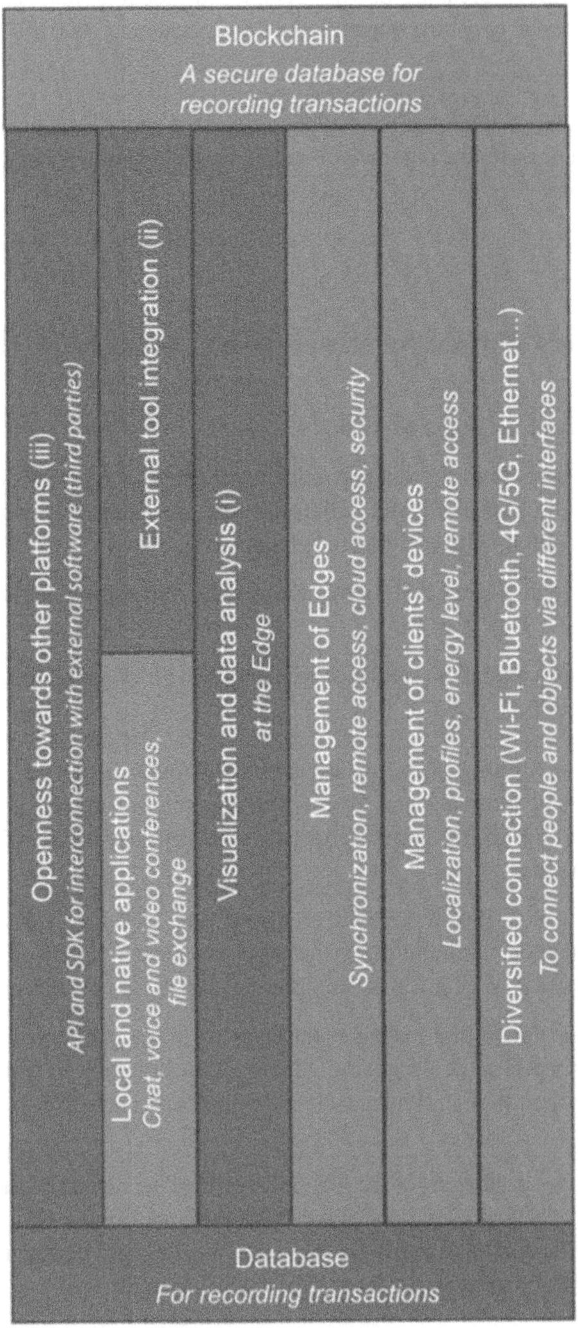

Figure 10.3. *Architecture of the Green PI platform (green color for what we provide and blue color for third party tools). For a color version of this figure, see www.iste.co.uk/alagha/networking.zip*

– Local and native applications: this layer proposes applications to facilitate teamwork and communications with the objects. Several applications are already integrated into IoE, such as chat, distributed storage, video streaming, audio conferencing, etc., with a distributed mode to manage the arrival or disappearance of edges in the system. The audio and video system will provide a local alternative to applications such as Zoom, Teams, etc. With IoE, you'll even be able to connect to it from multiple locations. Covid-19-related lockdowns have shown the power that this type of application can have in terms of data protection.

– The other layers correspond to (i) the openings of the platform to the data processing by the applications of the IoT system use cases that use our IoE, (ii) the integration of additional tools to the needs of the IoE user and (iii) SDKs and APIs to connect our IoE to external platforms. We already offer the tools necessary for these integrations and interconnections.

– Database: this is a database that the IoT user can install to store their data on Edge machines. This database is not the responsibility of Green PI and is left to the platform user who can install the database best suited to his applications. The database is accessible from all other levels, hence its vertical position.

– Blockchain: this is a distributed registry of transactions that can be recorded on Edge machines or in the distributed IoE infrastructure.

The blockchain serves as a tamper-proof ledger to record all transactions that take place on the IoE. It is distributed and uses a PBFT-based consensus algorithm to elect a leader among the infrastructure nodes to record transactions without conflict.

The blockchain is positioned vertically on the architecture so that any level can access it to record possible transactions.

10.5. Use cases: IoT in constrained environments

Green PI brings IoT applications into deep indoor environments, tunnels, ships at sea and other isolated areas to perform video surveillance, fire detection, intrusion detection, maritime pollution monitoring, etc. The main market applications are defense, public safety, etc.

The Green PI IoT platform can be battery-powered and carried on person, or it can be integrated into a buoy and powered by solar panels. Thus, the platform can be deployed in a minute and without the need for external resources in tunnels, buildings, ships and at sea for temporary or permanent IoT applications.

System life can be further extended with Green PI's Start-and-Stop (SaS®) feature that turns a platform off and on when needed.

Smart objects (cameras, sensors, devices, etc.) connect to the IoT platform using different interfaces (Wi-Fi, Bluetooth, Ethernet, 4G). The autonomous IoT services and applications can be hosted locally on the edge cloud of the IoT platform. The Edge Cloud enables data correlation at the source, providing fast server response time, high bandwidth and resilience to Internet disconnections. High-level data generated at the Edge can be sent to a remote decision center via the IoT platform's gateway. Greater correlation capability can be provided by federating multiple edges deployed at different locations through Green PI's scalable IoE functionality.

Figure 10.4 shows an example of a deployment for maritime pollution monitoring. Connected buoys detect pollution from a nearby boat using their embedded sensors and send alerts and images to a remote site through a meshed network of boys equipped with a 4G gateway.

Figure 10.4. *IoE in maritime pollution monitoring. For a color version of this figure, see www.iste.co.uk/alagha/networking.zip*

10.6. IoT in motion

Green PI connects fleets of moving objects and provides them with shared intelligence for swarming, collaboration and autonomous vehicles. The main market applications are transportation and logistics, automotive, defense, public safety, etc.

Green PI's IoT platform can be integrated as software or embedded as a module on smart robots, drones, vehicles and wearable devices (Figure 10.6). A group of objects connected by Green PI benefits from direct broadband and autonomous communications within the fleet. The fleet also shares an Edge Cloud with Edge-based applications for fast data synchronization, swarming, collaboration, etc. Greater synchronization capabilities can be provided via Green PI's IoE, which federates multiple fleets operating at different locations.

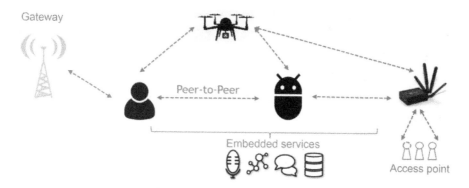

Figure 10.5. *IoE as a heterogeneous swarm of drones, robots,*
vehicles and people. For a color version of this figure,
see www.iste.co.uk/alagha/networking.zip

10.7. Massive IoT

Green PI is a large-scale edge solution for IoT applications deployed across multiple locations. Key market applications include healthcare and telemedicine, manufacturing, utilities, smart cities, etc.

Green PI connects different types of smart devices to its open IoT platform. If the amount of smart devices is high and requires wider coverage, additional IoT platforms can be deployed. These platforms will synchronize with each other and act as a single access point. IoT devices will be able to move from one platform to another seamlessly.

Smart devices connected to Green PI's IoT platforms share a common Edge Cloud. The Edge Cloud hosts mission-critical applications and services close to the data source to guarantee access, sufficient speed, fast response, resilience and data privacy.

Green PI synchronizes Edge Clouds deployed in multiple locations to create an IoE. The IoE allows you to interact with any user, object and program on the IoE as if they were nearby.

Thus, a doctor located in their office can interact with their patients and the patients' sensors located at home. A surgeon in hospital A can interact with robots in hospital B. These interactions happen with a dedicated infrastructure and no data going to any external cloud (Figure 10.6).

	Existing IoT platform	IoE platform
Architecture	Vertical to a central Cloud.	Horizontal from Edge to Edge.
Services	Centralized in a remote Cloud, regional Cloud (MEC) or Fog node.	Distributed in Edges.
Scaling up	Localized or extended using hierarchical architecture.	Scaling by tunnels from Edge to Edge.
Mobility	Moderate: mobility of objects only through a fixed antenna network including 5G infrastructure.	Complete: mobility of objects and infrastructure. With an integrated platform and synchronization system that supports splits and merges of resources at the Edge.
Autonomy	NO. Platforms depend on a node: a central Cloud, a MEC or a Fog.	YES. Services are distributed across Edges without a central node.
Sovereignty	NO. The platforms are based on regional, national or international data centers owned by operators or large companies.	YES. IoE allows you to deploy IoT applications with all data staying at the Edge and without going through any central node.
Opening	Proprietary with partial openness (open-source operating system, SDK, development environment development environment).	Agnostic, it is possible to add interfaces and services and connect any type of object and Edge.
Blockchain	Based on a fixed infrastructure with known resources in advance.	Supports mobility, partition and merging of Edges resources.
Carbon footprint	Will contribute 30% of the global carbon footprint by 2027.	Will save up to 25% of energy.

Table 10.1. *Benefits of the IoE platform*

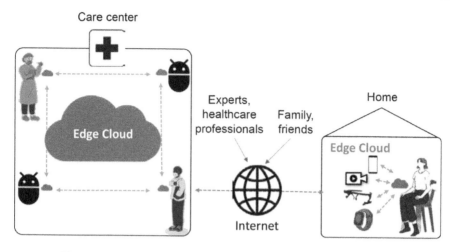

Figure 10.6. *IoE in smart hospitals and telemedicine. For a color version of this figure, see www.iste.co.uk/alagha/networking.zip*

10.8. The advantages

Table 10.1 shows a comparison between cloud-based IoT platforms and an IoE. We see the benefits of the IoE over the Cloud in terms of mobility, autonomy, sovereignty, openness and energy consumption.

10.9. References

Al Agha, K. (2011). Method for turning off routers in a communications network and router implementing this method. Patent, US9450835B2, EP2727403B1, JP6113157B2, WO2013000996A1.

Al Agha, K. (2012). Green Communications : réseaux low cost très économes en énergie et de haute qualité de service. *Techniques de l'Ingénieur*, IN152.

Al Agha, K. (2014). Device-to-device for wearable communication in 5G networks. *IEEE COMSOC MMTC E-Letter*, 9, 45–47.

Al Agha, K., Cavallari, N., Claveirole, T., Gawedzki, I. (2013). Distributed system and method for sharing capacity in an ad hoc network. US Patents, FR3011159B1, JP2015065653A, US9491088B2, EP2854467B1.

Cerovic, D., Del Piccolo, V., Amamou, A., Haddadou, K., Pujolle, G. (2018). Fast packet processing: A survey. *IEEE Communications Surveys and Tutorials*, 20(4), 3645–3676.

Cordova Morales, D., Velloso, P., Guerre, A., Nguyen, T.M.T., Pujolle, G., Al Agha, K., Dua, G. (2021). *Proceedings of SIGCOM*, 82–84.

11

Deployment of the Participatory Internet

In this chapter, we will describe the deployment of a participatory Internet using the example of Green Communications. This deployment is almost instantaneous. Quickly, nodes of the participatory network can see each other and form an Edge. This Edge contains nodes that are in the direct vicinity and others reachable through intermediate nodes. The Edge consists of an *ad hoc* or mesh network with embedded services offered to the network's clients.

We will also discuss the scaling of the participatory Internet to form an Internet of Edges (IoE) and the different possible approaches to reduce the energy consumption of the nodes of the participatory Internet to meet the needs of mobility.

11.1. The deployment

Green Communications' participatory Internet is composed of a set of embedded computers called Your Own Internet (YOI). Figure 11.1 shows a YOI router which consists of an electronic device equipped with two Wi-Fi interfaces and an Ethernet interface. YOI's power consumption is minimum (5 W) allowing it to be battery powered and to have wearable applications.

The deployment consists of simply positioning the nodes and powering them on. Fixed nodes can be powered by an electrical source, mobile ones can be battery powered. The network forms automatically without any manual intervention and is

Edge Networking,
by Khaldoun AL AGHA, Pauline LOYGUE and Guy PUJOLLE. © ISTE Ltd 2022.

ready for use as soon as all nodes have recognized their neighbors. The time required to start the network is expressed in seconds or tens of seconds at most.

Figure 11.1. *YOI router (©Green Communications). For a color version of this figure, see www.iste.co.uk/alagha/networking.zip*

Figure 11.2 shows an example of a deployed participatory Internet. It shows six routers forming the network with the links between the routers and then the clients, users or objects, connected to the network.

The participatory Internet contains a set of automatic discoveries of node characteristics such as temperatures, voltages, battery status, storage space, etc.

11.2. The Green Cloud

Once the participatory Internet is deployed, Green PI's Edge Cloud, *aka* the Green Cloud, then becomes available to the nodes connected to the network. The Green Cloud is embedded and distributed in all IoT platforms. It is resilient to network splits and merges. This resiliency allows the network to accommodate new nodes joining or leaving without affecting the Green Cloud data.

The Green Cloud is accessible via a local Web page (Figure 11.3) that offers applications and services hosted in the network (Chat, Storage, My Network, Setup, etc.). The Green Cloud hosts native applications provided by the participatory Internet and provides the tools for additional applications to be integrated into the Green Cloud. The native applications are the following.

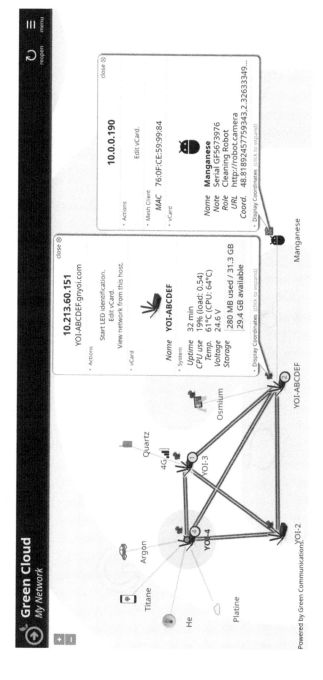

Figure 11.2. *A deployed participatory Internet (©Green Communications).*
For a color version of this figure, see www.iste.co.uk/alagha/networking.zip

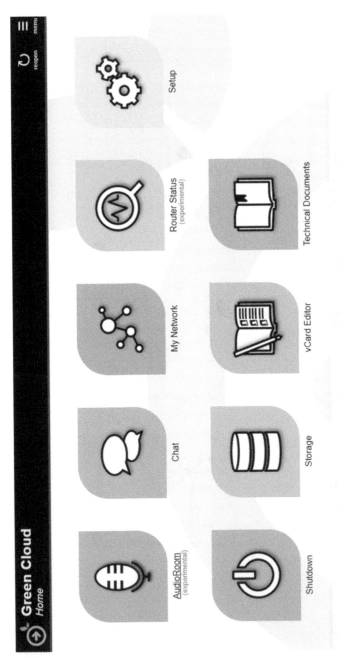

Figure 11.3. *Green Communications' Edge Cloud: the Green Cloud (©Green Communications). For a color version of this figure, see www.iste.co.uk/alagha/networking.zip*

11.2.1. *My Network*

My Network (Figure 11.4) is an application for viewing the status of the participatory network in real time. The application offers different information depending on whether the user is registered as an administrator or not.

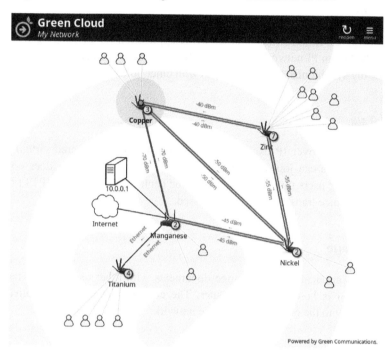

Figure 11.4. *The My Network application (©Green Communications). For a color version of this figure, see www.iste.co.uk/alagha/networking.zip*

The following information is visible to users:

– Location of the user in the network: materialized by a green disk around the router to which the user is connected.

– The number of connected clients: represented by a value affixed to each router.

– Router information: name, image, IP address, power supply voltage, CPU temperature, etc.

– Gateway location(s): when a router is a gateway to the Internet or another network, it is connected to a Cloud or a computer.

– The quality of the network links: the signal quality is indicated in dBm on each radio link of the backhaul network. The application also uses color-coding to visualize the quality of the network links.

11.2.2. *Chat*

Chat (Figure 11.5) is an instant messaging application for exchanging with other users on the Green PI network. The application is hosted on each router. The routers automatically synchronize their chat rooms with other nodes on the network.

11.2.3. *Talk*

Talk is a voice-over IP exchange application. It provides shared virtual rooms that multiple users can join to have a conversation. The application does not send audio by default; users must click and hold the central Push-To-Talk (PTT) button, which allows voice transmission when pressed.

11.2.4. *Storage*

This is an application to exchange documents with other users on the network. The application is hosted on each router. The content of Storage is automatically synchronized with the other routers on the network.

11.2.5. *vCard Editor*

It is an application that allows you to create a profile for the clients and platforms of the Green PI participatory network. The profile is a vCard that offers the possibility of associating attributes such as name, surname, ID, URL, photo, contact information, etc., to an object.

11.3. Scaling up

Scaling up to large networks does not support hypersecure or very high-performance networks as the number of clients increases and so do the vulnerabilities. To continue to benefit from all the advantages of the participatory network environment, it is necessary to consider that a large network is an association of independent Edges. Several solutions can be used to realize this set of interconnected Edges or an IoE.

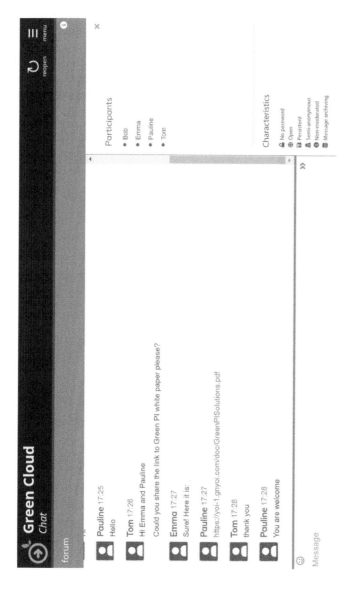

Figure 11.5. *The Chat application. For a color version of this figure, see www.iste.co.uk/alagha/networking.zip*

The network must be divided into Edges that can be tactical bubbles or independent, smart spaces. The Edge functions as a participatory Internet. It is necessary to decide, through a distributed election, a master node that represents the Edge. This election can use different algorithms existing in the literature like Paxos or RAFT. The master node can change over time for various reasons, such as a new election every x s, the disappearance of the master node, a change of Edge, etc.

Figure 11.6 illustrates the scaling with the different Edges that may be adjacent or remote. Secure tunnels are installed so that the Edges together form an IoE. Nodes in the Cloud (physical or virtual) can also create an Edge that the IoE can integrate as an additional Edge.

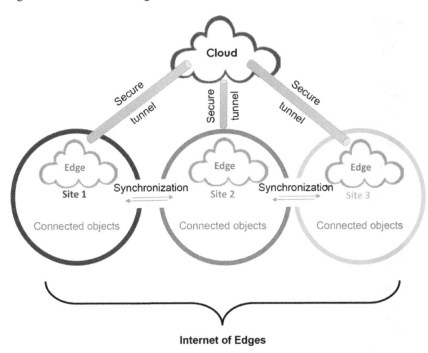

Figure 11.6. *Green Communications IoE. For a color version of this figure, see www.iste.co.uk/alagha/networking.zip*

11.4. Energy savings

Energy consumption is one of the most important criteria in the construction of new IT environments. The participatory Internet must provide a strong response to this demand. To achieve this, the network and the Edge data centers must consume as little energy as possible in order to be able to operate on battery power with a minimum of one day's continuous operation, which can be extended to several days or even much longer.

There are two main ways to save energy and achieve fully autonomous Edges, mobile or not. The first is to choose low-power, yet computationally powerful components, combined with optimized software and routing algorithms. The second solution is to use a Start-and-Stop (SaS) technology, which allows resources to be put on standby to reduce power consumption and achieve long battery life. Node standby is easily achieved by using a utility function. When this function is equal to 0, the node is no longer useful. This function takes into account the one-hop connections but also the importance of the node in the available paths of the network. The complexity comes from the reactivation that must take place automatically if the node becomes useful again. A simple solution is to turn on the power every 30 s, for example, test the usefulness of the node and turn it off again if the node is not useful.

Green Communications' approach for energy saving is the SaS, whose functionality turns a node on/off based on its utility to the network. This usefulness can be measured by several metrics such as supporting the transfer of data traffic, maintaining network connectivity, etc.

If sufficient conditions are met, the node saves its state to RAM or disk and goes into sleep mode to reduce power consumption. The node then wakes up as needed, using an interrupt (such as Wake-on-LAN) if this feature is available. Otherwise, a timer is programmed to turn on the node periodically, and it continues to measure its utility to decide whether to shut down or stay awake. Figure 11.7 shows an example of an ad hoc network. In this figure, node D can go into sleep mode if it is not forwarding network traffic, and it is clear that D is not an articulation point for splitting the network. Nodes G and E must remain awake to continue their role as routers for other nodes.

In a static network graph, the hinge points remain the same over time. In an IoE, the nodes may be mobile and, therefore, the network topology changes very frequently due to node mobility, the wireless channel and links quality. The hinge points can change and a node must constantly look at its status before going into sleep mode.

To determine changes in network topology, nodes use a routing protocol such as OLSR, AODV, etc. In proactive protocols like the OLSR, each node contains a partial view of the topology that is updated periodically by the routing protocol. SaS exploits the topology information so that each node in a distributed fashion can decide whether to shut down or stay awake.

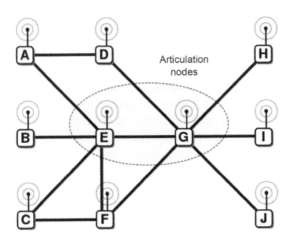

Figure 11.7. *Example of a network topology*

An IoE node using the OLSR routing protocol takes three verification steps to decide whether to turn it off or not:

– It ensures that it is not being used by a client or running an application that generates traffic to the network.

– The node verifies that it is not relaying any data traffic for all other nodes.

– It verifies that the node is not an articulation point for the whole network.

A node *i* creates a network graph G using topology information from the OLSR routing protocol and uses an algorithm to decide whether it is an articulation point or not. The node enters standby if the result of the algorithm shows that it does not disturb the network's connectivity.

In a network, topology information is propagated periodically through the routing protocol. If more than one node decides to go into sleep mode at the same time, they are not aware of each other's state, that is, changes in the network topology.

In this situation, the calculation of the articulation point control may result in an incorrect decision. For example, in Figure 11.7, if nodes D and E both decide to go into sleep mode at the same time, the connectivity between nodes A and G will be broken. This is because each of nodes D and E in their audit knows that the other can maintain A's connectivity to the network.

To avoid this, SaS technology introduces a backoff system to desynchronize the shutdown of nodes in the network. Instead of immediately going into sleep mode, each node waits for a random period of time. If a node receives a message indicating a shutdown, it avoids going into sleep mode. Otherwise, it broadcasts a shutdown message and goes into sleep mode.

Figure 11.8 shows the transition state diagram that governs SaS. The SaS state diagram has five states and eight transitions.

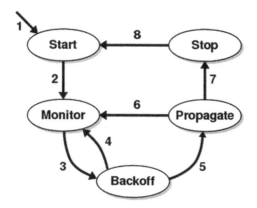

Figure 11.8. *State diagram showing the possible states and transitions for Start-and-Stop*

COMMENT ON FIGURE 11.8.– *The following are the transition definitions: (1) Initial transition to the startup state; (2) After the SaS process starts; (3) At the end of the monitoring period; (4) Upon receiving a shutdown message or the node is an articulation point; (5) At the end of the interruption period; (6) When a shutdown message is received, or the node is an articulation point; (7) When the propagation period ends; (8) When switching from standby to wake-up mode.*

Each state has its own set of instructions to check the state of the network and decide which transition to choose. Here is a description of each state:

– Start: this is the initial state of the SaS. After initialization, the process switches to the Monitor state to start its monitoring activity.

– Monitor: in this state, the process monitors the traffic status of the nodes and the network periodically. If there is no user activity and the node is not a source of data traffic, the node is assumed to go into sleep mode and the process switches to the Backoff state.

– Backoff: in this state, the process waits a random amount of time and checks the state of its articulation point before switching to the Propagate state. The process returns to the watch state if it finds itself as an articulation point or receives a message from any other node that goes into sleep mode.

– Propagate: this state is designed to take into account the propagation delay of messages in the network. When it reaches this state, the process sends an ex-turn-off message to all other nodes in the network.

– The process returns to the monitoring state if it receives a hibernate message from other nodes or if it is found to be an articulation point. Otherwise, the process goes to the standby state.

– Stop: in this state, the process goes into Stop mode. During this period, the node stops all its activities to save as much energy as possible.

Figure 11.9 shows the amount of energy expended for different numbers of flows in the network. We note that the energy consumption increases with the number of data flow in the network. The reason is that the increase in the number of flows also increases the data traffic load on the network. This increase in traffic load increases the number of transmissions, receptions and interferences, resulting in higher energy consumption. This contributes to an increase in the time to stay awake for each node, that is, to stay in the monitor state. The results show the efficiency of SaS by achieving average energy savings of 56–67% compared to the network without using the SaS mechanism.

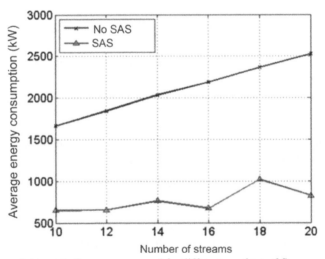

a) Amount of energy consumed for different numbers of flows.

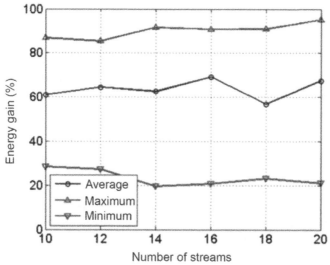

b) Amount of energy gained with the Start-and-Stop mechanism.

Figure 11.9. *SaS performance results. For a color version of this figure, see www.iste.co.uk/alagha/networking.zip*

The second part of the figure shows the minimum and maximum amount of energy gain found during the studied scenario. This amount varies from 19% to 91%, depending on the network topology.

11.5. Security

Security on the Green Communications IoE is provided on several levels:

– At the network level, wireless communications are WPA2/WPA3 encrypted for access and link. Remote access is provided via secure IP tunnels.

– At the application level, the embedded services use Transport Layer Security (TLS) and HTTPS cryptographic protocols to guarantee the confidentiality and integrity of data on the network.

– At the operational level, embedded services such as a local Internet can be confined and physically isolated from the outside world. No remote cyberattacks can then occur.

– At the configuration level, the platform uses SNMP's Privauth mode for exchanging configuration commands between the platform's nodes.

– The platform is open for the introduction of an additional security level if needed.

A blockchain distributed across all nodes in the network is available to record transactions securely. This blockchain uses a consensus algorithm to elect a leader for recording a transaction on the blockchain. Consensus avoids conflict between nodes when recording the validation of a transaction.

11.6. Wi-Fi and LTE hybridization

Hybridization is a technique that allows equipment with two or more network interfaces to connect to different technologies in a dynamic and automatic way. The multiple connections bring diversity that offers the possibility to benefit from the advantages of these technologies.

Wi-Fi and LTE technologies connect billions of people and objects around the world. Each has its own specificities, advantages and disadvantages. There are supporters and opponents of both technologies. It is impossible to show that one is better than the other and *vice versa*. Each out-performs the other in a context for which it has been optimized. Hybridizing the two technologies offers the advantages of each while eliminating their shortcomings. It consists in studying the environment and modeling a metric that allows switching from one technology to the other. All the complexity comes from the definition of this metric which must separate the technologies knowing that the technologies have nothing in common and do not define the qualities in the same way. Another essential constraint in the definition of the metric is the simplicity to facilitate its implementation in a product. A complex metric makes switching from one technology to another long, even impossible or counterproductive.

Wi-Fi is a simple, inexpensive technology that can be deployed without any infrastructure or planning. It offers a direct mode to exchange between types of equipment without going through access points. The drawback of Wi-Fi is that it uses free bands and, as a result, it can suffer from uncontrolled interference. A Wi-Fi user can have an excellent throughput and then, without being aware of it, be subject to interference from other users who are close to him and thus reduce his throughput.

LTE is a complex and, therefore, expensive technology. It also uses a licensed band, making it more expensive. An operator must deploy this technology with planning and studies that are also expensive. Technologically, it offers the direct mode to communicate from vehicle to vehicle without going through the operator's infrastructure, but for the moment, this mode remains in the specification without a real product that can be deployed on a large scale. On the other hand, it has the advantage of being able to offer reservations and quality of communications, especially if they are critical.

If one hybridizes Wi-Fi and LTE, then one can enjoy the benefits of both technologies. Wi-Fi can provide a direct mode for vehicle-to-vehicle conversation, and LTE can be used as a carrier network to communicate when direct mode does not provide good coverage but also when reservation of network resources is required.

Green Communications has specified, developed and implemented a hybrid solution based on Wi-Fi and LTE. It combines Wi-Fi using the direct mode with mesh extension and LTE using the infrastructure mode installed by a public operator or as part of a private network (tactical bubble, for example).

Figure 11.10 shows the Green Communications solution. A vehicle carries a YOI-4G router. It consists of a lightweight, low-power consuming box. It can be powered by the vehicle's 12V battery. This router contains two interfaces: Wi-Fi and 4G. The Wi-Fi interface is positioned in direct mode (the ad hoc mode of Wi-Fi), and the 4G interface can operate on public frequencies of operators as well as on private frequencies for organizations that have a license for private use.

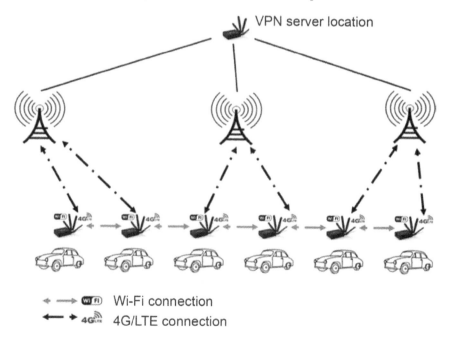

Figure 11.10. *Hybridization technique of Green Communications. For a color version of this figure, see www.iste.co.uk/alagha/networking.zip*

The routers incorporate an OLSR routing protocol that takes care of calculating routing tables to decide which interface (Wi-Fi or LTE) the packets should exit through. This routing protocol also does mesh and, therefore, Wi-Fi links can be used for direct transmission or over multiple hops to reach the destination.

Since LTE is managed by an operator that does not allow access to its network by an outside actor, we opted for the solution of installing a YOI router in the Cloud, then the LTE links are wrapped in VPN links between the mobile routers and the one in the Cloud. With this method, the router, when calculating its routing table, can compare Wi-Fi links and LTE links based on the radio quality of the links.

The metric used to choose between Wi-Fi and LTE is a Boolean that allows you to choose one or the other. This is because the two technologies do not measure link quality in the same way, and therefore, it is impossible to compare link quality. The idea is to choose one technology over the other. For example, a connected vehicle operator may decide to use a telecom operator or to use Wi-Fi links.

If technology A has priority, the solution is to measure the radio quality against a switchover threshold. If this threshold is crossed, then the routing protocol updates the routing tables to change the interface, and if not, the same output interface is kept. For example, if Wi-Fi has priority and the switchover threshold is –75 dBm, the Wi-Fi links are used as long as the route only contains links whose quality is higher than –75 dBm. If this condition is not met, we switch to LTE. The solution was tested and validated on the use case described in Figure 11.11.

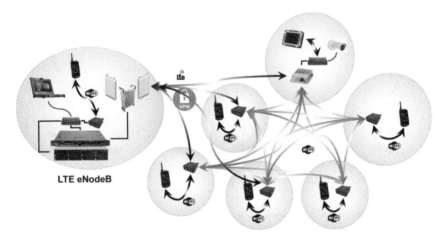

Figure 11.11. *Example of use. For a color version of this figure, see www.iste.co.uk/alagha/networking.zip*

The figure shows an LTE private network consisting of an eNodeB and an EPC. On this network, a YOI node is connected to act as a VPN server. Then six mobile nodes connect multiple devices: smartphone, camera, audio device (microphone and headsets), etc.

The eNodeB is installed about 40 km from the nodes that had direct Wi-Fi links. In the figure, the links in black are LTE links, and the links in green are Wi-Fi links. The routers also operated a Wi-Fi access point to connect mobile users' devices.

The scenario worked well by running various applications simultaneously: Push2Talk, video streaming, instant messaging and web exchanges.

Participatory networking technology has many advantages that depend on the application for which it has been chosen.

We must insist on the aspects of energy consumption, security by allowing the isolation of a participatory network from the Internet, resilience thanks to its totally distributed system and its agility to support applications with very short response times.

Participatory networks are expected to become very popular with the return of distribution in place of increasingly excessive centralization.

11.7. Conclusion

In this chapter, we have shown a concrete example of a real deployment of an IoE platform offering low latency, security and local data storage for increased protection.

The major advantage of such a platform is its speed of deployment, low power consumption and the way it adapts to interconnect with other deployments at the Edge or with instances in the Cloud.

11.8. References

Allal, I., Mongazon-Cazavet, B., Al Agha, K., Senouci, S.-M., Gourhant, Y. (2017). A green small cells deployment in 5G – Switch ON/OFF via IoT networks and energy-efficient mesh backhauling. *IFIP Networking Conference (IFIP Networking) and Workshops*, IEEE, Stockholm, Sweden.

Amokrane, A., Zhani, M., Langar, R., Boutaba, B., Pujolle, G. (2013). Greenhead: Virtual data center embedding across distributed infrastructures. *IEEE Transactions on Cloud Computing*, 1(1), 36–49.

Amokrane, A., Langar, R., Boutaba, R., Pujolle, G. (2014). Energy efficient management framework for multihop TDMA-based wireless networks. *Computer Networks*, 62(7), 29–42.

Amokrane, A., Langar, R., Boutaba, R., Pujolle, G. (2015a). Flow-based management for energy efficient campus networks. *IEEE Transactions on Network and Service Management*, 12(4), 565–579.

Amokrane, A., Langar, R., Zhani, M.F., Boutaba, R., Pujolle, G. (2015b). Greenslater: On satisfying Green SLAs in distributed clouds. *IEEE Transactions on Network and Service Management*, 12(3), 363–376.

Diallo, E., Al Agha, K., Dib, O., Laubé, A., Mohamed-Babou, H. (2020). Toward scalable blockchain for data management in VANETs. *WAINA*, 233–244 [Online]. Available at: https://doi.org/10.1007/978-3-030-44038-1_22.

Dilla Diratie, E. and Al Agha, K. (2020). Hybrid Internet of Things network for energy efficient video surveillance. *WF-IoT*, 1–6 [Online]. Available at: 10.1109/WF-IoT48130.2020. 9221241.

Laubé, A., Martin, S., Quadri, D., Al Agha, K. (2016). Optimal flow aggregation for global energy savings in multi-hop wireless networks. *ADHOC-NOW*, 9724, 124–137.

Laubé, A., Martin, S., Quadri, D., Al Agha, K., Pujolle, G. (2017). FAME: A flow aggregation metric for shortest path routing algorithms in multi-hop. *Wireless Networks, WCNC*, 1–6.

Laubé, A., Martin, S., Al Agha, K. (2019a). A solution to the split & merge problem for blockchain-based applications in ad hoc networks. *8th International Conference on Performance Evaluation and Modeling in Wired and Wireless Networks (PEMWN)*, Paris, France, 26–28 November 2019.

Laubé, A., Quadri, D., Martin, S., Al Agha, K. (2019b). A simple and efficient way to save energy in multihop wireless networks with flow aggregation. *Journal of Computer Networks and Communications*, 2019, 059401.

Mohamed, K.S., Alias, M.Y., Roslee, M., Raji, Y.M. (2021). Towards Green Communication in 5G systems: Survey on beamforming concept. *IET Journal*, 15(1), 142–154.

Shrit, O., Martin, S., Al Agha, K., Pujolle, G. (2017). A new approach to realize drone swarm using ad hoc network. *Med-Hoc-Net'2017*, IEEE, Budva, Montenegro.

12

The Future

12.1. The short-term future

We can imagine many uses of the participatory Internet or the Internet of Edges that are only waiting to be multiplied. The first example comes from the participatory Internet between neighbors, in ad hoc mode, to pool sufficient resources to realize a common private Cloud in which data is shared or not. The data can be encrypted to keep the necessary confidentiality while supporting generic applications that can be easily shared between all the partners of the participatory Internet.

For security reasons, companies can protect themselves from cyber-attacks and set up highly personalized information systems. The company's employees no longer have access to Internet services but only to those services offered internally. Today, there are already a large number of Internet applications in a distributed form, and these will only increase in the coming years. In addition, it is always possible to use Web services that are easily implemented on the participatory Internet.

Smart vehicle networks are also a source of many relatively short-term applications that allow vehicles to simply share resources. This solution allows passengers to share real-time games and to meet at home or the office.

Smart spaces are also an area where the participatory Internet is needed to realize a digital infrastructure with smart infrastructure services and to give the necessary computing and storage power to implement analysis and machine learning algorithms.

Another movement that gained momentum in 2021 was the rapid increase in the power of terminal equipment. After a relatively slow increase over the years

Edge Networking,
by Khaldoun AL AGHA, Pauline LOYGUE and Guy PUJOLLE. © ISTE Ltd 2022.

2015–2020, Moore's Law accelerated to a doubling of processor power every 18 months instead of every two years in the early 2010s.

The back-and-forth between centralization and distribution has been alive and well for decades, and while the late 2010s saw a return to centralization, distribution is now regaining power thanks to the power of processors, particularly ARM architectures that allow, among other things, a very large number of cores. The Skin data centers should quickly become a standard and allow the Edge to take an important place in the alliance between large and small data centers.

12.2. The medium-term future

The medium-term future of computing and networking is expressed in two very different ways when looking at current studies and research. A rather centralized solution, pushed by the telecommunication operators and a distributed solution thought by the Web industry and the supporters of the Internet of which the participatory Internet is a part.

The first centralization solution is based on SDN-type technologies with virtualized controllers in data centers that can be either in the core network or in the Radio Access Network (RAN). SDN networks are being deployed, and, for this, the development of east-west interfaces between controllers is mandatory in order to move to large networks and not remain on small networks with a very limited number of nodes. Some form of distribution, between centralization and distribution, should be imposed thanks to a standardized interface between controllers, which would allow the SDN architecture to scale. The interface that is emerging and should become the de facto standard for controller interconnection is the SDN interface (SDNi). It corresponds to the east-west interface of the OpenDaylight controller. Underlying, the SDNi uses BGP4. This interface should allow the realization of a rather strongly decentralized SDN environment. Such an environment is described in Figure 12.1.

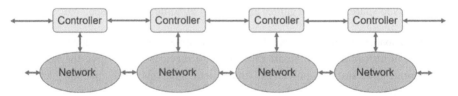

Figure 12.1. *A distributed SDN environment. For a color version of this figure, see www.iste.co.uk/alagha/networking.zip*

The second solution comes from participatory networks that coexist with highly centralized systems. The urbanization algorithms for virtual machines and containers are becoming more and more precise and will make it possible in the years 2020–2025 to deploy Internet of Edges-type architectures with a combination of an Internet of core networks. This solution is described in Figure 12.2.

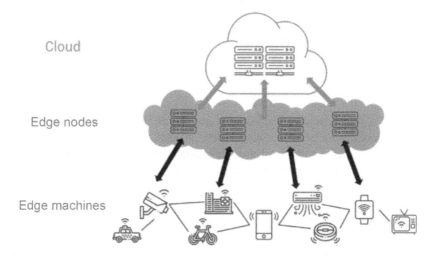

Figure 12.2. *Medium-term solution on the Edge. For a color version of this figure, see www.iste.co.uk/alagha/networking.zip*

12.3. The long-term future

Reflections on 6G started in 2020 with many R&D laboratories in the world with more than 50 engineers. The first proposed architectures are grouped as before in two main directions.

The first direction leads to centralization at the level of the MEC data centers and thus to a distributed cloud or a smart central data center (cognitive data center). Complete virtualization of the equipment is carried out to realize the digital infrastructure. Centralization at the MEC level is in line with distribution via controllers that interconnect via east-west interfaces. Associated with this centralization, many proposals emanate from researchers working on 6G, such as the number of antennas on the base stations, which could carry several million directional antennas with the transition from the MIMO 1024 of 5G to a MIMO 1M, with a thousand times more antennas. This solution leads to one antenna per user, extended by a network per user and per application, forming a horizontal slice. To achieve control of this excessively complex environment of antennas and slices, a control center is proposed with all the necessary intelligence.

The second direction is, on the contrary, totally distributed, of the type of the participatory Internet and globally of the Internet of Edges. This solution could be realized with a re-start of the solutions that allowed the Internet to begin and brought its success. The difference with the Internet comes from the consideration of mobility, digital infrastructure and distributed computing on the Edge. In addition, the Internet was available to users for transport, whereas the new generation of the participatory Internet provides networking, storage, computation, security and intelligence through network nodes.

Perhaps 6G will come to fruition with billions of autonomous nodes owned by users, enterprises and telecom operators, interconnected with each other but without any command center. The basic idea of the Internet that made it so successful is back in the spotlight. The reasons for this fluctuation between centralization and distribution are easy to guess: we centralize when distributed intelligence is insufficient to solve problems, and we distribute as soon as collective intelligence can be obtained in a distributed way. The 2010s saw the arrival of intelligence, but in a centralized form. The years 2025–2030 will be the years when control of networks will again be distributed thanks to the power put into the Edge. The years 2020–2025 are a transition from one technology to another.

12.4. Participatory Internet and IPV6

The participatory Internet can be seen as Airbnb, Uber, or any other model that allows the owner of a resource to make it available to others for a fee. This is in order to complement the offers of operators: hotels for Airbnb or cabs for Uber.

You own a car or an apartment, and you want to make this resource available to others from time to time in a participatory way. When someone wants to borrow it for a given period of time, you just have to connect to the platform to use this resource.

Everyone has a resource such as a smartphone, a computer or a tablet. If we want to create a participatory Internet to complement the offer of telecom operators and Internet providers, we can then make this resource available to others.

Making the resource available to others to complement the operators' offer means that the IP network routing protocols will integrate the physical links established by the local resource (smartphone, computer, box, etc.).

Consequently, when information circulates, it will choose the best path according to a metric, and optimization will automatically be put in place to avoid the information traveling thousands of kilometers to get back to its proximity. Figure 12.3 shows an example of resource sharing between objects and operators. In this figure, the information can choose a horizontal path from the object to object or pass through the antennas of an operator network.

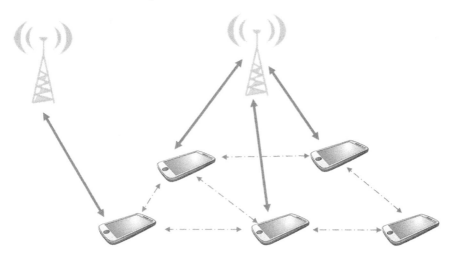

Figure 12.3. *Horizontal and direct communication versus operator network communication. For a color version of this figure, see www.iste.co.uk/alagha/networking.zip*

Network customers can also set up servers to offer services in the Edge instead of putting them in the Cloud. One service can be smartphone camera streaming. Nowadays, a lot of video streaming is done from phone cameras. These streams are uploaded to Cloud servers like YouTube, then people who want to watch the video connect to the YouTube server to receive the video. If the server were located directly on the phone, there would be no need to go through YouTube. Again, thousands of miles in both directions (to and from the YouTube server) can be avoided to go directly between the client who wants to watch the video and the server that authorizes the camera on their phone. In addition, the person streaming the video retains ownership of their data instead of leaving it to the cloud server.

These techniques of direct routing and server creation on user objects cannot be done without the use of a unique public identifier of the object. Indeed, at present, Internet and Cloud users' devices use the IPV4 protocol, which does not have the capacity to offer a public address to each device. Thus, one public address addresses dozens, hundreds or even thousands of devices, making it impossible to uniquely identify each device in the network.

The arrival of IPV6 removes this constraint that prevents the participatory Internet from flourishing. With IPV6, each device will have its own unique address in the network, and we will be able to install a whole set of services on our devices.

Take the example of an exit from a stadium after a soccer match: 80,000 people rush to the exit at the same time. The metro is saturated, and vehicles leave the parking sometimes with only one person on board. If these drivers want to offer carpooling to others and avoid the crowded metro, they will have to use cloud platforms such as Blablacar. Not only will the information go into the Internet and the Cloud, but probably the Internet will be saturated with these 80,000 people wishing to connect. The participatory Internet allows drivers to activate a server to propose a carpooling place that a client can acquire directly and without going through the already saturated networks.

IPV6 is becoming more and more established on terminal objects. Thus, all home boxes have IPV6 addresses. More and more smartphones are equipped with IPV6. Today, in France 100% of Bouygues Telecom phones and 60% of Orange phones are already connected to the IPV6 network. The evolution of the situation in France can be observed on the ARCEP[1] website. The acceleration has taken off and, in a few years, IPV6 will replace IPV4, making it possible to have a participatory Internet in addition to that of the operators.

In the longer term, the operating systems of devices such as iOS and Android will integrate by default to the participatory Internet and give everyone the possibility to offer their phone to contribute to improving the performance and especially to lower the energy consumption of the Internet and Clouds.

Platforms that allow for the counting of resources made available by some and their use by others will provide the business models necessary for the implementation of the participatory Internet. For example, when a person or company X makes a phone's resources (battery, memory and processor) available to another person or company Y to improve data transfer, Y will spend a sum of money that will accrue to X.

The Green Communications solutions described in Chapters 10 and 11 are already ready to implement the participatory Internet everywhere. Today, these solutions are done on an embedded and portable device, but, eventually, with the

---

1 http://arcep.fr.

arrival of IPV6, they will be able to be deployed on a larger scale and directly in terminal devices such as tablets or phones.

12.5. References

Abbasi, M., Shahraki, A., Barzegar, H.R., Pahl, C. (2021). Synchronization techniques in device-to-device- and vehicle-to-vehicle-enabled cellular networks: A survey. *Computers and Electrical Engineering*, 90, 106955.

Avasalcai, C., Murturi, I., Dustdar, S. (2020). *Edge and Fog: A Survey, Use Cases, and Future Challenges*. John Wiley & Sons, Hoboken, NJ.

Chen, M., Yang, Z., Saad, W., Yin, C., Poor, H.V., Cui, S. (2021). A joint learning and communications framework for federated learning over wireless networks. *IEEE Transactions on Wireless Communications*, 20(1), 269–283.

Chowdhury, M.Z., Hossan, M.T., Islam, A., Jang, Y.M. (2018). A comparative survey of optical wireless technologies: Architectures and applications. *IEEE Access*, 6(98), 19–40.

Dang, S., Amin, O., Shihada, B., Alouini, M.S. (2020). What should 6G be? *Nature Electronics*, 3(1), 20–29.

Giordani, M., Polese, M., Mezzavilla, M., Rangan, S., Zorzi, M. (2020). Toward 6G networks: Use cases and technologies. *IEEE Communications Magazine*, 58(3), 55–61.

Gui, G., Liu, M., Tang, F., Kato, N., Adachi, F. (2020). 6G: Opening new horizons for integration of comfort, security, and intelligence. *IEEE Wireless Communications*, 27(5), 126–132.

Gupta, R., Shukla, A., Tanwar, S. (2020). BATS: A blockchain and AI-empowered drone-assisted telesurgery system towards 6G. *IEEE Transactions on Network Science and Engineering*, 8(4), 2958–2967

Gyongyosi, L. and Imre, S. (2019). A survey on quantum computing technology. *Computer Science Review*, 31, 51–71.

Huang, T., Yang, W., Wu, J., Ma, J., Zhang, X., Zhang, D. (2019). A survey on green 6G network: Architecture and technologies. *IEEE Access*, 7(175), 758–768.

Khan, L.U., Yaqoob, I., Imran, M., Han, Z., Hong, C.S. (2020). 6G wireless systems: A vision, architectural elements, and future directions. *IEEE Access*, 8(147), 029–044.

Letaief, K.B., Chen, W., Shi, Y., Zhang, J., Zhang, Y.J.A. (2019). The roadmap to 6G: AI-empowered wireless networks. *IEEE Communications Magazine*, 57(8), 84–90.

Li, T., Sahu, A.K., Talwalkar, A., Smith, V. (2020a). Federated learning: Challenges, methods, and future directions. *IEEE Signal Processing Magazine*, 37(3), 50–60.

Li, X., Wang, Q., Liu, M., Li, J., Peng, H., Piran, J., Li, L. (2020b). Cooperative wireless-powered NOMA relaying for B5G IoT networks with hardware impairments and channel estimation errors. *IEEE Internet of Things Journal*, 8(7), 5453–5467.

Lu, Y. and Zheng, X. (2020). 6G: A survey on technologies, scenarios, challenges, and the related issues. *Journal of Industrial Information Integration*, 19, 100158.

Lv, Z., Qiao, L., You, I. (2020). 6G-enabled network in box for Internet of connected vehicles. *IEEE Transactions on Intelligent Transportation Systems*, 22(8), 5275–5282.

Manzalini, A. (2020). Quantum communications in future networks and services. *Quantum Reports*, 2(1), 221–232.

Piran, M. and Suh, D.Y. (2019). Learning-driven wireless communications, towards 6G. *IEEE International Conference on Computing, Electronics and Communication Engineering*, London Metropolitan University, 22–23 August 2019.

Qiu, T., Chi, J., Zhou, X., Ning, Z., Atiquzzaman, M., Wu, D.O. (2020). Edge computing in industrial internet of things: Architecture, advances and challenges. *IEEE Communications Surveys and Tutorials*, 22(4), 2462–2488.

Rout, S.P. (2020). 6G wireless communication: Its vision, viability, application, requirement, technologies, encounters and research. *11th International Conference on Computing, Communication and Networking Technologies (ICCCNT)*, Kharagpur, India, 1–3 July 2020.

Shafin, R., Liu, L., Chandrasekhar, V., Chen, H., Reed, J., Zhang, J.C. (2020). Artificial intelligence-enabled cellular networks: A critical path to beyond-5G and 6G. *IEEE Wireless Communications*, 27(2), 212–217.

Shahraki, A., Taherkordi, A., Haugen, O., Eliassen, F. (2020). Clustering objectives in wireless sensor networks: A survey and research direction analysis. *Computer Networks*, 180, 107376.

Shahraki, A., Abbasi, M., Piran, M.-J., Taherkordi, A. (2021). A comprehensive survey on 6G networks: Applications, core services, enabling technologies, and future challenges. *ArXiv preprint*, 2101.12475.

Sliwa, B., Falkenberg, R., Wietfeld, C. (2020). Towards cooperative data rate prediction for future mobile and vehicular 6G networks. *Proceedings of the 6G Wireless Summit*, 1–5.

Tariq, F., Khandaker, M.R., Wong, K.K., Imran, M.A., Bennis, M., Debbah, M. (2020). A speculative study on 6G. *IEEE Wireless Communications*, 27(4), 118–125.

Viswanathan, H. and Mogensen, P.E. (2020). Communications in the 6G era. *IEEE Access*, 8(57), 63–74.

Zhang, L., Liang, Y.-C., Niyato, D. (2019a). 6G visions: Mobile ultrabroadband, super internet-of-things, and artificial intelligence. *China Communications*, 16(8), 1–14.

Zhang, Z., Xiao, Y., Ma, Z., Xiao, M., Ding, Z., Lei, X., Karagiannidis, G.K., Fan, P. (2019b). 6G wireless networks: Vision, requirements, architecture, and key technologies. *IEEE Vehicular Technology Magazine*, 14(3), 28–41.

List of Authors

Khaldoun AL AGHA
LISN
Université Paris-Saclay
Gif-sur-Yvette
France

Pauline LOYGUE
Green Communications
Paris
France

Guy PUJOLLE
Green Communications
Paris
France

Index

Y, Z

Printed and bound by CPI Group (UK) Ltd, Croydon, CR0 4YY

27/10/2024

14580731-0003